THIS

MAGNETIC

NORTH

THIS MAGNETIC NORTH

CANDID CONVERSATIONS ON A CHANGING NORTHERN MICHIGAN

TIM MULHERIN

Michigan State University Press | East Lansing

Michigan State University Press
East Lansing, Michigan 48823-5245

Library of Congress Cataloging-in-Publication Data
Names: Mulherin, Tim, author.
Title: This magnetic north : candid conversations on a changing Northern Michigan / Tim Mulherin.
Description: First. | East Lansing : Michigan State University Press, 2025. | Includes bibliographical references.
Identifiers: LCCN 2024038611 | ISBN 9781611865363 (paper) | ISBN 9781609177850 | ISBN 9781628955484
Subjects: LCSH: Grand Traverse Bay Region (Mich.)—Environmental conditions. |
Environmental protection—Michigan—Grand Traverse Bay Region. | Grand Traverse Bay Region (Mich.)—Population.
Classification: LCC GE155.M45 M85 2025 | DDC 977.4/6—dc23/eng/20241112
LC record available at https://lccn.loc.gov/2024038611

Book design by Anastasia Wraight
Cover design by Erin Kirk
Cover art is *Cherries over Grand Traverse Bay*, by Emily Daimler

Visit Michigan State University Press at *www.msupress.org*

CONTENTS

vii   Preface

  1   Chapter 1
      A Migration Story

 11   Chapter 2
      An Indigenous Perspective

 29   Chapter 3
      Welcome Wagon

 53   Chapter 4
      Settlers

 79   Chapter 5
      A Taste of Northern Michigan

113   Chapter 6
      Invasive Species

145   Chapter 7
      America's Most Beautiful Place

173   Chapter 8
      Protecting Paradise

201   Chapter 9
      Eyes to the Skies

229   Chapter 10
      Every Day Is Earth Day

261   Epilogue

267   Acknowledgments

269   Notes

PREFACE

The week before the 2022 Labor Day holiday, I stopped by Habig Garden Shop a few blocks from our home in Indianapolis, on the north side of the city. Habig features a popular fruit and vegetable stand in late summer into early fall. Its prominent location on Eighty-Sixth Street, one of the city's most highly trafficked east-west arteries, pulls in plenty of customers.

With some fresh tomatoes and a half-dozen ears of corn in hand, I queued up in the improvised line, two older women ahead of me, perhaps in their late seventies or early eighties, and a fortyish woman falling in line behind me. The two elders were chatting while having their selections weighed and rung up. While waiting my turn, I overheard one say that she and her husband had just returned to Indy after summering in Michigan. I had been staying at our cabin in Cedar, about fourteen miles northwest of Traverse City, since the third week in April and would be returning on Saturday during the Labor Day weekend, Michigander wannabe that I am. Curious, I interrupted, "Where in Michigan?"

The woman beamed and answered with some obvious distinction, "Why, Leland." That was my opening for a greater conversation. I mentioned the book I was currently promoting—*Sand, Stars, Wind, & Water: Field Notes from Up North*, a nonfiction collection of essays and stories about my time in northern Michigan during the past thirty-six years, an expression of my love for its awe-inspiring outdoor beauty and my longing to live there;

to be an actual Michigander. I then went on about my research project that resulted in my new book—an exploration of the impact of the pandemic, climate change, and tourism on northwest lower Michigan—a story of migration and how the Grand Traverse region is handling such profound change and is just a microcosmic example of what's happening all over Great Lakes coastal areas. The snow-haired woman, second in line, shared, "We just got back from our usual time up in Northport." Not to be left out, the younger woman behind me blurted, "We had our first vacation in Traverse City in July. Went to the Cherry Festival with the kids. Loved it!"

Four of us, strangers all, standing in a random line together buying produce in Indianapolis, and all of us having spent time that summer in northwest lower Michigan. What were the odds? As I mulled over this remarkable coincidence on the drive home, I was struck by what that said about the human pressure on northern Michigan and throughout the Great Lakes region, comprised of eight states and two Canadian provinces, with 4,530 miles of coast.[1] Those who relocated during the pandemic; those coming from areas where climate change was devastating their former homelands, such as those on the West Coast who've endured wildfires, drought, and heat waves, let alone the risk of earthquakes and tsunamis; and the ever-increasing numbers of tourists, especially those visiting the region for the first time and are completely smitten by its wondrous natural resources. Sand, stars, wind, and water indeed.

....

In mid-July 2021, I was giving an author talk at the Leland Township Library. My first book had just been published and I was embarking on an author tour, making the rounds to libraries and other venues throughout Michigan's lower peninsula. The hourlong talk had just concluded. About a dozen people attended; a decent crowd, given it was one of those magical early summer evenings in northern Michigan. Once the question-and-answer session began, before I knew it, something of a townhall meeting broke out. All the attendees, save one, were locals, the majority businesspeople in the area involved in tourist-servicing industries. They were already edgy, and the summer season still had another six weeks to go. Several complained, understandably, about being short-staffed—one of many pandemic impacts, about the swelling numbers of visitors overwhelming tiny but oh-so-lovable Fishtown (Leland's historical harbor area, with its many retail shops, charter boats, and the Manitou Island Transit ferry; it's also another popular name for the village at large), but mostly, about the rudeness of a few too many of the tourists they were accommodating. I listened, fascinated, by how the Q&A had taken on a life of its own. After about ten minutes of the attendees sharing horror stories of what they had experienced thus far this summer, one turned to me and, as if a spokesperson for the rest, asked pleadingly of me: "So what are we supposed to do?"

I paused before answering, then deadpanned, "I didn't write that book." That got a good laugh.

Then the woman who posed the question said, "Well, maybe you should." This conversation would become a consistent theme throughout my author talks across the region, as the tension that existed between making a living from Up North tourism while patiently enduring the ever-swelling number of tourists was quite palpable, as I would come to discover for myself during my stay throughout the entirety of the summer season in 2022.

The book I had just concluded talking about had largely been written during the pandemic, when an outburst of creative energy occurred the world over as part of the phenomenon of the Covid-19 health emergency. During the early days of and throughout the height of the pandemic, I had been the chief executive officer of a K-12 public charter school on the east side of Indianapolis. These were incredibly confusing, fractious, stressful, and exhausting times for all, no less for school leaders. So once the weekend mercifully came around and I felt recovered enough from my workweek, I would go to my mental happy place and write stories and essays about my beloved northern Michigan—also beloved by an ever-growing number of many others. Within a year, I realized that I had accumulated the makings of a book-length work. This was not my original intention, as the writing was therapy during this once unimaginable, prolonged event. Yet at the encouragement of my wife, Janet, and several friends and relatives who knew what I had been up to and had read some sample pieces, I contacted a Michigan publisher in 2020, and that book came to fruition in June 2021. Unbeknownst to me at that time, the die had been cast for another book-writing project, suggested so presciently by that local shopkeeper at the Leland Township Library.

....

Northwest lower Michigan has an amazing coterie of writers who readily support one another in their labors of love. One I've had the good fortune of getting to know is Dave

Dempsey. Dave has made a career of environmental policy work, much of it focused on the Great Lakes. He currently serves as the senior advisor for FLOW: For Love of Water, a nonprofit based in Traverse City specializing in protecting the public's legal right to access and use the Great Lakes. He's also a prolific writer, with books covering Great Lakes conservation, a notable biography of former Michigan Gov. William G. Milliken, and several memoirs relating his affection for the Great Lakes, Lake Huron in particular. Dave and I meet for coffee or breakfast on occasion and talk about politics, the craft of writing, nature (both of us amateur birdwatchers), and environmental issues affecting the region, such as the looming threat of a catastrophic spill from Line 5, the aging oil and natural gas pipeline system running along the bottom of the Straits of Mackinac, and the host of invasive species destabilizing the Great Lakes.

One warm late September morning in 2021, Dave and I met for coffee at Morsels on Front Street, just east of Traverse City's main drag in the downtown area and well within sight of West Grand Traverse Bay. We were sitting outside as a pandemic precaution but also to enjoy another glorious early autumn day in northern Michigan. The Boardman-Ottaway River happened to run just behind Morsels. I'm easily entranced by fish, and the spawning Chinook and coho salmon were putting on a show, intermittently thrashing the surface. Dave looked over his shoulder occasionally when we heard a loud splash, and we would pause to appreciate the *Salmonidae*'s existential drama playing out nearby.

As we talked, he mentioned a curious term I was unfamiliar with: *pandemic and climate refugees*. Immediately, the salmon jumping faded into the background. I wanted to know more.

Dave explained that there had been a steady wave of migrants coming to the Great Lakes regions during the pandemic. These were not distressed, impoverished, endangered people fleeing political strife, violence, pestilence, or catastrophic weather events. They were largely lifestyle migrants, and many of them younger white-collar and tech professionals who realized they could virtually work from anywhere, and employers were allowing them that latitude. Why not in a stunning location away from big cities and their millions of people living together in congested coexistence?

Dave mentioned a friend who had moved back to Michigan due to climate change impacts experienced in northern California. Intensifying in frequency and extent over time, wildfires had become a constant threat to life and property each summer. After years of increasingly enduring sweltering heat, choking wildfire smoke, and keeping a go-bag ready at her front door—which she had to use several times when fleeing her home—enough was enough. And so she returned to her native Ypsilanti in southeast Michigan. Here in the Great Lakes State (a.k.a. the Wolverine State), the infamous Midwestern danger of tornadoes is rather uncommon, earthquakes are unheard of, wildfires infrequent, hurricanes and volcanoes nonexistent, and the long winters and their typically heavy snow, especially the farther north one goes, are just a part of life that also present multiple opportunities for outdoor play (and notably, clearing snow from roads actually occurs in a timely manner in northern Michigan—out of necessity). "When it comes to natural threats, we've got it pretty good up here," Dave remarked.

I continued to chew on the *pandemic and climate refugees* term. I had written about my high regard for the region, especially for its extraordinary scenery and seemingly endless outdoor diversions: The strenuous challenge of climbing a more than three-hundred-foot sand dune for the reward of a striking panoramic view of Lake Michigan. The shining-like-diamonds light of the Milky Way visible to the naked eye (something unviewable in the light-polluted night skies of Indianapolis, where I live but just can't bring myself to call home). Sailing on a nimble nineteen-foot Flying Scot on Lake Michigan with a dear friend and capable skipper, from Leland to the Manitou Islands, and from Charlevoix to Beaver Island, an approximately thirty-two-nautical-mile voyage. And the fresh, clean, cold water of inland lakes and trout-filled streams in the deep woods. People coming to the region for experiences like this, and wanting to stay, was completely understandable. For me, relocating here had been almost an obsession ever since I first saw West Grand Traverse Bay in the mid-1980s, when the region, though popular with tourists yet at a much more manageable rate—not the summer stampede it's become—was still somewhat sleepy. These more recent inputs are worth examining more closely, as they stand to dramatically affect and reshape the region for years to come.

The next time Dave and I had coffee a few weeks later in October, as the fall color slowly made its way south, I mentioned how my curiosity had grown about pandemic and *climate migrants*, which I considered a more accurate, less escape-oriented term in representing the majority of folks currently relocating to the region. (Keep in mind, however, that *climate refugee* may someday become more apropos.) "Somebody should write a book about that. Seems really timely."

Dave looked at me in his usual serious mien. "I agree. Why not you?" It seemed less of a question and more of a challenge, if not an assignment. "You have the unique perspective of being an outsider—with all due respect—but with an appreciation for the insider's point of view, gained over decades of visiting the region." There were just too many signs for me to ignore.

Why not me, indeed.

So here it is.

....

One of the best ways to define something is to first determine what it is not. In this case, this book is not a policy-rich, scientifically data-driven tome guaranteed to cure insomnia. It is, however, my personal exploration of the relocation phenomenon that's occurring in northwest lower Michigan, which exemplifies what's happening all along the "Third Coast"—the Great Lakes region—and in areas across the country where the landscape is magnificent and spacious, the promise of prosperity beckons, and the threats from climate change are minimal, at least for the near future.

Central to my research, I interviewed more than seventy-five experts in their fields, including representatives of some of the many environmental organizations in the Grand Traverse region, public safety officials, winery owners, orchardists, local business owners, government officials, tourism and commerce leaders, outdoorsmen, writers, and members of the Grand Traverse Band of Ottawa and Chippewa Indians—the present-day blood relatives of the region's First Peoples. As I've experienced and heard for myself, the significant, if not irresistible, gravitational pull toward the great outdoors in northern Michigan is indeed both understandable and problematic—right now and in days to come. Moreover, the people who have long called the area home, often over many generations, are some of the kindest, most generous, and caring folks I have ever met, friendliness being another attribute of the region, even among those who openly criticize what they call an "invasion" of outsiders. Which makes for an intriguing complication.

During my nearly six-month stay at our cottage in Cedar in 2022 from late April through early October, my time was largely spent on a book tour and researching this book as well as immersing myself in just being present in the region—going for long strolls through the countryside and along Lake Michigan, hiking woodlands and dune trails, bicycling Leelanau County's hilly terrain, fishing trout streams and inland lakes, and just generally indulging in that Michigander sensibility of outdoor appreciation. But I met many people along the way, most notably during morning walks at Good Harbor Bay beach. My conversations while standing in the wave-washed sand with these fellow beach walkers who, like me, were enchanted by the unparalleled setting, always offered perspective that resonated with me as I constructed this multifaceted story. Migrants all, helping each other along the way.

This book is not about declaring answers with unflinching certitude as to the challenges of the region brought on by the increasing interest in it from "outsiders." It's about immersing the reader in the phenomenon of northwest lower Michigan's current migratory experience now shaping the area and the factors defining it, which necessarily includes some historical context. I will take you along on my journey—interviews, observations, and personal experiences—and you can draw your own conclusions, alongside those I've arrived at through this literary journalism exercise, as to how the people of the region should best proceed to manage the significant change that's underway. And as we all know, change, for humans, generally doesn't come easy.

Shall we?

CHAPTER 1

A MIGRATION STORY

The planet isn't going anywhere. We are.

—George Carlin in *George Carlin's American Dream*

I first laid eyes on Grand Traverse Bay in August of 1986. I was thirty at the time and had just graduated from college, late bloomer in all things that I am, having entered the academy four years earlier while managing a popular bar on the north side of Indianapolis. I had been invited by a good friend and former bartending colleague who lived on Old Mission Peninsula in Traverse City to come check out his part of the world. I drove my new 1987 Honda Civic about four hundred miles north, cruising along listening to the fusion jazz of the Pat Metheny Group and Jon Luc Ponty winding through the car's cassette deck, as the trusty four-banger strained from time to time while climbing the hilly stretch on M-72 west from Kalkaska. As I reached the apex of a ridge while approaching Acme, the suburban town just northeast of Traverse City, suddenly East Grand Traverse Bay appeared. "Whoa," I uttered, dazzled by the sight. I pulled the Civic over to the shoulder, put it in park, and got out, taking in the vast expanse of water in all its bejeweled blueness. Then and there I said aloud to myself, "I think I'm finally home." Having lived in Indiana for twenty years at that time, I never accepted the appellation of "Hoosier." Seeing the bay, and over the course of that introductory weekend, getting a whirlwind tour of Traverse City and Grand Traverse

County, including the Boardman-Ottaway River and Ranch Rudolph, I began to devise a plan to relocate, just like many people who came Up North and saw this magnificent area for the first time. Its splendor was irresistible.

In August 1988, my wife, Janet, and I joined my friend and his wife on a camping outing on South Manitou Island. Janet and I had never been camping together—and she had never been camping before—an adventure in and of itself. We sailed out of Leland, a charming, tourist-attracting, Norman Rockwell-ish, no-stoplight village about twenty-five miles up the Leelanau Peninsula from Traverse City. My friend's wife drove us there on scenic M-22 along West Bay on a postcard-perfect northern Michigan mid-July afternoon. Janet couldn't take her eyes off the closest thing she would ever come to the Mediterranean, the aquamarine and navy-blue waters mesmerizing. "Wow, it's so gorgeous," she would involuntarily repeat along the way.

My buddy, a skilled planner of outdoor diversions, was ready and waiting. The sailboat was prepped for the trip; we just had to stow our gear and back the pickup truck onto the concrete boat launch and slip the boat into the water, and away we went, leaving the protection of Leland Harbor's jetty and entering open water, a sheer thrill for us landlocked Hoosiers. We landed on North Manitou Island first, some twelve nautical miles from Leland, walking the deserted sandy beach beneath the towering dunes, our captain and I scanning for choice stones and fossils, pausing to examine the ones that silently invited us to pick them up for a closer look, determining whether to retain or toss aside, as our wives got better acquainted. For the first time, Janet and I were experiencing island consciousness: that unique state of mind in which the binding of civilization falls away, left behind on the mainland, responsibilities and worries with it, while geography and weather, birds in flight, and the very act of breathing stir one's awareness. In a word, liberation, if only for a precious interlude.

For three days on South Manitou, we hiked about the island, cooled off in Lake Michigan, sailed some more, fished for yellow perch on inland Florence Lake, cooked over open fires, stargazed, and slept like the rocks we pocketed from the beach as the onshore winds whispered in the boughs of the cedar trees surrounding our campsite. Northern Michigan was making quite an impression on me, and central Indiana seemed like a bad dream—both of which I could not shake.

....

During the summers of 1992–1995 we rented a house in Leland, just a block from South Beach off Reynolds Street. We would stay in Leland for two weeks each August: week one was for de-stressing from the demands of careers and raising children, for gradually taking the edge off; week two was a period of unscheduled, spontaneous fun with the emphasis on relaxation. We spent most days on that beach, reading, rockhounding—largely hunting for Petoskey stones, multicolored beach glass, and "Leland Blues," the highly sought sky-blue to blue-green slag from the Leland Lake Superior Iron Company's foundries in the late 1800s[1]—bodysurfing when the tides were up, tossing Nerf footballs and Frisbees while wading in the great lake, dozing while catching rays that we really didn't need, and, inevitably, daydreaming about what it would be like to actually live here; if not in Leland then nearby Traverse City would be just fine.

A few years later, in 2000, we shopped for a slice of northern Michigan heaven with Coldwell Banker Realtor Sam Abood. Sam, a former bartender, drove us to points hither and yon on several house-hunting trips with another Indianapolis couple we introduced to the region. (In years to come, we would stop raving about the wonders of Up North, realizing, belatedly, that we were recruiting more visitation, irrationally wanting, like so many others who discover the area, to keep it to ourselves, along with those who had already made it in before the figurative door could be closed.) After looking at several fixer-uppers in Traverse City—a Boardman-Ottaway Riverfront home that I alone fell in love with at first sight, an unaffordable empty lot on Lake Leelanau, and dozens of other possibilities pushing our modest price range—we landed on a six-hundred square foot cottage set on an acre with one hundred feet of frontage on Spider Lake just southeast of Traverse City. The 450-acre all-sports lake had everything we wanted in a getaway: clean, clear water for fishing, kayaking, swimming, and boating, with nearby woodlands for hiking and birdwatching.

We made an offer on the property. The owners, a couple of retirement age, wanted $140,000; we offered $136,000. They insisted on the asking price. Sam, protecting just my interests as it turned out, told the insistent sellers, "There are a lot of properties for sale in northern Michigan, and we don't have to have this one." Although I loved his hardball approach, this thoroughly upset my partners—most notably the one I cohabited with— who were more than willing to pony up the advertised price. To me, and to Sam, holding out was a matter of principle. But one should never underestimate fate. A year later, the home was still on the market; we repeated the same offer, and they met us halfway. Sold! We now owned that slice of northern Michigan we were after, shared though it was.

Our kids were young adults at the time with other preoccupations that didn't include us (which we viewed as a win-win situation), so Janet and I ended up staying at the cabin five to six times a year by ourselves, spread throughout late spring, summer, and into October, alternating holidays with our partners. (After the first Fourth of July, we gladly relinquished that particular holiday rotation, turning it over permanently to our partners, as we did not find much joy in the battlefield-like munitions resounding throughout the night, our Lhasa Apso wholly concurring, while they reveled in the explosive outburst of patriotism.)

During every visit, without fail, I got that gnawing feeling of never wanting to return to Indy. Most people in central Indiana were quite content living side by side with nearly two million others. To me, with northern Michigan longingly in the rearview mirror, it was suffocating.

So with my wife's reluctant permission, I ended up making several attempts to relocate us to Michigan, landing two jobs there a few years apart, both in healthcare management, both in hospitals: in Chelsea, a bedroom community near Ann Arbor in southeast Michigan, and in Grayling, approximately fifty miles east of Traverse City. Yet in both cases, I had to fold up my tent and return to Indy, Janet unwilling to leave her native state, her grown children, her parents and sisters and extended family, and her long-standing dental hygiene patients. *For better and for worse*, I kept reminding myself. What we do for love.

In 2006 we sold our interest in the Spider Lake property to our partners. And I thought that was it: I was resigned to ending my northern Michigan relocation dream, fatigued by my unsuccessful attempts.

Then came Cedar. Two years later, while we stayed for a week at a rental home in Leland along M-22 just north of town in early June, Janet went seasonal house hunting with Sam, despite my reservations, and they found what would become our current home-away-from-home in Cedar, a small, historically Polish-Catholic town in south-central Leelanau County. It was a 1,200 square foot three-bedroom chalet featuring let-the-sky-in quarter-moon front windows, located on a slight hill and heavily wooded lot, a mile from the long-closed Sugar

Loaf ski resort. Summoned to check it out, I reluctantly entered the house—then instantly felt at home. Forty-eight hours later, our offer was accepted. My visceral connection to northern Michigan—a constellation of spiritual, emotional, psychological, and physical associations—had been restored.

For the past fourteen years we've made good use of our modest retreat, as have our children and their families. Owning property in Leelanau County and being just two miles from the north end of Sleeping Bear Dunes National Lakeshore, with its thirty-five miles of contiguous Lake Michigan shoreline, has been a dream come true. Yet for me, it's never enough: I want to *live* here. Just like many who experience the area. And for me, even in winter. Like, well, some people. That hasn't happened, and most likely never will, due to marital circumstances previously noted. However, thanks to Dave Dempsey's provocative challenge to pursue an exploration of the changes that are overtaking northwest lower Michigan, with the most predominant driving influences of the pandemic, climate change, and tourism, I spent most of nearly six months—from mid-April to early October 2022—working out of Cedar conducting research. It also gave me the chance to experience firsthand what it's like to actually be a Michigander in this region as spring transitions into the busy summer, and to observe more closely behaviors that the locals tend to complain about from outsiders, as well as that of the general population itself.

Waking up each morning in Cedar was paradisical. From late April and throughout the month of May, I frequently heard new birdsong in our yard and throughout the neighborhood, the migrating birds returning in waves. One chilly morning during the last week in April, I poked my head outside and noticed tiny birds moving through our lot, zigzagging from tree to tree. When I dialed in my Nikon 10×42 binoculars, I spotted scads of ruby- and golden-crowned kinglets. A few days later, I heard the haunting stop-and-listen song of multiple wood thrushes while out on a walk in the neighborhood. In early May, the buoyant call of several rose-breasted grosbeaks filled the air. Then, a week or so later, flashes of the fiery orange feathers of Baltimore orioles in flight became common sightings, as they returned to nest here. Meanwhile, numerous warbler species moved through the area as if in shifts, some traveling farther north, passing through on their migratory route; others, like the sweet-singing American redstart, staying to nest. Eastern wood-pewees took up residence, their unmistakable *pee-a-wee* calls starting up just before sunrise and lasting into dusk. The sandhill cranes arrived in noisy numbers, their unmistakable alien croaking inviting all below to search the skies for them, the seven-foot-wing-spanned birds often landing in nearby farm fields in huge numbers for an overnight stay. And on and on.

Northern Michigan has many picturesque small towns, from north of Grand Rapids right up to Mackinaw City at the tip of lower Michigan's "mitten," and across to Lake Huron in the east and Lake Michigan in the west. Idyllic places where children grow up surrounded by nature, and parents just might worry less. On the Leelanau Peninsula alone, scenic towns like Suttons Bay, Northport, Leland, Glen Arbor, and Empire imprint an elusive, deeply desired contentment on visiting city folk. During my nearly six-month stay, every time I returned to Leelanau County and drove up our gravel driveway, then paused on the front deck, day or night, and looked up into the crowns of the sixty- and seventy-foot sugar maple trees and the sky beyond, I felt completely at home. *Home.* The soulful locus where one can ultimately just be, the place that speaks to us at our core, and all that factors into that sensibility, the obvious and the mysterious. Finding this special sense of place is a quest we are all on, at one time or another in our lives, something of a genetic existential imperative. Once found, keeping it the way we like it—sometimes in the face of momentous change—is a never-ending preoccupation, subject, of course, to one's interpretation of home.

....

On Monday, September 26, 2022, I drive from Cedar to pick up Janet and Benny, her Pomeranian (emphasis on "her"), at the Cherry Capital Airport, about a half-hour trip. Their 9:30 p.m. arrival on a Delta jet from Detroit, the flight originating in Indy, is on time. Traverse City is dead, in the best sense of the word, with scant vehicles on the street. My drive from Cedar is unencumbered, and I sail into the airport unimpeded, immediately finding a spot in the short-term parking lot, and walk across the street and enter the terminal. Ten minutes later we're driving out of the airport. That simple.

Throughout the week she's here with me we go for daily walks. Among them, I take her to the four-mile Boardman Lake Loop Trail, just completed in July. For years we had walked the two-mile leg of the trail that runs along the east side of the lake, starting at the Traverse Area District Library. Now the circuit is complete. Of course, each day we spend several hours at a time at Good Harbor Bay beach, interrupting our reading or contemplation or dozing with intermittent strolls along the shoreline. Fall is here in its earliest stage, the maples starting to show some flash of color, the mercury beginning to loosen from its summer hold, the winds now up more often, signaling the seasonal transition, and Lake Michigan more frequently agitated. Change is in the air, quite literally. Intensified by the profundity of autumn, looking at the visible edge of this inland sea from the mainland beach is indeed like gazing into infinity, a perspective unavailable to me in Indianapolis; even the city's sky has its limits, the Milky Way imperceptible (as it is to nearly 80 percent of North Americans[2]). In central Indiana, once the beginning of the westward tallgrass prairie, such a bracing view is now obstructed by mile after mile of dense neighborhoods, acres and acres of concrete and asphalt, retail strips and malls, warehouse-sized schools, stadiums. What cities require. Beyond the Circle City's suburbs, corn and soybean fields stretch to and beyond the horizon. This immensity of citified civilization is precisely why I'm here, now, in Leelanau County. In this, I am not alone.

The spell is broken when we leave Good Harbor Bay beach for the last time this year. I pause at the trailhead for one more lingering say-goodbye look; I always do. Once back at the house, we resume the several days labor of tidying up and getting ready to decamp. Nearly six months of bachelor occupancy demands closer scrutiny than usual in closing the cabin. Before Janet arrived, I went so far as to wipe down the inside of the refrigerator, trying to make the very best impression, though I left the redworm and earthworm bait containers alone. After so many years of me keeping live bait fresh in the fridge, a once clandestine maneuver, she's become accustomed to seeing it there and no longer flinches at the sight.

While touring the house one last time, I pause to feel the emptiness of each room and the spectral aura left behind by our loved ones who spent time there this year. Then I walk the property, saying quiet goodbyes to the trees, the birds who are heading south and those staying for the winter, such as the chickadees, titmice, nuthatches, blue jays, and the varieties of woodpeckers: the downy, hairy, red-bellied, northern flicker, and especially the striking pileated woodpeckers. Lock the shed, lock the house, start the car, take a deep breath, sigh, take in this bittersweet moment, then drive off in gratitude.

Four hundred miles later, once back in Marion County, southbound on multi-laned Interstate 69—a poorly disguised dragstrip—then onto the I-465 beltway—a virtual fifty-three-mile racetrack—my aggravation at returning to the city becomes a full-blown gale. We're once again exposed to reckless, distracted, rude scofflaws comingled with thousands more who just want to get to wherever they're going in one piece. Where's the Buddha when you need him? Or an Indianapolis Metropolitan Police Department officer with a radar gun.

Finally arriving at our house on Broadway Street in Nora, our northern Marion County neighborhood, we spend the next hour lugging in our gear and putting it away, sorting through the mail, filling up bird feeders, watering the flower gardens, reorienting ourselves. We're tired. I'm cranky. I take a shower. Then we sit on the back deck, me sipping a beer, Janet with Benny on her lap. The two of them are glad to be here. Me, well, not so much. It will take a few days to settle back into a routine. It's not that I don't want to be here with my wife; it's that I don't want to be here in Indy. Or any other large metropolitan area. Northern Michigan calling.

....

During my lengthy stay in Cedar, I would check the goings-on in Indy on my iPhone before bedtime—an always sobering exercise. The headlines suggested a shooting gallery in progress, that perhaps yellow crime scene tape should be permanently wrapped around the city. "Shooting, attempted robbery leaves Indianapolis funeral director dead."[3] "Attendees pepper sprayed after fight breaks out during Indy funeral."[4] "Indianapolis: Dutch commando dies after shooting outside US hotel."[5] Even the Starbucks on Monument Circle has closed due to safety concerns.[6] And then there's this: "Indiana announces 'Air Quality Action Day' for Sunday."[7] High ozone level warnings are broadcast, which children and older adults and those compromised by respiratory issues should especially heed. Summertime in the city.

Of course, these days such seemingly interminable problems are just part of the program for every major metropolitan area in the country; it's not just Indianapolis. And those that have the wherewithal to make a move are thinking twice about staying put in such painful places.

As for me, there are extenuating personal circumstances I must accept. My wife's parents reside in Indianapolis. Our children and six grandchildren are here. Janet is still working (although she could undoubtedly do so remotely if she pushed it). And, unlike me, my wife is no fan of colder, longer, snowier winters, an annual victim of Seasonal Affective Disorder. In the face of such a gravely disordered urban existence (to be clear, this is my unshared-as-a-couple personal view), along with the irresistible pull of the magnificent natural beauty of northern Michigan, nonetheless, the above-noted factors overrule. So for now, it's Basecamp Indy until spring (with a monthlong timeout on the Gulf Coast of Florida in the winter for morale purposes). But for others who can make a much cleaner, permanent northbound break, they aren't hesitating. How many more will migrate north to the Traverse City region in the next several decades? Is the "welcome mat" out for everyone so inclined to relocate? What impact are these newcomers having on the area—on its economy, culture, and environment? Many questions remain. Yet the answers are certainly beginning to appear.

This microcosmic look at northwest lower Michigan in the face of a sea change exemplifies what's happening now throughout the Great Lakes, as well as in other areas of the country renowned for their outdoor appeal. This loose migration is attracting those desiring a lifestyle change who are familiar with the Grand Traverse region through previous tourist experiences or repeated seasonal stays. Notably, this relocation movement has been sharply driven by the pandemic. It's also beginning to be influenced by climate change impacts felt most acutely along the West Coast (flooding, extreme heat, wildfires), in the Southwest (drought, wildfires), and in the Southeast (rising seas, more tropical storms, and hurricanes).[8] And it includes those natives boomeranging their way back home. They have come, are coming, and will continue to come. Their stories vary, the factors are many, and the reality is one that just can't be ignored.

CHAPTER 2

AN INDIGENOUS PERSPECTIVE

As Original Man walked the Earth, he named all of the ni-bi' (water).
He identified all the rivers, streams, ponds, lakes and oceans. . . . These
are the veins of Mother Earth. Water is her life blood.

—Edward Benton-Banai, *The Mishomis
Book: The Voice of the Ojibwe*

In 1990 I was a journalism graduate student at Indiana University—Indianapolis. In one course, I embarked on a research project on the Miami Indians of Indiana's attempt to regain their tribal recognition from the federal government. I can't recall my rationale in deciding on this subject, although as a white man, I did—and still do—have an abiding interest in Native American history and culture. Back then, I had read quite a few books about the near genocide/cultural annihilation of the First Peoples in North America, such as *Black Elk Speaks: Being the Life Story of a Holy Man of the Oglala Sioux* by John G. Neihardt, *Bury My Heart at Wounded Knee: An Indian History of the American West* by Dee Brown, and *Custer Died for Your Sins: An Indian Manifesto* by Vine Deloria Jr. I had grown up with the contrived, acceptably racist, Manifest Destiny–infused, white man cowboy hero movies of John Wayne and his ilk. I had seen *Dances with Wolves* in the theater, the Western starring Kevin Costner released in 1990 that appeared to be a decent attempt at a more accurate portrayal of Native American life and the U.S. Cavalry's brutality in pushing Natives to the brink of extinction. But all this was secondary to the fact that I had never met a Native American, an authentic interaction that was essential to the legitimacy of my research goals, and no less, my personal development.

This changed in the fall of 1990 when I drove up U.S. 31 to Peru, Indiana, about seventy miles north of my Indianapolis home, and made a cold call on the Miami Nation of Indians of Indiana's tribal office. There I met Lora Siders, the office administrator and tribal historian. Thanks to her, I later interacted with several key members of the tribe, notably Tribal Chairman Ray White and spiritual leader Wap Shing, and was taken on a tour of Miami historic sites, including weathered cemeteries and the Seven Pillars along the Mississinewa River, a remarkable limestone formation carved by the river's currents over thousands of years. This had served as a sacred space where the Miamis traded and conducted council meetings and is used yet today for tribal ceremonies. A decade later, I invited members of the tribe to spend a day at a summer camp for children with bleeding disorders at YMCA Camp Carson in Princeton, Indiana, which I coordinated for the Indiana Hemophilia & Thrombosis Center. The Miami participants brought and played their tribal drum, had a linguistics expert teach the campers Miami words and common phrases, and made dream catchers with the kids during a craft session. My long-ago graduate school research project and its lingering effects had certainly influenced the way I *see* America, in that its Indigenous Peoples were no longer invisible to me. Yet they unfortunately seem to be to many white folks I know, and are considered something of a novelty, wrongly, whenever the subject comes up.

The Anishinaabek, Michigan's Original People

As I undertook the research for this book, it made great sense to me to include voices from the Grand Traverse Band of Ottawa and Chippewa Indians (GTB) as the First Peoples in northwest lower Michigan. My initial contact was with JoAnne Cook, chief appellate court judge for the band and an outreach educator. Cook sometimes teaches an adult education course at Northwestern Michigan College, "The History of the Anishinaabek." Her historical overview incorporates cultural and spiritual aspects of the band, and she covers the legal issues involving treaties (which are still ongoing) leading up to tribal life in modern time and the efforts to restore and advance Native traditions. She is also in demand for presentations to civic groups and libraries throughout the region, most notably in the six adjoining counties that comprise the band's service area: Benzie, Charlevoix, Grand Traverse, Leelanau, Manistee, and Antrim. According to Cook, the GTB has approximately 4,600 tribal members.

Cook, fifty-five, grew up in Peshabestown just south of Omena, toward the tip of the Leelanau Peninsula. When we speak by phone in mid-June 2022, it is not so much as interviewer to interviewee, but reversed somewhat, as teacher to student.

Historians have determined that the Anishinaabek—meaning the "Original People" who claim Algonquin heritage—have been in the Grand Traverse region for thousands of years, Cook says. They migrated to the Great Lakes region from northeastern North America coastal areas, following the St. Lawrence River inland.[1] Bemusedly, she mentions that researchers recently found proof of Native presence in the Grand Traverse region reaching back thirteen thousand years ago. Yet Anishinaabe oral tradition pushes that estimate even farther back, she notes, to "time immemorial." She adds, "Even though we know the story, science is catching up with us."

Early into our conversation I ask about the GTB's concerns about environmental threats to the region, exacerbated by the influx of visitors and relocators. Cook responds by bringing up the Anishinaabe creation story and how humans came to be placed on Earth as the last species by the Creator. "So then, what does that mean?" she asks as a prompt to provide the answer: "You know your place. Our whole philosophy is about living in balance, and that means with everyone and everything in creation: animals, plants, water." Among the Anishnaabek, respect for animal life was honored long before such modern-day progressive movements espousing love of Mother Earth and all its creatures. "All Anishinaabe people believe and know that she is our mother," Cook emphasizes.

She asks if I have read or heard of *The Mishomis Book: The Voice of the Ojibway*, written by Eddie Benton-Banai, an Anishinaabe Ojibway, and notably, one of the founders of the American Indian Movement in the late 1960s. I had not. She explains that Benton-Banai wrote it in the style of a children's book for all his people, members of the Three Fires Confederacy, which includes the Ojibwe/Ojibwa (Chippewa), Ottawa (Odawa), and Potawatomi (Bodowadomi).

In the origin story, Earth experienced a worldwide flood, which sounds remarkably like the story of the cataclysm in the Christian Old Testament's book of Genesis. "The original people turned away from our way of life and started to war and not to take care and be good Anishinaabe. So, the Earth was destroyed—flooded—and all of the First Peoples were gone," Cook relates. As I, she thinks such uncanny parallel cross-cultural stories are "amazing." After the flood, Turtle Island—a new Earth built upon the shell of a great turtle—was created.

I purchase a copy of *The Mishomis Book*, and as I discover, it's a must read for anyone interested in Anishinaabe tradition, mythology, culture, and history. I pay particular attention to the Seven Fires prophecies. These prophecies predate the European arrival in North America and were revealed to the Anishinaabek before they arrived in the Great Lakes region by seven visiting prophets. As written by Benton-Banai, the Seventh Fire itself predicts a new people's emergence, described as the Light-skinned Race:

> It is at this time that the Light-skinned Race will be given a choice between two roads. If they choose the right road, then the Seventh Fire will light the Eighth and Final Fire—an eternal fire of peace, love, brotherhood and sisterhood. If the Light-skinned Race makes the wrong choice of roads, then the destruction which they brought with them in coming to this country will come back to them and cause much suffering and death to all the Earth's people.[2]

The Ojibwe and other Indigenous North American people have interpreted these two roads as being technology and spiritualism. Benton-Banai continues: "They feel that the road to technology represents a continuation of the headlong rush to technological development. This is the road that has led modern society to a damaged and seared Earth. . . . The road to spirituality represents the slower path that the traditional Native people have traveled and are now seeking again."[3]

Cook tells me that we are now in the time of the Seventh Fire prophecy. This second-to-last Anishinaabe prophecy says that the light-skinned race will approach the First Peoples wanting to learn more about Native life—which is already happening. Says Cook, "Lighting the Eighth Fire will be dependent on the choice that the non-Native people choose: the road of technology or the road of saving our Earth and understanding the importance of it." It appears that we may well be transitioning now to the time of the Eighth prophecy.

I ask her what the band thinks about all the people coming to the area, not just ever-increasing numbers of tourists but those who have moved here during the pandemic and now, though a trickle, due to climate change in their previous states of residence. "We've had concerns about that for about six hundred years now," she quips, laughing with me as I recognize the shortsightedness of my question. She notes, "We lost our land in Leelanau County because people kept moving in." Then she adds, "You're not going to stop the influx of people here. But the more you can educate them on the region and the history of where they're moving to is really beneficial."

Cook is certainly paying attention to the increased migration to the region. This correlates with a rising interest in newcomers wanting to learn about the history of the Anishinaabek, especially as it relates to Indigenous culture's innate reverence for the environment.

Documentarians covering environmental stories pertaining to northern Michigan are now including the Anishinaabe perspective. "When I was growing up, that was not happening," Cook says of this recent development over the last decade or so. The new sign project along the stretch of the Boardman-Ottaway River—a.k.a. the Ottaway River to the Anishinaabek—that winds through Traverse City is indicative of the upsurge in interest in Native history by non-Indigenous people, whether long-time locals, newcomers, or visitors.

The Kchi Wiikwedong Anishinaabe History Project (named after the original place name given by the region's first inhabitants, the Kitchi Wikweedong Odawa; Kitchi Wikweedong translates to "around the big bay") is being spearheaded by Emily Modrall, forty-two, who is notably not Indigenous but does hold a doctorate in Mediterranean archeology from the University of Pennsylvania. Modrall initially got involved in the project when she noticed three peculiar trail markers within the Traverse City limits. The markers, numbering 31–33 in Traverse City, are simple gray plaques mounted on white-painted stones that read, "OLD INDIAN TRAIL CADILLAC TO TRAVERSE CITY." This triggered her archeologist's curiosity, and she soon discovered that there are thirty-three such markers running from Lake Mitchell in Cadillac to West Grand Traverse Bay in Traverse City, the last one located near West End Beach along the Traverse Area Recreation and Transportation Trail. Frank Ettawageshik, United Tribes of Michigan Executive

Director, placed them there in the eighties as part of the 1987 Michigan Sesquicentennial Celebration. "This trail was part of an intercontinental transportation system where we transported trade goods," Ettawageshik told 9&10 News in January 2022.[4] Although no longer navigable, the Old Indian Trail was part of an extensive trail network throughout Michigan used for thousands of years by the Anishinaabek.[5]

According to Modrall, the markers were "overlooked acknowledgements that there is a longer history to Traverse City, that things happened here before Captain (Harris) Boardman showed up and cut down all the trees in the 1840s." The new signs are bilingual, in English and Anishinaabemowin, the Indigenous language of the First Peoples in the region. The first marker was installed at the Traverse City–owned Brown Bridge Quiet Area in late 2023, and others were put in place in Leelanau and Grand Traverse counties in the months following. To be overlooked no more.

We Are on Native Land

While enjoying a comfort food lunch at the Cedar Tavern in May 2022 with Gary Howe, a former Traverse City Commissioner, I mention my interest in the region's Native Americans and their rightful place in the migration story of northern Michigan. He immediately refers me to Mark Wilson, a former Grand Traverse Band of Ottawa and Chippewa Indians Tribal Council member. Wilson, forty-two, served two consecutive four-year terms with the band and was elected to the Traverse City Commission in November 2021. He owns his own business, New Leonard Media, in which he creates "audio and video content for environmentally and socially responsible organizations." He's also been a DJ for many years and is an afficionado of hip-hop.

I meet him at his home in the Traverse Heights Neighborhood on a sunny mid-June morning. We walk back to his garage, where his Chevy Volt plug-in hybrid is housed, then enter a studio in the back of the building for our conversation.

Wilson has a thoughtful, serious demeanor. Early on it becomes clear that he's passionate about his Anishinaabe heritage. It doesn't take long before he shares that everyone on his father's side had been removed from their homes and sent to Catholic boarding schools. "This was a public policy effort to assimilate all of the Native peoples across the continent," he explains. Wilson tells me that the last boarding school in Michigan closed in the eighties (and one of the last to close in the country), Holy Childhood of Jesus in Harbor Springs,[6] which astonishes me: that was only yesterday. I confess my Catholic background and long-time struggle with the church in trying to stay Catholic, with so many embarrassments to contend with, such as the ongoing priest pedophilia scandals and the church's role in trying to separate Native American children from their culture through religious boarding schools. He says sympathetically, "That's okay, I'm half Sicilian and attended Mass many times." I appreciate the grace shown, but it still doesn't feel okay.

Wilson goes into the background of the formation of the GTB, notably the achievement of reclaiming tribal recognition by the federal government in 1980, which was wrongly terminated in 1872 by then-Secretary of the Interior Columbus Delano.[7] Now federally recognized, the band is governed by a seven-member tribal council and chairman that oversee the GTB's economic development, which centers upon legalized gaming which, in turn, provides crucial financial independence. "The resort and gaming operations are the economic engines for our tribe because we don't have a tax base," Wilson comments. The tax base is small due to the loss of land over the years, with just twelve acres owned by the GTB in Peshawbestown in the early eighties, that parcel now the site of tribal administrative buildings. Today the GTB owns Turtle Creek Casino & Hotel, Leelanau Sands Casino & Lodge, and Grand Traverse Resort and Spa, along with approximately one thousand acres of agricultural land.[8]

At this point he mentions the "second coming of the Removal Act." This urban relocation program began in 1953, continuing the diaspora of the Indigenous population by encouraging them to participate in this voluntary relocation to large metropolitan areas, ostensibly for career training, yet far from their ancestral homelands. The Bureau of Indian Affairs also promised to assist with housing and employment. Wilson's father participated, attending a Native American trade school in Milwaukee, where he met Wilson's mother. According to the United States Census Bureau, prior to the urban relocation program, just 8 percent of American Indians lived in cities. By 2000, that number had risen to nearly 64 percent.[9]

Wilson's father eventually became a conservation officer for the band during a time that was "pretty dangerous," he says. In the eighties and nineties, unfriendly whites were known to say, "Spear an Indian and save a fish," he recalls. (In fact, at that time this malicious slogan could be found on bumper stickers throughout the region.) This racist attitude came from fears that Native Americans would decimate the fishing in Lake Michigan once treaty rights were reaffirmed in federal court.

As a child, Wilson dreamed of being a professional skateboarder. "But I realized I was too afraid to do what it really takes," he says, smiling for the first time in our discussion. During his teenage years he became attracted to hip-hop music. "I learned how hip-hop as an art form is an American subculture that actually helps give identity to those who have had their cultural identity stripped from them involuntarily," whether in the case of Native Americans, through African slavery, or for those emigrating to the United States. Hip-hop appeals to him because, he maintains, "It's an inclusive culture, as well as a socio-political movement."

Wilson is conflicted about those who migrate to the region, yet he's refreshingly honest about his reservations. He tries to be "inclusive" and doesn't want to be a "gatekeeper." He tells a story that exemplifies the word-of-mouth referral chain that has in no small part contributed to the area's growth. "A good neighbor ended up here twenty years ago," he recounts. "She fell in love with it. Met a gentleman from New Jersey and moved him here and they had a couple of babies. He brought his brother. His brother met a girl from here, married her, then his brother brought his cousin and she's getting married to a gentleman from here. It's just the way it is." He adds, "I love all of them and believe they have a right to be here."

He suggests another category to characterize some of the migrants coming into the region: "There are cost-of-living refugees here too. Yet people complain about how expensive it is here." He comments that his modest middle-class home in Traverse City "is a million-dollar house in Silicon Valley." Now that working remotely has boomed and is likely here to stay, as accelerated dramatically by the pandemic, those white-collar workers no longer have to struggle to pay exorbitant prices on leased or purchased homes, for example, on the West Coast and in large metropolitan areas such as Chicago. Wilson observes, "People flee to towns like this where they can have plenty of space. We see them at our casinos. Why be an average rich person when you can be a pretty big fish here?"

When Wilson ran for the city commission, a long-time local family signed his petition to get him on the ballot. "They were so proud of how long their family had been here," he recalls. "Abraham Lincoln himself gave their great-great grandfather their lot on Old

Mission Peninsula." He holds my gaze and says, "You realize that was a stolen lot. Right up to the water's edge was our treaty territory. Those peninsulas [including Leelanau] were meant to be held in trust for tribal allotments [per the Treaty of 1836]. We gave up fourteen million acres of land [in the Michigan Territory] with certain stipulations: that our way of subsistence remained and that we agreed to reside in certain areas on our reservations; in 1836 part of that was Old Mission Peninsula."

He mentions the renegotiation of that treaty, the Treaty of 1855 (a.k.a. the Treaty of Detroit), when around that time many of the Anishinaabek on Old Mission Peninsula moved across Grand Traverse Bay to Omena on the Leelanau Peninsula. "And over time those lots were stolen as well." By 1900, the vast majority of the eighty-seven-thousand-acre reservation the Ottawa and Chippewa Nations were allotted in Leelanau and Antrim County per the Treaty of 1855 had been illegally acquired without compensation by land speculators and white settlers, made possible by Congressional acts and corrupt Bureau of Indian Affairs agents, then whittling the promised land down to seven hundred acres.[10] Wilson says that in the 1860s and 1870s, the Indians in the area traveled south for the winter to their seasonal hunting grounds, as they had for thousands of years. When they returned, their land had homes being built upon it by white settlers because the Indians had "abandoned" their parcels. "Simply put, our land had been stolen," Wilson declares.

In light of this disastrous treaty history, Wilson notes an interesting contemporary twist. When winter comes, many of those who have retired to northern Michigan for magnificent late spring through summer weather turn into "snowbirds," leaving the region in the fall to winter in Florida and other warmer southern destinations. He says the inside joke among the band is, "I'm not sitting in their house here going, 'You abandoned your lot. You haven't been here for eight months—where've you been?'" He adds, "We want our day in court with the federal government and we want our settlement." In 2021, the GTB began a process to file a lawsuit against the United States government for compensation for the stolen land, based upon the worth of the land at that time plus interest. The first step in that process is to obtain a congressional reference bill to enable the band to sue the federal government.[11]

I mention that a friend of mine's great-great grandfather landed in Good Harbor Bay around 1855 and secured a large parcel of land—several thousand acres—as a homesteader. All that property was eventually sold off over the years, a point of considerable regret among the current-day family members, who are well aware of the worth of land in Leelanau County in today's skyrocketing real estate market. Wilson connects the dots for me: "They are definitely the benefactors of stolen land if they're out there seven generations. And they may not realize that at all." And once again he magnanimously says, "It's okay." Yet clearly, winning a tribal settlement would go a long way in righting this longstanding egregious wrong.

Wilson tells me he's interviewed people who want to serve on various neighborhood board committees and public service commissions. "I read their letters, and they say that they moved here in 2018. Well, that's cool; you want to get involved. But then sometimes my head is like, you just got here, and you want to have influence on what we do here. But at the same time, there's nobody else putting their name in the hat [to serve]. Meanwhile, 2018 is four years ago, so they've been here long enough to say, 'I like it, but. . . . '"

When asked how his people, the Anishinaabek, are regarded in the region they have called home for thousands of years, he gives his own personal account. "I'm Native American, so my skin is slightly browner than yours. I'm half Sicilian and have a lot of my mother's genetic qualities, so I don't look as Native as my father or sisters." He often hears that he "doesn't look Indian," especially while on the GTB reservation. But when he was younger, that distinctly wasn't the case. "The kids at Silver Lake Elementary School and West Middle School were sure to remind me that I wasn't white."

Importantly, Wilson is the first person of color to serve on the Traverse City Commission. This step, he says, is indicative of the effort the community is putting forth to recognize diversity. The success of the band's two casinos, Turtle Creek and Leelanau Sands, helps to ease how Native Americans are viewed by the predominantly white population in the region. According to U.S. 2020 Decennial Census data, Leelanau County is 90 percent white (20,039 citizens out of 22,301); Grand Traverse County 91 percent (86,508 out of 95,238). The Native American population of Leelanau County is 672 (3 percent); Grand Traverse County is 969 (1 percent). Moreover, the biracial population of Leelanau County is 1,100; Grand Traverse County is 5,249; for both counties, this would include a significant number of people with Native American ancestry.[12]

According to Wilson, the GTB employs approximately two thousand people, and notably, 2 percent of gaming revenues go to local units of government. The tribal council entertains requests for grant funding from the area's nonprofits, as submitted through local government, and decides on these requests. He says, "So now that we're seen as a funding source, I think people treat us differently." Though racial discrimination "is not as bad as it was," it exists, nonetheless. He maintains, "It's just not in your face."

Once a wrong-way teenager, Wilson dropped out of high school, got involved with drugs, became suicidal. But he found the strength to turn his life around. He obtained his GED, attended community college, and recently earned a master's degree in public administration from Central Michigan University. Proudly, he notes, his sons will be the first in his family to graduate high school. Wilson has set an example for them as he continues to rise in his leadership roles, first with the GTB and now for Traverse City. His own internal migration—from down-and-out to being elected to prominent leadership positions for the band and the city—is in its own special category of surviving and now thriving, and is a role model for his sons, tribal members, and the people he serves throughout the region.

One of the most challenging aspects of serving on the city commission involved the decision to reconstruct Grandview Parkway to handle the increasing traffic, especially during the busy summer season, and introducing more crosswalks for pedestrian safety in traversing the busy thoroughfare. The nearly $25 million project, completed in October 2024, was funded and overseen by the state of Michigan in cooperation with Traverse City government, as it involved rebuilding a section of U.S. 31/M-72/M-37.[13] "Some people dream of this utopia where we all walk and bike everywhere we go and then the parkway is completely gone and what used to be the parkway is now a park," says a pragmatic Wilson. "That's beautiful, but. . . ."

How to slow-grow Traverse City, and in turn, Grand Traverse County, and handle urban sprawl in the process are among his preoccupations as a city commissioner. Given his leadership role, he is also front and center on the dispute pertaining to the height of buildings in the city, now limited to sixty feet/six stories, which could block precious views of the bay and increase density, versus spreading outward to preserve water views yet contributing to sprawl.[14] Looming in the background is how the region will manage growth in the coming decades—and developing a sense of urgency in planning for it. Wilson says the only obstacle that currently exists to moving Up North is nothing new but is more difficult to surmount: affordability. "But the people are still coming, and so we should be prepared for it."

I part company with Wilson after an hourlong conversation. As we leave his garage studio and reenter the bright sunshine, he asks me to wait a minute. He goes inside his house and returns with a copy of *The Eagle Returns: The Legal History of the Grand Traverse Band of Ottawa and Chippewa Indians* by Matthew L. M. Fletcher, a law professor at Michigan State University, who is also the director of the Indigenous Law and Policy Center there. Wilson keeps copies on hand for those he meets who show a willingness to learn more about the history of the Anishinaabek and what they have gone through since the incursion of European settlers in the region leading up to present day. "This might be useful to you," he says as he makes a present of the book and shakes my hand, the passionate advocate for Indigenous rights now smiling warmly. There is no word for goodbye in Anishinaabemowin; I do hope our paths cross again.

Michigami Morning

On Friday, June 3, 2022, I stop by the Arthur Duhamel Marina in Peshawbestown, just off M-22, home of the Ed & Cindi John Treaty Fish Company. I'm hoping to schedule a ride on their Lake Michigan (i.e., *Michigami* in Ojibwe, meaning "Great Water") commercial fishing boat to learn more about their work. It's about 4 p.m. and Cindi just sold five pounds of fresh-caught lake trout to a regular customer who, squeezing by me in the doorway, "highly recommends" I pick some up as well. After I introduce myself, Cindi—apron on, filet knife in Latex-gloved hand—tells me that this is their busy season, when they go out on Grand Traverse Bay twice daily to set and retrieve their gill nets. They also have a booth at the Sara Hardy Farmers Market in downtown Traverse City each Saturday. Yet kindly indulging me in my request, she promises to look into getting permission for me "to go out on the boat." She keeps talking as she quickly guts and cleans her way through a bin containing large fresh-caught lake trout, that razor-sharp knife making me nervous—for her. But she's working on well-practiced muscle memory and welcomes the unexpected company as she expertly slices away. Fifteen minutes later I excuse myself, but not before I buy a pound of just-fileted lake trout for $10. That night I dine like a king. The trout is succulent, flaking easily with my fork. In foodie parlance, this is a splendid trout-to-table experience.

Weeks go by. Then on the evening of Tuesday, July 19, I receive an unexpected text message from Cindi, inviting me to come out for an interview the following morning. I report to the marina just before 10 a.m. The Johns, who are in their mid-sixties, pull up in their nothing-fancy pickup truck, so common and essential in northern Michigan. Cindi says hello and promises to be right back as she disappears inside the marina's processing building to retrieve something, and Ed waves as he heads directly to their fishing boat, the forty-six-foot *Linda Sue*, named after Cindi's deceased sister. Their son, Alex, thirty-two, visiting from Atlanta, Georgia, pulls up in another pickup truck and introduces himself. "Do you want anything to drink?" he politely asks, as he's making a run to a nearby convenience store. I'm good.

As I wait for Cindi and Ed to join me for our interview, I walk over to the docked *Linda Sue* and gaze out into the bay. Overhead it's partly cloudy, the prevailing southwest summer wind is moderate, kicking up two- to three-foot waves, nothing the *Linda Sue* and her crew can't handle. Cindi approaches and instructs me to go ahead and board the *Linda Sue*. Although I did request this opportunity when we first met, I was under the impression that we would be interviewing onshore today. Apparently, there's some confusion, as another writer, "some local reporter," had requested a boating experience with the Johns, which had already been cleared by the band's Natural Resources Department. Realizing the mix-up, she calls the Grand Traverse Band's conservation officer, who pulls up to the marina in his truck within minutes. He checks my identification and approves the boat ride. "Enjoy," he says, quickly driving off, one and done in mere minutes. I haven't exactly dressed for a fishing outing, wearing a golf shirt and shorts on this seasonably wonderful northern Michigan summer morning, but hey, who cares; we're goin' fishin'.

The crew of four, including Alex and me, motor out of the marina and away from the protection of the seawall. As we chat, Cindi warns me of "a bit of a chop" and recommends that I sit in the cabin with Ed as he navigates out to their fishing grounds, about twenty minutes away. Ed, a lean man who doesn't look his age—life on the lake has been good to him—keeps his eyes fixed on the water ahead, saying little. I do the same. The loud hum of the diesel marine engine and the sound of the displaced water streaming by the hull are soothing, and talk is nonessential to this meditative moment. Besides, the Johns have a job to do, and I'm happy just to be along for the ride. I deeply inhale the clean air and take stock of being out on the bay. I have never been seasick, and this trip doesn't break that stretch of good fortune.

The boat's pilothouse is up front, with a tent-like awning covering the fish harvesting workspace immediately behind it. Large oval and rectangular dark gray bins, some filled with shaved ice for keeping the upcoming catch fresh, surround us. On the *Linda Sue's* starboard side is a hydraulic gill net lifter for reeling the netted fish up from the depths and into the boat. Ed and his son wear green foul weather bib pants; Cindi is in orange. Her hair is pulled up, ready for work. Once on the fishing grounds, Ed will keep the boat steady, and Cindi and Alex will handle the fish retrieval. "It's a wonderful, one-of-a-kind boat," Cindi says with pride. "A naval engineer from Cheboygan designed it."

While preparing for this morning's harvest, Cindi provides me details about the Johns' commercial fishing way of life. She views talking with reporters and writers as their family's opportunity, if not obligation, to be goodwill ambassadors for the band. About halfway out to their fishing grounds on West Bay—the location of which I am asked not to reveal—I leave the pilothouse and stand in back near the lifter, where the action will be, finding my sea legs and eager to see the overnight haul of fresh fish.

Minutes later, Ed cuts back the engine; we're now on the fishing grounds, bobbing in 250–300 feet of water. Alex and Cindi prepare to raise the gill nets. The lifter is activated, and the green nylon monofilament nets begin winding into the boat. Within thirty seconds a lake trout in the ten-pound range is pulled from the lake; its gunmetal gray and white marbled skin "are really beautiful," Cindi remarks to agreeable me. About every five seconds or so another fish is raised from the depths, Alex skillfully guiding the nets into one of the large bins, the fish piling up there. He's mindful of his work, as the mechanical lifter, with more than a few years on it, whines as it steadily rotates, sounding tired. Should Alex not pay attention, catching his hand in that contraption would be unforgiving, and I quickly dismiss that awful thought. I'm reassured in that the Johns are old pros at this labor of love, and they respect the hazards involved in commercial fishing, "one of the most dangerous occupations in the United States," according to the Centers for Disease Control and Prevention.[15]

The mother-and-son team work quickly and diligently, dropping the lake trout into the bins to be pulled from the nets and iced down once they're finished hauling up this morning's catch. Every few minutes Alex grabs a shovel and covers the flopping fish with ice. Seagulls gather around the boat, like clockwork, no doubt. Cindi smiles at them. "I love seagulls," she tells me while glancing at the opportunistic birds. "I can't imagine what this world would be like without them." As if she's reading my mind, she explains, "We're allowed to keep fifteen pounds of undersized fish, which we hardly ever get." The gulls, no doubt, are waiting for the rejects that need to be returned.

The Johns typically fish seven days a week. Sometimes they fish during the winter if the ice holds off and the collective seasonal allotment set annually by the Michigan Department of Natural Resources (DNR)—as dictated by the 2000 Great Lakes Consent Decree, an agreement between the state and five Native American Tribes, including the GTB—has not been reached. (The decree covers tribal fishing rights per the 1836 Treaty for 18,730 square miles of lakes Superior, Michigan, and Huron.)[16] Cindi explains that the current shared lake trout limit among commercial, tribal, and charter fishers on Grand Traverse Bay is one hundred thousand pounds for 2022.

I inquire about their take on climate change impacting Grand Traverse Bay. "We're not really sure what we're seeing," Cindi admits, then mentions Lake Michigan's high water levels in 2020, which approached the record set in 1986, a debate associated with climate change she doesn't expand upon.[17] As to the greater subject, she remarks, "We're not really sure why it's happening and how it's ultimately going to affect us." Then she grins and says with almost cosmic deference, "It's bigger than us."

As for the health of the fishery, she has more to say. The lake trout, Treaty Fish Company's predominant and nearly exclusive catch, are "healthy and amazing and vibrant." In recent years their taste has dramatically improved due to the lake trout's preference for eating the invasive round gobies. Therefore, she sees this invasive species as beneficial to their business. Another plus, this one for the lake's ecology: the bottom-feeding gobies like to dine on young zebra and quagga mussels. "We're just grateful that the goby got here and made the fish delicious," Cindi remarks. "The lake trout didn't used to be delicious, unless smoked. They were very greasy because they ate the alewives." As we chat, a strange-looking creature spills into the collection bin. The nearly two-foot-long fish with long dorsal and anal fins bears mustard-colored, camouflage-like markings. As Ed removes it from the net, I ask what kind of fish it is. He holds it up for me to examine, answering, "Burbot: poor man's lobster," a member of the cod family. "You want it?" If it tastes like lobster, absolutely.

Ed says at one time they couldn't sell their whitefish because "they were all bruised up inside like they had some kind of disease." The Johns spoke with a Great Lakes biologist who suggested the flesh of the whitefish was discolored due to the lake trout ramming them away from their spawning beds, apparently a high-contact sport. "The meat was good, but it didn't look good because it had those red marks." Whitefish are bottom feeders, and lake trout eggs are part of their diet.

Cindi shows me a photo on her phone of a lake trout they caught with a lamprey wound. "Here is where the lamprey tried to stay attached as it slid all the way down the side of the trout." The lamprey, eel-like parasitic fish with round, toothy, horror movie–style mouths that attach to fish to suck their blood and bodily fluids, are not the plague they once were in the Great Lakes due to the efficacy of control measures, though they do persist in smaller numbers.

The Johns catch some whitefish on occasion; none shows up in the nets this morning. The Lake Michigan (and Lake Huron) whitefish population has been declining for years, and marine biologists and commercial fishing operators tend to place the blame on the invasive quagga mussels that have colonized the bottom of Lake Michigan and overwhelmed much of their invasive sister zebra mussels.[18] (Both zebra and quagga mussels were inadvertently introduced to the Great Lakes through the ballast tanks of ocean-going freighters.)[19] Whitefish, native to the Great Lakes, thrive on plankton as their primary food source. Cindi concludes, "the water got too clean," meaning it's no longer cloudy with this near-microscopic life, the mussels decimating the whitefish's food source by filtering the water and consuming voluminous amounts of plankton. "When you know that a population of fish that has been here for eons is almost completely gone—you've seen the ratio of whitefish to lake trout that we get—it's not good at all what's taken place." Despite all the human-introduced threats to the health of the Lake Michigan fishery the Johns rely upon for their sustenance, Cindi remains in awe of this great lake's resilience. "It's amazing what the environment can handle."

....

As Fletcher writes in *The Eagle Returns*, during the 1970s and 1980s, Native commercial fishers contended with frequent harassment from their white counterparts. Their equipment was vandalized, and on occasion shots would be fired at their boats.[20]

Arthur Duhamel, a pipe fitter who helped build the Mackinac Bridge in the 1950s, returned to his home in Peshabestown in 1972. There he began to fish commercially. By the mid-1970s, the Michigan Department of Natural Resources had banned gill net fishing in Grand Traverse Bay. Nonetheless, Duhamel doggedly continued to fish—even after being arrested several times and jailed, and while enduring continuing vandalism and other provocations—under the claim of exercising his tribal fishing rights.[21] Duhamel's perseverance eventually led to the establishment of successful Native commercial fishing enterprises on Grand Traverse Bay, per a federal court decision reaffirming the Treaty of 1836's provision ensuring tribal fishing rights (and use of gill nets), overriding regulations established by the state.[22] This decision was influential in the GTB's federal recognition being reinstated in 1980.

Ed John got his start crewing for Duhamel in the mid-seventies. In 2000, the Arthur Duhamel Marina opened, the home port for the GTB's tribal fishing. The dock and fish processing facility are owned and operated by the band.

Ed recalls, "When we first started selling our fish at the markets, I actually had confrontations with people as to why we get to use gill nets. It was interesting." The couple named their business with great intention. "We call it Treaty Fish Company because that's the protection we get to do what we do," Ed elucidates. In those early days of their commercial fishing business, the Johns lost some of their initial farmers market customers who found gill net fishing to be an unfair advantage over trap netting, the method non-Native commercial fishing operations had to use. "But most of them came back," Ed says, smiling.

....

Ninety minutes later we're back at the marina. Inside the processing facility, Cindi weighs their morning take, which comes to about two hundred pounds, "an average catch," she assesses. Her day isn't done until all the fish are cleaned, filleted, and packaged. Once again, she's skillfully working that "very sharp" knife. As I ask my remaining questions, she removes the roe from a sizable female lake trout, setting it aside rather than tossing the egg mass into the nearby commercial kitchen–sized trash can. "Caviar?" I guess correctly. The Johns have some Ukrainian customers who live in the area who favor the delicacy; they sell the lake trout roe to them for $5 a pound.

I ask Cindi what she thinks about all the migrants in the region of late. She believes it will never become a tidal wave of newcomers. "This area has winters, and it has its other challenges. This will probably keep them being seasonal. But I don't blame them for wanting to be here." When she moved back to the area as a child, relocating to Peshabestown in the seventies, her earlier years spent in Indian River and near Ann Arbor, she recalls that "it was like driving through a painting: it was just so stunning. It is for everyone who visits."

I take the opportunity to ask Cindi about their unique livelihood from a spiritual standpoint. She stops cleaning fish for a moment and turns to me. "It's something that God created for us. It's very special to be able to go out on the boat, to go out on the lake, as often as we get to. It's really touching to know that when we're out there, we're smelling the same stuff that our ancestors smelled. We're having that same feeling, which is really good medicine. So yes, it's definitely spiritual."

I drive back to Cedar, glad—if not privileged—to have accompanied the Johns this morning to gain insight into the life of the Native commercial fishers on Grand Traverse Bay. Then I slap my thigh and curse to myself: *I forgot the damn burbot.* That "poor-man's lobster" dining experience will just have to wait.

CHAPTER 3

WELCOME WAGON

We've got great beaches and pie, but we've got
a lot more than that.

—Warren Call, president and CEO,
Traverse City Connect

I have an aversion to large crowds. It's not what I'd call an agoraphobic fear. It's just that I prefer to be in a more controlled environment, around a minimal number of people, and that those few in proximity to me are well behaved. This condition took a while to come on. Like decades.

When I mixed drinks for a living, most nights I was surrounded by hundreds of party monsters. By the mid-nineties, my bartending days were done. From then on, I had zero interest in being among a horde of strangers gathered for the common purpose of having fun in public. A more sobering look at my surroundings, brought about by the impatience of age, perhaps, did in this more carefree part of me. As a result, my kids didn't get to go to Walt Disney World in Orlando, Florida—at least with their parents; a kind and concerned grandmother took care of this traditional family rite of passage for them. So our children weren't damaged for life, and I couldn't be criminally charged with abuse and neglect. Later, when we stayed in Leland during the National Cherry Festival week, we avoided downtown Traverse City, just as many locals do. Too many people. Too much traffic. Too much like what I was escaping from in Indy.

Cherry Festival Walkabout

Overcoming my reluctance, on July 6, 2022, I'm finally going to the National Cherry Festival—on a field research trip, and certainly not alone. A few days earlier, I asked my friend Mary, who lives about a mile from our chalet in Cedar, if she would like to accompany me. She gave me a *you've got to be kidding me* look. I pleaded for backup. "Coward," she laughed. "Okay, I'll cover you. Should be fun."

It's a picturesque northern Michigan early summer afternoon, the kind of day the tourists anticipate and festival vendors count on. Sunny, no-sweat low humidity, light onshore wind. We rendezvous at Oryana on Tenth Street, the health food co-op where Mary works. "It's a nice day, let's walk," she insists. And so we head north on foot toward the festival.

The closer we get to the downtown area, the more people we see, the louder the collective hum of human activity. We wait at the crosswalk at Cass Street and Grandview Parkway (M-72) with dozens of other Cherry Festivalgoers, as if we all got the memo and are wearing shorts, T-shirts or tank tops, and sandals or sneakers—unofficial National Cherry Festival attire. Our first stop: the midway. "Let's make this fast, Mary," I suggest, half joking. "This ain't pretty."

"Got that right," she agrees. "But it is pretty damn funny." And it is an excellent cultural anthropology study.

I fail to understand the attraction to carnival rides. Flirting with death via poorly camouflaged astronaut-training simulators, which could well result in a bout of vertigo or even public embarrassment from upchucking—while *paying* for the experience—never struck me as fun. Clearly, though, I'm in the minority. The midway is swarming with thrill-seekers. Many of them are of middle- and high-school age.

We decide to check out the nearby Duncan L. Clinch Marina. It's the height of boating season, and many of the slips are occupied with sailboats, tugs/trawlers, yachts, and the occasional cigar boat. So much wealth floating in front of us. Per Mary's guidance for enjoying myself today, I suspend my usual what-the-world-needs-now judgment and simply admire those who have the means to spend it on vessels to traverse the inland seas of the Great Lakes. Good for them. After a few minutes leaning on the fence surrounding the marina and daydreaming about the sailboat I'll never have, Mary nudges me. "To the beer tent, matey, to drown our plebeian sorrows," she orders, taking me by the arm. I protest not.

As anticipated, "Pete the Pin Man" awaits us. Mary knows Peter Garthe, who's been selling the Cherry Festival's commemorative pins since 1993,[1] and introduces us. Smiling and radiating goodness, Pete relieves us of some cash and hands us our pins, informing us he's intent on selling a million of them (which he's on track to do). I take a photo of Mary and Pete for posterity. After interacting with such a fine ambassador of the festival, I feel even better about the beer I'm about to drink.

We buy several poker chips for a round of adult beverages, as there are no cash sales—easy math for everybody. I have a Bell's Two-Hearted Ale on draft, and Mary finds herself a canned hard seltzer at another serving tent. We find a cocktail table to stand at and enjoy our drinks. Half of the tables are empty; the rush will be tonight. The invigorating breeze picks up slightly as we gaze at the northern horizon toward Power Island. The view of Grand Traverse Bay is achingly beautiful. "So nice," Mary says, beaming.

We finish our drinks and Mary decides to take our fieldtrip another direction: "Let's go look at all the cherry-themed merch we're not gonna buy." She steers me into the Official Cherry Festival Souvenir Tent. Of course, it's brimming with cherry-themed items, and I naturally gravitate toward the T-shirts. With Mary's help, I repel temptation and reluctantly leave empty-handed. "Don't look back," she commands, pushing between my shoulder blades as she ushers me out of the tent. "Had enough?" The beer has made me sleepy. We head back to Oryana at about 5 p.m. But now we're going against the late afternoon tide of festivalgoers coming our way.

As we cross Grandview Parkway, standing in the middle of South Union Street is a solitary soul, an older man wearing a wide-brimmed fishing hat, FBI-agent-dark sunglasses, blue jeans, and a white T-shirt with a black-printed message: "Don't let morals get in the way: kill those babies." I can't resist taking a photo with my iPhone. Lots of people around us are looking at him uneasily; he's definitely a downer. The silent evangelist seems to be looking right at me. His oversized black sign that stands perhaps eight feet tall, as if his cross to bear, declares assuredly, in reverse white and red type, that "ALL SINNERS WILL BE DESTROYED." I'm glad to see that he cites his source: Psalm 37:38.

"Creepy," Mary says as we move on.

At the next stoplight, another divinely inspired geriatric Jesus Freak leans toward me and says, "Are you ready for the Lord? He's coming, you know."

"Oh, for sure," Mary responds for me. "Gotta run. Have a nice day." The fellow smiles at us like he knows something we don't. Then we hear that stomach-churning sound of a metal-on-metal collision out of view on the parkway. We step over vomit on the sidewalk. Figuratively, it suddenly feels as though a storm cloud is passing over us. But as I look out at the sun-kissed crowd of happy people eagerly heading for the festival, I readjust. The party is on.

Back at Oryana, I'm not ready for the afternoon to end, but end it must. "Thanks for letting me tag along, Tim," Mary says appreciatively. "I haven't been to the festival in years, and it really was fun." As I turn toward my car, she calls out, "Hey, keep in mind there's a strong chance that you and I may just burn in hell." And we part company, both of us laughing wickedly.

Cherries Jubilee

Kat Paye holds a distinctive position in the Grand Traverse region as the executive director of the National Cherry Festival. Of course, I just had to talk to her, with Traverse City being renowned as the "Cherry Capital of the World." (Notably, Michigan grows approximately 75 percent of the nation's tart cherry crop.)[2] Because of the festival's small full-time staff of six and the fact that it's responsible for three other major annual events in the region besides the Cherry Festival—the November Bell's Iceman Cometh Challenge mountain bike race, the CherryT Ball Drop on New Year's Eve, and the Leapin' Leprechaun 5K footrace in honor of St. Patrick's Day—Paye isn't that easy to track down. But then I receive a phone call days after trying repeatedly, and it's well worth the wait. She's accommodating and pleasant, an expert in public relations. Everything that the head of the National Cherry Festival should be.

Paye, forty, had previously served as the Cherry Festival's operations director. She became the executive director in 2016. Remarkably, she's also participated in and attended the festival since she was eight years old.

In 2020, the pandemic tabled the Cherry Festival. In 2021, a limited version was held, without the premier event, the airshow. Thankfully, in 2022, the festival went full bore once again. Because the festival isn't gated, an attendance count can only be estimated, which the festival says amounted to roughly 750,000 *visitor days* in 2022 (an estimate determined by survey) for the weeklong celebration. "We're an open festival," Paye explains, "and 90 percent of what we do is free to the public."

The festival is by far the largest event held in the region, as is its economic impact. "The Economic Assessment of the 2022 National Cherry Festival," authored by researchers from Grand Valley State University, reported:

- There was a total of 323,500 [actual] festival visitors in 2022, 73 percent of them from outside of Grand Traverse County, with more than thirty states and ten countries represented.
- The total economic impact estimate for the 2022 festival reached $33.4 million.
- The majority of festival attendees said they would be returning, and 94 percent indicated they would be recommending visiting Traverse City to their friends.[3]

The festival is a green event. Paye says everything that can be recycled is, proudly sharing that "we put nothing into landfills." An independent recycling auditor through Green for Life Environmental (GFL) helps the organization ensure that it's the best environmental steward it can be. "This is the first year we've achieved 100 percent," she says, referring to their recycling score per GFL. "Everything you see onsite—from the cups in the beer tent to the spoons in the ice cream tent—are fully compostable materials." All vendors are required to be fully compliant.

Of course, not everybody in Traverse City is a fan of the Cherry Festival. (Although they should be used to it by now, as the first Cherry Festival took place in 1925, formally known as the Blessing of the Blossoms.)[4] Indeed, Paye is hyperaware of that. "A lot of the things we hear is the air show is too loud, the traffic is too much, the festival is too long." Paye's business may be cherries, but she knows a thing or two about turning a lemony situation into lemonade. Every complaint she fields is viewed as an opportunity to promote the festival and gain converts. For example, when a resident called about the Blue Angels flyovers above his house shaking his walls and knocking over and breaking his TV, Paye delivered a check for replacement costs and provided straps to secure the new TV to his wall. "We listen. We apologize. And we try to make things right where we can."

She'll tell such naysayers, "You might not like the air show, but your kids might love the parade. We have 150 events over eight days, and 90 percent of them are free to the public. There is something for everyone. People forget that." She also lets everyone within reach know that the foundation's events contribute to the well-being of the community. For example, the Leprechaun 5K fundraises for the Munson Medical Center's Family Birth Center and neonatal intensive care unit. As well, the CherryT Ball Drop raises money to help alleviate food insecurity. "We combat the negative with the positive," she notes.

Paye and staff maintain a sense of humor about the more irritating aspects of the festival for some locals, evident in the festival's new signature ice cream flavor developed by Moomers Homemade Ice Cream in Traverse City. It's called the Cherry Traffic Jam: vanilla ice cream with tart cherry swirl and graham cracker crunch. Her favorite cherry food is, no surprise, the official cherry crumb pie featuring Montmorency tart cherries made by the Grand Traverse Pie Company.

In 2022, when the ninety-sixth National Cherry Festival rebounded from the impact of the pandemic, it was a special time for Paye. Her three-year-old son accompanied her in a convertible along the July Fourth parade route in downtown Traverse City. Paye says he was "super excited, waving at everyone. It was beautiful, and I was overwhelmed by the people who were clapping and cheering and thanking me for keeping the festival alive and that we were back—I get teary-eyed thinking about it. The street was lined with people three deep. It was this huge moment of relief, that 'oh my gosh, we made it. We survived the last couple of years.'"

The National Cherry Festival's executive director feels fortunate to have grown up in Traverse City. She went away to college, returned, and has been here ever since. Because of her upbringing, she doesn't take the region's natural resources for granted. "My mother always said, 'Other people visit; you're lucky enough to live here.'"

Tourism Is Not a Four-Letter Word

Traverse City Tourism (TCT) knows how to put its hometown on the map. For example, my wife, Janet, has a subscription to *Midwest Living* magazine. The publication promotes tourism throughout the Midwest. When she received the fall 2022 issue, Janet called me to the kitchen to show me the inside cover's two-page spread advertisement for Traverse City, a TCT-sponsored ad. "That's pretty cool," she said. I had mixed feelings. Does the region really need to spend money on out-of-state advertising to attract vacation visitors anymore?

The *Midwest Living* ad shows a photo of a lighthouse, an iconic northern Michigan image. A couple in their late thirties or early forties are shown on a beach, happily hurrying toward what appears to be the Lake Michigan shoreline. They're holding hands, laughing, ecstatic. She has on a casual jacket and pants; he's wearing a North Face puffer vest, sweatshirt, and blue jeans. It's autumn. The headline declares, "Exactly where we should be." The supporting ad copy is brief: "When you're true to who you are, you're true to where you are. Come join us."[5] Admittedly, the ad works: I'm ready to start packing right now.

TCT's website states: "Organized in 1981 as the Traverse City Area Convention and Visitors Bureau, Traverse City Tourism (TCT) is a nonprofit corporation that serves as the area's official destination marketing organization. Our focused mission is to stimulate economic growth through the attraction of convention business and leisure tourism development."[6] In short, TCT primes the region's tourism pump.

I call Trevor Tkach, Traverse City Tourism's president and CEO for the past five years, on Thursday, September 1. He cheerfully greets me in a Mister (Fred) Rogers–like way: "It's a beautiful day in Traverse City, my friend." I tell him that I'm in Indy for the Labor Day weekend, though I'd much rather be Up North. "I think everybody wishes that in the summertime. There's no better place."

Tkach, forty-five, who previously served as the National Cherry Festival's executive director, maintains that the Cherry Festival "was tourism before tourism was tourism. Its roots were in pairing agriculture and tourism to drive economic growth. They've been a big player in that over the years and often don't get the credit they deserve for putting Traverse City on the map, really driving a lot of interest around the state and nationally about the region."

TCT is intent on spreading tourist demand over the course of 365 days a year, thus diversifying the tourism calendar, Tkach says. "We are not a seasonal community; we do not board up the shops on Labor Day weekend." A few years before the pandemic, that used to be the case. Not anymore.

Although it almost seems counterintuitive, TCT is sensitive to the area being overrun, especially during the summer's peak tourism season, and the "value proposition," as Tkach puts it, taking a hit due to overcrowding and poor visitor experiences as a result. The supporting service industry is one such area of concern. "Where we're strapped mostly right now is the workforce. That's inhibiting our ability to grow thoughtfully. Collectively as a community, we continue to work on this issue." Affordable housing is impacting the area's workforce, contributing to the shortage the service industry has seen in the region since the start of the pandemic, if not earlier. The scarcity of affordable childcare is an added complication. Therefore, interest in working in the hospitality industry has suffered as another ramification of the pandemic. Tkach says, "Twenty-seven percent of all jobs lost in the state of Michigan [during the pandemic] were hospitality and leisure-related jobs. And a lot of those people aren't going to come back." He acknowledges the challenge this presents both now and in impacting "the whole industry for a generation." Rebuilding a pool of service workers is high on the region's economic development agenda.

It's no secret that many businesses in the Grand Traverse region rely on summer tourism to keep them in business year-round. Tkach says that it's typical for such businesses to have a negative operating budget for several months during the winter. "That's just the nature of this area. We'd love to see a day when that's not the case and cash flows year-round and we're not so reliant on summer." Before the pandemic, "one in six jobs was in the hospitality and leisure space in the five-county region" (which includes Grand Traverse, Leelanau, Benzie, Antrim, and Kalkaska counties).

The pandemic's initial impact on tourism, recalls Tkach, resulted in "an immediate dip." So TCT responded with a "Happy Places, Wide Open Spaces" campaign. This helped kickstart a "pretty quick return around Memorial Day weekend of 2020," he says.

"When [the pandemic] first hit, like most others, we were looking at our numbers thinking, boy, we'll probably be out of business by September; this was in March 2020. What ended up happening, however, is that an influx of visitation in the summer months helped us throughout the rest of the year. We still dropped off precipitously in the fall because that's traditionally our conference season. So much like the big cities who lost huge trade shows and conferences, we were significantly affected by that." Yet as the pandemic wore on, northern Michigan tourism regained its momentum. When winter came, ski resorts saw significant demand, as did golf courses later that spring. The in-state and out-of-state draw to outdoor activities, for which the region is renowned, saved the day.

....

As with outdoor destination locations throughout the rest of the country, many visitors are now using Airbnb and Vrbo rentals for their short-term stays in northern Michigan. As quoted in the *Traverse City Ticker*'s November 20, 2022, issue, Tkach states, "We've seen significant growth in STRs (short-term rentals) over the past 5–10 years. In recent years, we're looking at probably about 20 percent increase in inventory in that segment alone."[7] He tells me that 25 percent of all short-term rentals in Michigan are in the Grand Traverse region, yet the area makes up but 2 percent of the state's total population.

TCT conducted a survey in 2022 to gauge people's sentiments on the short-term rental growth in the area. Although concerns remain due to the conduct of some short-term renters, he says, "You don't want to throw the baby out with the bathwater. Not every situation is a bad one. Ninety-nine percent of these are probably good experiences. It's when you get a loud bachelor party or trash is left behind or people stay up too late, they're more noticeable."

TCT holds the view that there needs to be some parity between regulations for hotels and those for people opening their homes as short-term rental properties. "We want to make sure that if you're going to do transient business, that you're creating a safe environment for a guest and following all of the same rules that a hotel would have to follow." This includes regulatory, zoning, and taxation issues that still need to be addressed—locally, regionally, and statewide. He goes on, "Short-term rentals continue to grow here. You can't stop it. I don't know that you want to. But there are going to be inherent challenges to that growth, and we need to be mindful about it and be planning now for what that looks like."

Tkach says the Grand Traverse regional community recognizes the critical role that tourism plays in driving the local economy. But there is also the matter of tourists being respectful visitors, which remains an ongoing community concern. Commendably, TCT is addressing this in its current branding. "We have three big words we use in a lot of our campaigns now, and that's *respect*, *connect*, and *celebrate*. This is our home. We're letting you into our home, so have respect for the space and the people in it. It's important." He notes that the pandemic not only increased interest in northwest lower Michigan but also raised the issue of visitor behavior. "We need to be more deliberate with the guests and make sure they understand rules of engagement and not overstepping bounds."

During the summer of 2022, several alcohol-serving establishments in northern Michigan went public with their fatigue about being fed up with poorly behaving customers and declared they weren't going to take it anymore. The *Detroit Free Press* picked up on a Facebook post from Short's Brewing Co. in Bellaire, Michigan, about this situation. The popular brewery had been experiencing "another 'relentless' wave of rude customers at its sprawling downtown Bellaire brewpub who 'swear, yell, laugh in our faces, name-call, belittle, bring us to tears, and threaten negative reviews or to never come back.'"[8] Similarly, just days earlier, the manager at the East Park Tavern in Charlevoix decided to close the tavern's kitchen early and posted a sign on the front door that said, "Due to the mistreatment of our servers our kitchen is closed." The manager, Larah Moore, wrote on Facebook, "I'm so incredibly disappointed and embarrassed by the Fudgies (northern Michigan tourists) we have this year. My staff took a *beating* all week. Last night was our last straw. Too many rude comments. Too many arrogant individuals acting like they can throw money at us to get their way. Too many cocky jerks."[9] The tavern was short-staffed and had been overrun with customers during the Venetian Festival, which attracts thousands of visitors each year, a perfect storm for patience wearing thin.

I mention these unfortunate examples of egregious customer behavior in abusing servers to Tkach and challenge the maxim that "the customer is always right." He responds, "I think things are shifting for the better. But you really have to be open with your staff and have them understand where the line is." R-E-S-P-E-C-T.

....

For all the somewhat understandable handwringing about tourism from a vocal minority of the local population, it's easy to overlook that Traverse City has been a tourist destination since the 1860s. One cloudy afternoon in late May 2022, I stopped by the Leelanau Historical Society Museum in Leland to peruse the tourism archives. Executive Director Kim Kelderhouse graciously took the time to pull artifacts from way back when about the industry. One, a yellowing pamphlet entitled, "Beauty Spots in Leelanau," featured black-and-white outdoor photos on its cover of "Northern Michigan Resorts on Grand Traverse Bay." The piece referred to itself as a "1901 Souvenir."[10] Kelderhouse also showed me a small poster promoting travel on the Grand Rapids and Indiana Railway "To All Points on Grand Traverse Bay." The G.R. & I. provided passengers a booklet, "Michigan in Summer," with the "names and rates of all hotels and boarding houses at the resorts."[11] In 1902, passengers traveled the G.R. & I. from Traverse City to Northport, on the northernmost tip of Leelanau County.[12] And notably, the railroad line assisted with the construction of the Grand Hotel on Mackinac Island. Indeed, tourism has been, and will always be, essential to the prosperity of the region. It shows no sign of abating, either, evidenced by the eight hotels now being built in Grand Traverse County. Tkach says that these construction projects will increase total hotel volume in the area in the next several years by 20 percent.

Tkach is confident that people will continue to seek out and settle in "a place where the weather is more temperate and there's water and there's natural resources and agriculture." Because of the lack of natural disasters affecting the area, Americans from places around the country that are experiencing such catastrophes in growing and alarming frequency are noticing. "They're going to flock to a place where they don't have to deal with those things anymore, not only on vacation but also with quality of life and long-term living arrangements."

Tkach bids me goodbye, needing to move on to yet another meeting in a day filled with them. I hope he has "another great day in God's country."

"Thanks, Tim; I always do."

Avoiding Aspenization

In late September, I speak by phone with Warren Call, president and CEO of Traverse Connect. The organization merged with the Traverse City Area Chamber of Commerce in 2019 and now serves "as the lead economic development organization for the Grand Traverse region."[13] Early in our conversation, I broach the pandemic. He surprises me with this: "Honestly, kind of sorry to say, we had a good pandemic. Obviously, our existing businesses had a very difficult time—especially our hospitality businesses, which had a very acute, very difficult period. We're still having some significant struggles in getting people back in the workforce, especially in those entry-level service jobs. But overall, we had several positive impacts from the pandemic; namely, one of the few things you could do would be to go outside and do something in nature, and we're one of the best places in the country, if not the world, for that. Right?" He knows his audience.

Continuing, Call emphasizes, "The sale of boats; the utilization of our trails and our ski resorts; the people that came to the beach in the summer here, the likes of which I had never seen—it was fantastic." Many local business owners, he says, claimed 2022 was their best year ever. The annual Traverse City Horse Shows became "the third largest in the country because of the pandemic." Because so many of the top riders in the world were in Florida and Kentucky when the pandemic hit, and many from South America and Europe were marooned in the states, "it was the perfect storm" to have them come to Traverse City during the summer. The show, established in 2015, takes place in nearby Williamsburg. The economic impact of the weekslong summertime Horse Shows came to nearly $353 million in 2021.[14]

Call, forty-three, is a boomeranger. He grew up in Benzie County on Crystal Lake's north shore and returned to the region in 2009 after living in New York City and Salt Lake City. He's been Traverse Connect's chief executive since 2018.

Traverse City's lead business development cheerleader refers to the region as a "thriving accessibly remote environment." People value the region for its slew of water-centric activities, its ski hills and bike trails, its dunelands and woods. Not only is northwest lower Michigan's exceptional outdoor recreation "what people want to do when they come Up North; increasingly, it's what people want to do everywhere in their spare time," he notes. Call loves the fact that he can leave his office in downtown Traverse City and get to a beach, on a trail, or down a ski hill in a matter of minutes. The healthy lifestyle that the relative remoteness of Traverse City brings, compared to larger urban areas downstate, is indeed easily accessible.

Traverse Connect's strategic plan focuses on attracting talent to the region. "We got really lucky," he says. "We were in the process of building that out before the pandemic struck." One of Traverse Connect's key strategic components for cultivating interest in relocating to the region is Michiganscreativecoast.com. There, potential relocators will find a job board, information on working remotely, business startup advice, and a freelance directory. Such an outburst of entrepreneurial activity and encouragement didn't exist here not so long ago. Once upon a time, people seeking to relocate to the Grand Traverse region would hear the disappointing refrain about "half the pay by the bay." Now talent can be paid their worth here. The Creative Coast website has testimonials aplenty from relocators who came during the pandemic and now work remotely or created a new business or secured gainful employment.

Call tells me his wife, Marina, who's from Southern California, thinks winter is oversold here. A video on the Creative Coast website, "Keenan & Kristen's Story," features some honest—and amusing—commentary on the northern Michigan winter. "Y'all, can you tell I'm, like, shivering?" Kristen Berlacher blurts, with a two-handed grip on her coffee cup. I can: she's visibly trembling. Berlacher is sitting outside with her partner, Keenan May, in what appears to be early springtime. They're both wearing winter coats and stocking caps. She works remotely for Airbnb in San Francisco. He works remotely as well for a tech company based out of Nevada. The cold weather notwithstanding, Berlacher declares they "decided this is where we wanted to be. It's been incredible." May continues to praise the four seasons. Then she interrupts, "Don't get me wrong, winter is brutal," but adds, "you figure out ways to enjoy it."[15]

Unlike his wife, Call is a fan of winter and offers plenty of good reasons. Fat-tire biking, cross-country and downhill skiing, snowshoeing, ice fishing, ice boating, and the growing interest in winter surfing on Lake Michigan—there are enough pastimes to keep most any outdoors-oriented soul happily engaging with nature all winter long.

For those on the fence about making a life-changing move to the region or recent arrivals who want to get plugged into the community, Traverse Connect also created a network of "Northern Navigators." The website lists twenty-five professional contacts—"regional ambassadors"—whom interested parties can reach out to with questions about living and working in the region. Whether fielding lifestyle-oriented queries, what to know about local schools, Realtor referrals, or where to go exploring the great outdoors, the Navigators serve as something of an intimate "welcome wagon" for those seeking their place as newbies in the community.[16] The Navigators themselves are boomerangers who have returned to the region as well as relocators who moved here either in the distant past or during the pandemic. They're more than willing to share their experiences with newcomers to help them get their bearings.

....

Technology firms and startups are finding a home in Traverse City. Why? The attraction of that accessibly remote environment is indeed a primary reason. And consider that the area will never attract smokestack industries. "That's just not our thing. You're talking about the types of work and jobs that can be done from anywhere; that's an area where we can really stand out as a great location," Call explains. "You can sit in an office in Traverse City and design software, do coding, web design, graphics, etc. that can be deployed out anywhere. . . . We can make it here—whether that's intellectual property, technology, value-added agriculture, niche manufacturing goods, whatever that might be, and then export it out to the world."

Regarding the tourism-heavy regional focus, Calls says, "We're kind of at capacity as it relates to importing tourists. Nothing to take away from that sector of that industry in general, but we need to look for other ways. That's why we focus on those tech, trade, and creative industries."

Traverse Connect has taken what some might view as a bold step in promoting diversity in attracting talent to the region. The organization's website features a webpage with content regarding "Diversity, Equity, Inclusion, and Belonging," with Traverse Connect referring to itself as a champion of these intertwined social movements.[17] "As you can imagine, that's not an easy topic to address," the chief executive says candidly. "We saw it as part of our duty. From a basic economic standpoint, we've got to make sure that this is an attractive place for talent. There will be two types of communities: those that are able to compete for talent in the future, and those that are not. If we're going to be one of those [successful] places, we have to foster a culture of openness and acceptance and creativity. For those people that aren't always comfortable with some of the diversity topics, we do try to remind them that the reason we're talking about this and so focused on it is from a standpoint of the need to be an attractive place long term for the next generation." Showing the courage of the organization's convictions, he adds, "We don't mind catching the lightning strikes every once in a while, because we do feel like it's our responsibility to be out there talking about it."

....

What will northwest lower Michigan look like in ten years from an economic growth standpoint? Call explains that the Traverse Connect strategic plan is not aiming for the region to become another Aspen or Vail, Colorado, or even Key West, Florida—high-end vacation destinations where housing and consumer costs have risen to levels beyond the reach of middle-class residents. "That's the biggest thing that we are concerned about," he says. "It's kind of the model not to be." Instead, the intention is to continue developing a diversified economy with a "world-class quality of life." Call notes that more college grads are moving into the area. The prime working population—thirty-five- to forty-nine-year-olds—once bleeding away, is now rebounding in the Grand Traverse region. Tech jobs are opening up. Wages are rising. The outlook is bright.

The Traverse Connect leader lets me go by sharing an anecdote from earlier in the day. He was on a "business attraction call" with someone looking to move his tech firm from *Scotland*. He asked how the caller obtained his contact information. "He said, 'I'm looking for what is going to be the best place to live over the next twenty to thirty years from a combination of quality of life, climate resiliency, growing workforce, and good demographics, and I found Traverse City.'"

Cherry Capital Airport, Gateway to Northern Michigan

In early August, I reserved a seat on Delta Air Lines for my wife to fly to Traverse City on Monday, September 26, 2022. When booking, I was surprised to learn there were three Delta flights that day from Indianapolis International Airport to Cherry Capital Airport (TVC). Moreover, I could have picked from United and American Airlines to get her here. About twenty years ago when I flew to Traverse City from Indianapolis, multiple daily flights from Indy to here on multiple airlines in late September certainly weren't happening. As I would learn in greater detail, the skies around Traverse City have become a very busy place.

On September 23, 2022, I met with Cherry Capital Airport's chief executive officer, Kevin Klein, in his office on the second floor of the terminal. It was dress-down Friday, and Klein, fifty-one, was dress-code compliant, wearing blue jeans and a blue logoed airport pullover and dress sneakers. His office features a view of the airport, a comfortable meeting area with a coffee table and chairs reflecting his welcoming demeanor, and, most striking to my inner-child, shelves surrounding his desk with models of aircraft. The display includes military and commercial jets, biplanes, and fittingly, a mini-replica of an MH-65 Dolphin United States Coast Guard helicopter, no doubt in honor of his neighbors, the USCG Air Station Traverse City.

The airport's chief executive is a lifelong Michigander, having grown up in Saginaw. Aviation was his focus from college on, as he earned a degree in aviation management from Western Michigan University. His second job post-college was with Johnson Controls at Teterboro Airport in New Jersey (famous for its involvement in the "Miracle on the Hudson" emergency landing of U.S. Airways Flight 1549 in the Hudson River on January 15, 2009).[18] Klein later worked at the Gerald R. Ford International Airport in Grand Rapids before coming to Cherry Capital Airport in 2002, eventually working his way up to CEO.

Of course, the Traverse City airport plays a key role in the transportation of visitors and businesspeople to and from the region. It is truly a regional airport, Klein says. "Acme Township and the Torch Lake area, historically, have been among our highest users of the airport," he notes. TVC draws passengers from across the region, "from the southern Cadillac area, all the way up to the [Mackinac] bridge, and all the way up to Alpena." Now with Allegiant Air operating out of Traverse City, passengers are driving in from as far as the Upper Peninsula to catch direct flights to Florida.

As expected, summer is the busy season for flying into and out of Traverse City. According to Klein, in July 2022, 112,000 passengers transited through the airport. Cherry Festival is certainly the big draw. The Traverse City Horse Shows accounts for "heavy air traffic coming in" as well. Klein mentions that during the Horse Shows, the airport can have more than one hundred corporate/private jets parked there.

Although Klein anticipated a very good 2022 for passenger volume at Cherry Capital Airport—and it was, with 582,908 departing and arriving travelers, its second best year—2021 holds the record, with 602,606 passengers passing through TVC's gates.[19] With major airlines pulling service from sixty-four airports nationwide, largely due to the current pilot shortage and other staffing shortfalls, with some flight cuts reaching as much as 60 percent, Klein says that TVC is only down between 10 and 15 percent. "People in the industry look at us like, no way. It's unbelievable. We're doing very, very well." With rising demand for air travel to and from the region, that success looks to continue.

The noteworthy increase in arriving and departing flights at Cherry Capital Airport during the past thirty years reflects the growth of the Traverse City region. In a follow-up email from Klein in September 2024, he provided a then-and-now comparison based on data from the Michigan Department of Transportation and U.S. Department of Transportation: "On a July day in 1994, [there were] twelve arrivals and twelve departures, for a total of twenty-four airline operations in a day. In 2024, we have thirty-one arrivals and thirty-one departures, for a total of sixty-two airline operations in a day." Yet there's more to the story, he points out, and it involves posteriors in seats. "The average number of seats per flight was approximately thirty-five in 1994. Today, the average number of seats per flight is ninety-six." Indeed, when it comes to options for traveling to and from the region, "727 Fly Don't Drive," the airport's address, is not only cute but telling.

Cherry Capital Airport is in "a great financial position," states Klein, having zero debt, a rarity for airports. He predicts a steady rate of 2–3 percent growth for the next five years, which, he notes, generally reflects the overall population growth rate in northern Michigan. Once the national pilot shortage has been resolved, he expects annual growth to climb to nearly 5 percent. "Some airline consultants have said that they feel our growth, from a percentage basis, is going to be in the top twenty-five to fifty airports in the country, and I echo that." TVC features five jet bridges and six gates, with expectations of at least doubling the number of gates in the next decade or so. Its two runways are over seven thousand feet each, so the airport can handle the largest passenger aircraft.

....

Change is literally in the air for the aviation industry, Klein, a frequent smiler, enthusiastically expresses. Electric aircraft will be the next major innovation. Drone air freighters for UPS and FedEx aren't far behind. Advanced air mobility will support the online ordering industry, with pharmaceuticals and Amazon deliveries conveyed by drone, and not implausibly, meals for shut-ins. This will be especially helpful to those living on the area's peninsulas, with drones crossing Grand Traverse Bay—by air or water—for such deliveries rather than today's more circuitous route by car. Essentially, he's saying that the largely rural makeup of northwest lower Michigan's counties benefitting from once-futuristic Jetsons-like drone technology is no longer farfetched. It will provide convenience, save lives, and help preserve the region's natural resources by reducing the carbon footprint. "And that's pretty cool."

Location, Location, Location

My interviewee this beautiful mid-May morning is a member of Real Estate One's Jack Lane Team—no less than Jack Lane himself. Several times during our conversation at Brew coffee shop in the historic City Opera House building on Front Street (rebranded and reopened in late 2023 as the Outpost, still a coffee-serving establishment), the Realtor is interrupted by a friend or business acquaintance or former happy-camper client. Lane, whom I had never met before, is easy to recognize from his website's photos and videos, except he's gone totally casual this morning, courageously wearing shorts on a cool, sunny morning, flip-flops, and a windbreaker-like jacket. He's already seated, waiting for me, and throughout our ninety minutes together drinks several cups of coffee. (I, however, am a coffee lightweight, and barely make it through a third of a cup.) Lane, sixty-seven, is imposing in his football-player size yet easily approachable, having a pronounced sense of humor, a trait good for cultivating prospects, closing sales, and retaining repeat customers. As of 2022, he's in his thirty-fourth year in the real estate business in the Grand Traverse region. A natural storyteller with a velvety voice, Lane has a Saturday morning radio show on WTCM-AM, Newstalk 580, called "Ask the Real Estate Guy."

Lane's sales territory is extensive, covering "Frankfort to the bridge." He can afford to be choosy about the properties he agrees to sell, having sold more than 1,700 homes in his real estate sales career.[20] "Anything south of Empire would probably have to be a million-dollar deal to draw my attention," he says flatly.

Lane's stepfather, Robert Chase, DDS, served as mayor of Traverse City in 1963. Perhaps that's where he gets his frankness from. As I discover within minutes, the man has a lot to say—and wastes no time saying it.

"There's a magical feeling to Traverse City and to the surrounding area," he starts off in his ambassadorial manner. "That's why people are coming here in droves." He expects thousands and thousands more to make landfall in coming years. That's a marked change from when he was a youngster in Traverse City. "When I was a kid growing up, the only thing that could kill you here was boredom." And because of that, once reaching adulthood, many went elsewhere.

Lane finds the NIMBYism (Not In My Backyard) of some of the region's residents stultifying. "There's nothing you can do about being one of the most in-demand cities in

America," he declares. Moreover, "you can't tell people they can't live here." He says this minority "shut-the-gate mentality has been here since 1900." Yet he believes that despite such regionalistic murmurings, "people that live here love this place, even though they love it a little bit differently. It's a good problem to have." At the time of our conversation, 1,200 active buyers were "chasing maybe a hundred houses" throughout his territory, bidding wars further driving up demand. (As of late February 2024, roughly the same number of buyers are pursuing perhaps two hundred homes in his market. He says that active buyers will pay up to the asking price, but paying above that is a thing of the recent past.) And no small number of them were prospective buyers from out of state.

The pandemic-inspired near-mania for real estate in northern Michigan, which technology has helped accelerate through online listings and virtual home showings, is evident by some of the more unusual phone calls Lane has taken over the past year from prospective buyers. He'll post a listing, it pings on a property-seeker's phone (given the respective search criteria), and he may well get a call from somewhere way out of state. "'I just saw the house you listed'—this was about twenty minutes after I listed it," he recounts of an interested buyer calling from Alaska. "Two weeks later, I put another house on the market. Twenty minutes later—Thailand." Playing futurist, a useful trait for a Realtor, Lane predicts that fifty years from now, Michigan may become "the most coveted state," perhaps only rivaled by Hawaii.

Judging from his experience, the climate change migration has begun. "I have people who have moved here because of California wildfires," he tells. "My baby sister lives in Bozeman, Montana. The last two years, all summerlong, the skies have been filled with smoke. No question we're getting [climate migrants]. And that will intensify as we get older."

When Lane first entered the real estate industry in the late eighties, out-of-state buyers typically came from Chicago, St. Louis, Cincinnati, and Cleveland. "It was rare back in those days to get somebody moving here from California. Now it's common." Remarkably, those California buyers find the real estate prices in the Grand Traverse region to be something of a bargain, which northern Michiganders can hardly fathom. "If you want to buy a three-bedroom, two-baths place in Aspen [Colorado], it's probably going to start in the $3 million range. So don't tell me, 'Oh my God, places [here] cost $575,000—hey, that's crazy!'" Lane says that in 2020 and 2021, home prices were appreciating annually by nearly

18 percent in the region due to low supply and very high demand. (As of midsummer 2022, largely due to high interest rates, home prices were leveling off in the Grand Traverse area.)[21]

Although Lane says that climate-wise, Michigan will remain a highly sought relocation target for people across the country fleeing natural calamities such as wildfires, earthquakes, and hurricanes, "the only thing that could harm our real estate market is environmental disaster." He mentions the threat of a pipeline spill in the Straits of Mackinac from Enbridge's Line 5, twin pipes that convey crude oil and natural gas to refineries in Detroit and Toledo, Ohio.[22] "Even though it's one hundred miles away, it would foul the water and it would foul the public perception of the water. But that's the only thing that could pull the plug." (Additional discussion on Line 5 is covered in chapter nine: "Every Day Is Earth Day.")

Lane, who stays in shape by biking fifteen miles almost daily, loves living in the Grand Traverse region. It's "the vibe on the street," which, he says, is different than anywhere else he's traveled to, which includes all forty-eight contiguous states and all ten Canadian provinces. "I come home, and I can't believe that I get to live here."

Festival Fatigue

I connect with former Traverse City mayor Jim Carruthers via Facebook, and he readily agrees to an interview. We met at Brew (of course) in late April 2022. Although I have a list of questions prepared, I discover that I really didn't need them, as Carruthers is off and running with his engaging, wide-ranging discourse, admittedly enlivened by his caffeine dosage. From the get-go, he mentions his husband; the fact that he's a (very) proud, fiscally conservative, social liberal Democrat; is cause driven and maintains that everyone should give back to their community; and believes in working with the other side of the aisle.

Carruthers, fifty-nine, is a transplant to the region, moving to Traverse City in 1989, when he drove from Boston to paint his grandmother's hundred-year-old cottage on Old Mission Peninsula (purchased in 1938 for $4,000, the property worth millions now, Carruthers remarks). "I'm from people that started coming here in the 1800s as tourists," he says. "My grandmother tells stories of taking the train up here." And if she came by auto, "sometimes the drive was three days, and there were dirt roads north of Grand Rapids. It wasn't an easy place to come for vacation, but it was a place to escape the heat and to be Up North in this beautiful outdoor environment."

Carruthers never intended to stay in Traverse City, yet he's been here ever since. He recalls renting a five-room trailer upon his arrival for $175 a month. Got a job with the Grand Traverse Regional Land Conservancy (GTRLC). Ran an HIV service organization. Became politically active, supporting campaigns for former Traverse City Mayor Margaret Dodd and city commissioners Anne Melichar and Ann Rogers, which he characterized as "helping to break the glass ceiling." Solicited public support for the Traverse City Light & Power wind turbine installed along M-72 in 1996, the largest utility-grade wind generator placed in this country.[23] And in 2015 became the mayor of Traverse City, serving three consecutive two-year terms.

When he first arrived in northern Michigan, breaking in with the locals proved to be a challenge. "Even if you were coming here for generations, it was hard to get involved," he recalls. "If you weren't born from the soil of Grand Traverse County at Munson Hospital, you were nobody." He mentions a decidedly different experience for his grandmother. "She used to always talk about how friendly Traverse City was. When she came up for the summer, they remembered her at Oleson's [Food Store] and Maxbauer's [Specialty Meat Market]." And today, it's even more hospitable, says the former mayor. "We are very welcoming and friendly. We engage here and say hi to people on the street. The locals are that way." But they do have their limits, he suggests, especially when tourist season arrives.

As noted in the *Traverse City Record-Eagle* in November 2021 in a story about Carruthers opting not to seek reelection, "Preserving the city's character has long been his goal, and that'll pose a challenge as the city reaps the benefit of years of tourism marketing." As to whether the city is at risk of "Aspenization"—becoming a town that caters to tourists at the expense of permanent residents and the working class who make it function—Carruthers thinks Traverse City is already there.[24]

He tells me, "Tourism kind of treads on us pretty heavily in the summertime. We don't get to use our parks; we don't get to have a quiet moment. Reservations for local restaurants need to be made weeks in advance." Sharing can be hard, especially when under the welcome yet disruptive influence of being a tourist destination. "We've become so popular that the conveniences of living in these great towns is gone because we have to make way for the tourism and the dollars that they bring."

There is also the phenomenon of migrants bringing aspects of their former homes with them, a human propensity from time immemorial. But this does disturb the regional homogeneity. People come to the area for its outdoor assets, its rural splendor. "But when they get here," Carruthers contends, "they want Walmart, they want Sam's Club—they want all the crap they left behind." Now Costco is here. A second Meijer store has opened in Grand Traverse County, in Williamsburg, approximately five miles east of Traverse City. And yes, there's a Walmart and a Sam's Club. To be sure, many locals shop at all these retail centers. Tourists here on vacation do as well, the convenience of buying in bulk for a week or two not lost on them. Small-town charm may take something of a hit with these giant warehouse stores spread throughout the city and its suburban areas. Yet in Traverse City proper and when visiting the enchanting villages throughout northwest lower Michigan, many of whom prohibit chain/franchise stores, both visitors and residents value their distinctly small, family business-dominant appeal. And modern conveniences remain within reach without compromising the stillness of the woods and the quiet of the lakes. It's arguably the best of both worlds.

Carruthers remembers when Traverse City was known for not having such big-city amenities (although the first Meijer store in Traverse City has been there since the nineties). "When I moved here, this was a boring little town. By 5 o'clock, it was tumbleweeds rolling down the street." There wasn't much nightlife, and just a few restaurants served food after 10 p.m. "You came here for the peace and quiet, the fresh water, the open spaces," he explains. "You came here to relax, to leave behind the stressors of urban living. But now we're growing and becoming a more urban area, so everybody wants what urban areas have in Traverse City, which is slowly changing what Traverse City is. I know we have to change, and we have to grow, but our brand is a small Up North town on all of this great freshwater. That's why people come here. That's why people live here. That's why we all want to be here. But all of us moving here is starting to slowly erode and ruin it." He summarizes his concern by saying, "I'm not anti-growth, but I don't want to kill what we have."

....

As I listen to the former mayor, it occurs to me, a sexagenarian, that younger generations are naturally driven to make their mark, to forge their own identity, to not keep things the same, to attempt to improve upon what is. They bring innovation. As their elders once did, they, too, deserve to have their moment in the sun. This includes trendsetting in fashion, art, music, architecture, industrial design, their take on organized religion, their rejection of the old ways of racism and sexual and gender discrimination—all manifestations of culture. This can be hard on the generation in power, as the threat of losing control sends both a subliminal and overt message that the end is near—in more ways than one. So we cling even harder to our version of the tried and true, not wanting to let go. Indeed, so much of the change that Traverse City is seeing is coming from outside of the area. Just like Carruthers. His election as mayor, and his repeat terms, ushered in a new era of equality that will leave its own historical mark for generation upon generation. Sometimes change can indeed be good for what ails us as a community.

....

Carruthers brings up "festival fatigue" in Traverse City, if not for the region. "We marketed this area heavily for tourism with the Cherry Festival and Film Festival and beer festivals and wine festivals, and over the years we've created our own mess by tourism." He asks rhetorically, "How much is too much? Why is every weekend a festival?"

Although that may be something of an exaggeration for Traverse City, it definitely isn't for the region. Kalkaska's National Trout Festival in late April. Boyne City's National Morel Mushroom Festival in May. Empire's Asparagus Festival and Leland's Wine and Food Festival in June. The Traverse City Film Festival and Charlevoix's weeklong Venetian Festival in July. Suttons Bay's Art Festival, Elk Rapids Harbor Days, and the Cedar Polka Fest in August. Northport's Leelanau UnCaged and Harbor Springs Festival of the Book in September. And let's not forget the Up North granddaddy of them all, the weeklong National Cherry Festival in Traverse City that runs over the July Fourth holiday. This list is not exclusive; there are many other festivals throughout the region, all with avid followings. Carruthers understands how some locals may complain, *Enough already!* Nevertheless, such cultural celebrations are real moneymakers, and are especially vital for small communities. "I think it all boils down to we can all talk and say that we want something different, but these are all revenue generating," he admits. "We're a tourist town that makes a lot of money off tourism. We can't ever take tourism away."

CHAPTER 4

SETTLERS

What we have loved, others will love, and we
will teach them how.

—William Wordsworth,
"The Prelude"

When I was interviewing Glen Chown, executive director of the Grand Traverse Regional Land Conservancy, while walking the grounds of the conservancy's new headquarters, he mentioned Marla Morrissey, one of the conservancy's major supporters. "That's someone you should talk to," he encouraged. Originally from the West Coast, with a home in Los Osos, California, and, until recently, a hobby farm in Oregon, Morrissey has fallen in love with northern Michigan.

Love Thy Neighbors

Morrissey spoke to me by phone from her second home near Kalkaska in October 2022, enjoying the autumn color display at her new Northwoods property. Once clearcut during the lumber industry's heyday in northern Michigan in the late 1800s, the woods on Morrissey's property are flourishing in their ongoing recovery. Reflecting aloud, she says, "I'm very lucky to be here. It's been quite a journey. How did this happen to me? Is it really about climate change? I'm still in the process of understanding it myself."

Morrissey, seventy, has been involved with the environmental movement since sixth grade. Back then she assisted with a campaign to protect the tule elk (native to California) from hunting "because there were almost none left." Her growing ecological awareness led her to support numerous environmental causes out West. One involved working on a marine sanctuary off the California coast to protect *Salmonidae*. "I'm a big salmon and steelhead person," she avers, an influence owing to her father, who was "quite the fisherman." (She'll be right at home here in northern Michigan). She adds, "I just got the fish conservation genes." Of note, Morrissey authored a proclamation declaring October as "Salmon and Steelhead Awareness Month" for San Luis Obispo County, which eventually went statewide. "We all want the fish to be there for our grandkids."

She was born in Los Angeles and, she says, didn't take to it at all from the get-go. "I probably wanted to exit the next day. So that was the beginning of my migration; it was like, get me out of here as soon as you can." Her father started a successful mini-storage enterprise in California—"before mini-storage was even a term"—in the sixties and she became involved in the family business, her son eventually taking the helm. In 2016, on the recommendations of her accountant and Realtor, and having never set foot in Michigan, she sold the business and restarted another: ownership of a commercial property leased to a CVS Pharmacy in Traverse City. Morrissey says 2016 "was a different world" then in northwest lower Michigan. "I had no idea about the influx of pressure that was about to come here."

Researching environmental groups in the Grand Traverse region, she learned of the work of the Grand Traverse Regional Land Conservancy (GTRLC). Later, in 2019, she made her first visit to the region. Kate Pearson, the conservancy's senior charitable giving specialist, took her on a walking tour of several conservancy projects. They included the Maplehurst Natural Area in Antrim County, Lower Woodcock Lake Nature Preserve in Benzie County, Mitchell Creek Meadows: The Don and Jerry Oleson Nature Preserve in Grand Traverse County, and the Upper Manistee Headwaters: The Milock Family Preserve in Kalkaska County. "I've worked with a lot of agencies on the West Coast doing environmental work, mostly habitat conservation, raising money to buy property to preserve it. I was just so impressed with everything the conservancy was doing here."

Afterwards, Pearson shared a listing for an 80-acre parcel that was for sale, adjacent to the nearly 1,300-acre Milock Family Preserve. While visiting the preserve with Pearson, Morrissey "just fell in love with it." She imagined, "Gosh, if I could be out here, how nice that would be!" Dream come true, she purchased the property in 2022. Morrissey will be living there from April through November, with longer-term plans to make it a permanent move. She'll be living on ten acres; the remaining seventy acres have been donated to the GTRLC.

....

Realizing a childhood dream, Morrissey kept her Oregon farm teeming with livestock and domesticated animals for children to interact with, including goats, miniature donkeys, and dogs. She also leased part of the property for rotational grazing for grass-fed cattle. But the impact of the twenty-two-year megadrought affecting Oregon—the worst in 1,200 years—told her that it wouldn't be sustainable.[1] Nor did she consider the farm to be "much of a gift to the world." When she read about the "Biomass distribution on Earth" study, published in 2018 in the *Proceedings of the National Academy of Sciences* journal—which found that "humans and their livestock now comprise about 96% of all mammal biomass on Earth"[2]—Morrissey says, "it disturbed me greatly." The farm was sold in 2022.

She mentions Lydia Millet, a climate novelist living in Tucson, Arizona, who works for the Center for Biological Diversity, an organization Morrissey has supported in the past. She shares a quote from a *New York Times* profile of the author published on October 6, 2022, a week before we spoke. It includes an excerpt from one of Millet's essays, which reflects her own experience in Oregon: "[S]he won't stay if the land 'begins to die too visibly—if I see its native life turn brown, as the drier, hotter seasons pass, and vanish around me.' The guilt of abandoning the place she loves would be bad, but it would be better than helplessly watching it turn to dust."[3]

Morrissey relates to Millet having a second home (Millet's in Maine). "Having these two houses, I'm dealing with that now too. My carbon footprint is higher [because of] that. So here we are part of creating a problem." Having the means to have both can be easily rationalized, in that one is fortunate enough to be in such an enviable position. As well, having the option to move to a more climate-favorable locale is an advantage, whether owning one or more homes. Morrissey's conscience is grappling with this in a very open, vulnerable way. "So there's a lot of stuff in there that I sure don't have figured out, but it bothers me. It's very complex what we're dealing with today."

Morrissey has a heightened sensitivity to her impact on the area as a newcomer. The day of our chat, she would be meeting a neighbor near her new home for the first time. She's concerned about how she presents to strangers who might well have been born and raised in the area. "How am I a threat? Maybe they don't want seventy acres going to the preserve. I don't know who these people are. How are they going to categorize who I am? How open can I be? All these thoughts have crossed my mind. Mostly, I just want to get along; I don't want to be a threat to anybody." She is also cognizant of being an outsider who has just purchased a home in the area, though one with a conscience. "I bought a house that now makes it harder for locals to have the money to compete with buying this kind of property."

When Morrissey was a child, her mother read her children's books by the early conservationist Thornton Burgess, such as *Old Mother West Wind*.[4] "They helped children see what the animals were experiencing," she relates. This empathic perspective took root then and is still playing an influence so many years later in her unfolding new life in northern Michigan. She asks herself, "As a neighbor to the preserve, how am I supposed to live here?" She believes that her non-human neighbors should be accommodated as well by her presence. She's already installed screens on the windows to prevent birds from flying into them. And she realizes what was once okay on her farm in Oregon isn't okay here. "I cannot let my dogs run around," Morrissey says, "even though there's all this space." She emphasizes, "I want to be attentive to what my effect is. It's wonderful for me that I get to be here. But what does it do to the animal life next to me? Should I put bird feeders out, and when?" Such considerations, she says, are an endless ecological puzzle to work through. "I'm realizing now as a migrant that getting more knowledgeable about where you are is pretty important, and how you can fit in to help enhance a place and not diminish it."

Wanting to reinvigorate her involvement in environmentalism, especially driven by what she's experienced with climate change on the West Coast, she feels as though she's back on track. The conservancy's new headquarters at Mitchell Creek Meadows will feature a library that Morrissey has taken a lead role in establishing, donating forty boxes of environmental books, a collection she's amassed over many years of environmental activism. Now as an official GTRLC volunteer, she'll be helping at the Milock Family

Preserve and in the library at the new conservancy headquarters in Traverse City. Through her interactions with visitors, she'll be raising consciousness about their role as members of a wider family in the northern Michigan ecosystem, and beyond. "It's an awareness process." She mentions to me that "normally, a conversation goes so quickly you never get to talk about who we are as a species and what's really happening." Not anymore. Morrissey is more than ready to have that essential conversation here in northern Michigan.

A Homecoming

I met Heather Nachazel Ford nearly two decades ago at her Uncle Greg's wedding at St. Joseph's Catholic Church on South Bohemian Road near Maple City. The little white wood-sided house of worship with its distinct bell tower, now used sparingly for weddings and an annual Mass on May 1 observing the Feast of St. Joseph the Worker, was built by Bohemian immigrants in 1884.[5] The wedding Mass in this idyllic rural northern Michigan setting honored not only the newlyweds but also their immigrant ancestors.

Heather, forty-three, would divorce at the age of twenty-four and strike out on a new life, attending Michigan State University (MSU) in Lansing, earning a degree in social work. Upon graduation, she received a commission in the U.S. Air Force. During her ten years in the military, she served in the Iraq War in 2010. Later, while stationed in Japan, she met her second husband, Greg, thirty-eight, who was also in the Air Force. In 2013, they returned stateside. Three years later, Heather, then a major, received her discharge. The Fords moved to Colorado Springs, Colorado, and later Seattle, Washington, where Greg pursued his career in the tech field and Heather worked as a licensed clinical social worker. While in Seattle with her growing family of two children (Jacqueline, now ten, and Christian, eight), Heather's homing instinct kicked in, and she began mulling over returning to northern Michigan. Eventually, amidst the pandemic, when so many Americans reconsidered their lives, she tired of the "rat race" in Seattle, a metro area of 737,000 residents.[6]

So in February 2021, Heather, with family in tow, not only returned to the Grand Traverse region for good, but the couple also purchased a property in Leelanau County in the heart of her Bohemian ancestors' homeland. Always up for a challenge, the Fords bought what is known locally as the Bicentennial Barn property, a historic landmark on the northwest corner of the intersection of M-22 and South Bohemian Road, once known as Shalda's Corners. The four-acre property, just a mile from Good Harbor Bay, abuts the Sleeping Bear Heritage Trail, which runs directly in front of their home and traces along M-22. "Returning pays homage to our ancestry," Heather says proudly.

While interviewing her at the Bicentennial Barn property in early May 2022, she shows me a precious family document: *Descendants of Wencil Nachazel & Miscellaneous Items* by Bob and JoAnne (Nachazel) Burkey, written in 2002. The Nachazels' American story began about the time of the American Civil War. Johann Nachazel, his wife, Mary (Koubek) Nachazel, and the first of what would end up being thirteen children, four-year-old Mary, came from Czechoslovakia. They were part of the Bohemian emigration to America in that era, first arriving by ship in Chicago around 1860, and several years later, in Good Harbor Bay on a hired sailboat, most likely a schooner, that "sailed to Michigan looking for Paradise."[7]

Soon after, the Nachazels ended up homesteading a large parcel "near Pyramid Bay, in deep forests never touched by human hands," helping to establish the village of North Unity. (The Fords' property is located on land that was once part of North Unity.) The family history notes that the Czech emigres' "first love was farming and particularly the growing of fruit. Apples, pears, peaches, strawberries, but especially cherries were grown in abundance."[8]

While reading the Nachazel family history, I unearthed several interesting nuggets. The first, family genealogist JoAnne Burkey remembering her grandfather telling her that "he would have to carry a shotgun to school because of the bears." Then this: "The Czechs have many sayings to promote beer drinking, but the claims are often dubious. One of the favorite ones is 'Beer makes beautiful bodies.'"[9] Unfortunately, try as I might, I have not found that to be the case.

....

Once I realized the Fords were my new neighbors, approximately three miles from our cottage in Cedar, I had several occasions to visit during the summers of 2021 and 2022, being invited to family events, including a reunion. The festivities at the Fords usually center around a bonfire, a cookout, copious alcoholic beverages, joyous conversation, and booming laughter well into the evening.

The farmhouse has been gutted for renovation, so the family had been living in a camper on the property during the warmer months while renting an area home through the winter. But enough of that, Heather informed me in the spring of 2023. The Fords purchased a second home in the area as they await the completion of the renovation and becoming permanent occupants of the Bicentennial Barn property in 2025.

During our interview, we both prefer to talk outside under a sunny sky, the temperature pleasant in the low sixties, with a cool, light wind stirring the smoke from the bonfire she's tending. "I'm a Nachazel, Tim, so you know we gotta have a fire to talk by," the short in stature yet physically capable millennial conveys in her military-honed command presence. Hadley, one of the Fords' three Labrador retrievers, keeps me company during the entire interview, occasionally soliciting a head scratch, while his colleagues dutifully bark at passersby.

Since moving to Seattle, Heather and her family had been coming to the Traverse City region every summer to vacation with her parents, her sister's family, and her many relatives in the area. "I wanted to be in the country. I really got sick of suburbia." The Fords also tired of the social unrest occurring in Seattle, as well as the other maladies affecting many metropolitan areas these days, including a growing drug problem and homeless population. She says that while in Seattle, her kids couldn't go outside and play without her worrying about their safety. "I just told Greg I'm not going to raise them like this."

During the pandemic they rented a house in Glen Arbor for six weeks in February to see if the northern Michigan winter weather would agree with them. "We had the best time of our lives," she recalls, "and that's when we bought this house." A proud Midwesterner (and ardent Kansas City Chiefs fan, Greg being a native Kansan), she says her new home means "everything" to her. And like every boomeranger I spoke with for this book, Heather confesses, "You don't realize how beautiful it is here until you live other places in the world. I lived in the mountains, and I love the mountains. But it's not *here*."

Having deep family ties to the region has helped the Fords' reception, which, she says, "has been really nice." For example, when Heather visited the local post office to establish residency, the postmaster noted, "'Oh, you're a Nachazel. Your postman's a Nachazel. We'll take care of you.' That's the small-town thing I've never had." As well, her uncles have readily pitched in with some construction work on the house. Her Uncle Greg, an artist, intends to paint a fresh mural to replace the weathered one on the post-and-beam barn. It was painted as the official National State Commemorative Bicentennial Landmark in 1976.[10]

Because theirs is an inholding property in the Sleeping Bear Dunes National Lakeshore, there are certain restrictions. Significant alterations to the exterior of their buildings are not permitted. Moreover, the property cannot be used for commercial purposes, such as a short-term rental or a barn wedding venue. They can, however, have a farmstand, selling produce raised in their own garden. "We had to get all of our plans approved by the park superintendent," she says, adding, "he loves what we're doing here."

The Fords are indeed getting back to the land. They've tilled a quarter-acre garden. A small greenhouse is destined for seedling starters. The first of their poultry livestock was delivered, and they've butchered and served them, a life lesson for their children. They also plan to raise horses and sheep. Heather says earnestly, "I want to work and live off the land, just like my ancestors." She and her sister, Meghan, spent a lot of time during their childhood on their grandfather's 160-acre farm in Kingsley—and a lot of it working there—an experience she treasures, if not at the time, then certainly today. "We want to keep it simple and have a simple way of life. We're getting back to our roots."

....

A few weeks after talking with Heather, on an unseasonably warm Saturday evening in mid-May, the temperature earlier that day reaching the low nineties, I stop by the Fords to say hello. No one is home except the barking Labs inside the camper. So I decide to drive over to the Cleveland Township Cemetery. It's within walking distance, next to the Cleveland Township Hall off M-22 at the former Shalda's Corners, which is also the site of a long-gone general store, dance hall, and icehouse. The white sign at the entrance declares that the cemetery was established in 1880. There is no gate, visitors apparently always welcome. I turn onto the two-track that winds through the grounds. The graveyard isn't a big draw on Saturday nights in May; other than the "residents," I'm alone. I park my truck in the middle of the two-track. M-22 is quiet, traffic sparse.

I stroll among the headstones searching for Nachazel markers. As I wander about, I come across some of the more common Bohemian names of the early settlers in the 1850s and 1860s, Shalda and Bufka among them. A carpet of tiny, low-growing lavender wildflowers covers many of the graves in the sunlit areas. Birdsong and spring peeper calls enhance my tranquility. About ten minutes after I begin my exploration of the cemetery, I walk up to the tombs of Anna and Joseph Nachazel, laid to rest in the late 1950s. Side by side, the couple's graves are shaded by a towering pine tree, most likely growing when the first Nachazels arrived in Good Harbor Bay so long ago. I say a prayer for them, the departed, and for me, still here. Fortunate that they were to have walked the Earth here in Leelanau County. As am I.

One Loud Cultural Influencer

The question is, who *doesn't* know the Loud brothers? Throughout my preliminary discussions with friends and acquaintances about my project and considering interesting, topic-germane people to interview, on more than one occasion I was asked, "Have you spoken with the Loud Brothers yet?" In their short time in Traverse City, the sibling tandem has made their mark as chroniclers of the area's cultural evolution. Through their *Boardman Review* website, I managed to connect with Nick, co-founder of the print and digital journal, along with his older brother, Chris. Always eager to meet with enthusiasts of Up North life, Nick readily agreed to get together in early August, at Brew (naturally). It was an overcast late morning, and the coffeehouse was overrun with locals and lots of tourists who wanted to hang out in a suitably trendy establishment, notably with an abundance of moms with middle school–aged kids. The din of happy campers provided an appropriate downtown Traverse City summertime ambiance for our conversation.

Nick, thirty-three, is a transplant to the area, having grown up in Ann Arbor. He was no stranger to the region, however. "As long as I can remember, my family came up to Northport and Glen Arbor and rented a cabin for a weekend or a week in the summer, and sometimes in the winter too." In 2002, his parents built a house in Northport. For seven consecutive years, throughout high school and college, he worked summers at a restaurant there. "It was definitely a way of falling in love with the area, meeting people, and making summer friends who are now my friends." Working in a restaurant gives one an intimate view of culture, and he managed to get "a good idea what Leelanau County was like and what Traverse City was like."

Nick attended Kenyon College in Ohio, earning a degree in filmmaking and psychology. Then he headed for Los Angeles to cut his teeth as a documentary filmmaker, staying in California for the next six years. He moved to Traverse City in spring 2017, joining Chris to launch the *Boardman Review*. Thematically, The *Review* has an Up North lifestyle focus that showcases the creative work of young professionals and established artists—fine artists, photographers, poets, fiction and nonfiction writers. Along with its travelogues and photo essays, the publication explores what makes the Grand Traverse region such a desirable location to not only visit but also to live and work in. Foremost, it celebrates the area's extraordinary natural resources as being the best reason for being here. If there would have been a *Boardman Review*–like publication when I first ventured Up North decades ago promoting the good life to be had in the region, as well as so much career opportunity that has emerged of late, chances are my family would have relocated way back then. No doubt the *Boardman Review* is influencing others right now to make that permanent move north.

During a period of extensive travel just before moving to Traverse City—including visiting Italy and living in Norway for several months—Nick developed the concept for the *Boardman Review*: the types of stories to tell and the multimedia methods of telling them—print and/or digital, videos and podcasts. It would be all of the above.

"When you're traveling and you start thinking about the place that you love, it really clears your mind," Nick relates. "It took me to what are my core values and what are the things that are most important to me about this area and the lifestyle. So that experience really helped me put together this publication's concept." When Nick arrived in Traverse City, he brought along a sense of urgency about launching the *Review*. He thought, "It's now or never. Someone else will do it if we don't and I'll be kicking myself." So it happened sooner than later, with the first issue published just months after he relocated here, in the summer of 2017.

....

In addition to covering stories that highlight the region's identity as a growing must-see if not must-stay destination, often focusing on pieces especially appealing to those in their mid-twenties to mid-forties, a nonprofit organization is highlighted in each issue. Reflecting the community-first values of the Louds, a portion of the proceeds of each issue is donated to the respective profiled nonprofit. Overall in the *Review*, "everything is centered on whether you're from this area or about being in this area," Nick explains. "It needs to have some sort of centric theme to it, as to why you chose to be here, whether you chose to stay here or you moved and came back, or you just moved here." He well knows, per his own experience, that "there is something about this area that draws people in." To be sure, it's the region's spectacular natural beauty and Traverse City's rapidly developing identity as a "cool town," he says. He makes it clear that the *Review* purposely stays away from "pissing contests"—controversial subjects—especially of the local political variety. "We try not to hit people over the head with an opinion. There's [already] plenty of that out there."

Nick, a handsome GQ-looking guy with a closely cropped beard and swept-back dark-brown coiffure, is part of the millennial influx in Traverse City that's altering the landscape. Enlivening night life. Expanding foodie culture. Refreshing seasonal festivals. Catalyzing entrepreneurial energy and innovative ideas, exemplified by the *Review* itself. This, as ever, threatens the status quo, "the establishment," as it was derogatorily called in the sixties and seventies. Nick recognizes this. "It's gotten to the point where some people feel that the change has gotten out of their control."

He hasn't ruled out involvement in local politics someday; meanwhile, he encourages others from his age group to become civically involved. Heeding his own advice, Nick now serves on the Leelanau Conservancy Board of Directors as, half-jokingly, "the token young person on the board." Most of the conservancy's board members are boomers and above the age of sixty. But that's not a condemnation. "They've been very welcoming of me bringing in new ideas. They think some of the thought processes should be evolving and changing; they're just not sure how to do that. They're open to change. That's really nice."

The cultural shift that is happening in the Grand Traverse region, with its to-be-expected occasional clash of values, is not all that unique. Some of it is a reluctant changing of the guard, a wariness of youthful gentrification. There's a more liberal, progressive orientation making its presence known among the more conservative traditionalists who have historically decided the direction of the region. But, according to Nick, there is a unifying saving grace at work here: "There is one common denominator: everyone loves the area. Everyone believes that they don't want to ruin certain things, whether environmental protection of the land or protecting the land from overdevelopment, as well as picking the right kind of development in the right place." *Bingo.* And so the essential open question facing the region remains: how can you love a place and invite others to love it, too, without destroying what attracted everyone in the first place?

Living elsewhere and returning to the area has a way of widening one's perspective. Nick realized he had been in his own "liberal bubble" before he got out into the world. He's observed that people who have relocated to the region—whether newcomers or boomerangers—"have a really good appreciation" for their new northern Michigan home. Whereas "people who have been here all their lives haven't been afforded a chance to live somewhere else, so they can get more into that cynical mindset. Those are the type of people who are afraid of new people coming in and change." Through the Louds' profiling of "all the cool things people are doing here," the *Boardman Review*'s founders hope to influence those more change-averse folks, publishing relatable stories for everyone. It's not just the wealthy who are migrating to the area that are "automatically outside of your sphere," as Nick puts it. There are young professionals integrating themselves and their families into the fabric of the region's culture and traditions, who care about environmental conservation and being a part of a thriving, caring community.

....

I'm old enough to be Nick's father. He's young enough not to want to spend time with me. But our conversation isn't limited by the thirty-three years' age difference. I don't want to be negative about embracing change, although I do try to discriminate between change for the better and mere change for change's sake. And I don't want to come off as curmudgeonly and change challenged. Nick observes, "Any younger generation throughout history is a little more hopeful about their lives." In a *but seriously* comment that doesn't escape me, he adds, "My parents might be complaining about something like too many people in Northport. I just remind them that 'you know, you guys are living an incredibly good, comfortable life.' And they go, 'Yeah, we know.' You get so used to your own little world. But it's good to have those reminders."

He continues, "Living here, it's good to do some of those stereotypical touristy things like going to Sleeping Bear Dunes and hiking to a great lookout spot so that you can remind yourself why you appreciate living here and why you chose to live here, and that you understand the value of living here. We're incredibly lucky to be in this area."

Before we part company, Nick gives me a copy of the *Boardman Review*, Issue 19. The cover photo looks to have been taken by a drone, an example of the popular airborne photographic angle of the past few years capturing that Up North magic from above, thanks to technology. The image is courtesy of Pure Michigan. A lone paddleboarder is floating above translucent water in what is most likely Lake Michigan. The shallows are a sandy brown and the water transitions into gradually darker bands of clear blue. It certainly makes me want to open the magazine. So I do.

Inside, the issue's six stories cover a writer's meditation on her lifelong relationship with water, the opening of a cannabis shop in Northport, the Traverse City Film Festival, the development of the new Chain of Lakes Water Trail through four Grand Traverse region counties, a local foundation that supports an artist-in-residence program with a guesthouse and studio design involving internationally renowned architect Peter Bohlin, and a husband-and-wife's adventurous spring bike tour of lower Michigan.[11] The topics—all celebrating the progressive vitality and natural splendor of the region—are intended to pique the interest of residents and visitors alike, with that special younger generations appeal. Old man that I am, I liked them too.

Last One in Shut the Door

When you first spend quality time on a freshwater lake, especially as a child—whether for an overnight stay, a long weekend, or extended vacation—be it a Great Lake or a small-acreage body of water you can easily see the opposite shoreline from, it gets imprinted into memory. As a child in northeastern Pennsylvania in the sixties, I had my first such experience when I was nine years old. Our next-door-neighbors in Scranton, the Walshes, invited me to spend a week with them at their cabin on a lake in the nearby Pocono Mountains. Another first—going out on an aluminum fishing boat with my friend's grandfather for an outboard-motor-propelled cruise, as I gripped the side in fear while exhilarated by being out on the water. Using flashlights to spot clots of baby bullheads wriggling along the shoreline at night. Listening to popular music of the day—the Beach Boys, The Beatles, the Stones—while sitting at a picnic table outside the clubhouse giggling as teenagers danced flirtatiously, an attraction we in our prepubescence had yet to comprehend. Fishing for eager yellow perch below us, under cover of a diving platform.

Chasing lightning bugs and ducking stunt-flying bats. So when I heard from Meridith Mulcahy in response to my posting on Nextdoor soliciting any newcomers to the area who might want to share their relocation story, and learning that she and her husband, Pat, live on Lime Lake just two miles from our cottage in Cedar, I couldn't wait to visit them.

As has been the case throughout the remarkable northern Michigan summer of 2022, the mid-August day we meet in early afternoon is perfectly scripted: sun drenched and in the upper seventies, with low humidity and a gentle southwesterly breeze. Meridith kindly brews me some tea, while their dog, Dune, a welcoming and playful Goldendoodle, waits beside me. When Meridith returns, now with Pat, who breaks away from a project in his garage workshop, Dune decides to get a bit closer to me. "I rarely see him lay his head on anyone's feet like that, so he must think you have a good soul," Meridith observes. "He's a good judge of character," I joke, and we press on.

We talk beneath umbrellas on their sprawling second-floor deck overlooking 670-acre Lime Lake, an unobstructed westward view. A pontoon boat slowly cruises northward, while a fishing boat with two anglers is anchored along the drop-off perhaps an eighth of a mile from the shoreline. As I soon discover, they are a delightful couple, often answering for each other and nodding in agreement.

The Mulcahys, both a youthful sixty, are now fully retired as a unit. Pat recently "semi-retired" as a trial attorney in Ann Arbor; Meridith left the workforce just before him after twenty-eight years as a high school Spanish teacher in Novi, the westernmost suburb of Detroit. Early in the pandemic, the couple hunkered down at their Lime Lake seasonal home, purchased fifteen years earlier, and Pat worked remotely. As with many trying out remote work during the pandemic, the experiment was successful. So, after thirty-four years in a house built in 1892 in Northville, just south of Novi, they decided to relocate permanently to Leelanau County, closing on the sale of their Northville home two weeks earlier. Says Pat, "So far, so good; I'm not really missing it."

Pat brought Meridith to the area in the eighties when they were in high school, and they would go skiing at Sugar Loaf ski resort (which was also a high school winter break destination for friends of mine in Indianapolis back in the early seventies). They returned to Leelanau County repeatedly over the years. Their two adult children, who now live on the East Coast, "would rather visit us up here than they would downstate," says Meridith. "This is where they spent the summers up here working at The Leland Lodge."

She mentions some northern Michigan friends who recently visited Scotland. "They had a great time," Pat reports. "One said to me when she got back, 'But we have this view here of the bay.' We've traveled a lot too, but really, some of the most spectacular views are right here."

The Mulcahys just completed their first year as residents on Lime Lake, and it's clear they've found contentment. It wasn't long into their new lakeside life that Meridith noticed Pat "was so happy" being here. "I always had my summer vacation. But he had never had this." And "this" is an immersion in nature, something many otherwise preoccupied urban dwellers have or make little time for. Perception deepens. Things otherwise ignored become captivating, such as dragonflies in flight, sunning turtles, cloud formations, starlight. The couple even noticed the day the ice completely disappeared from the lake's surface, that most assured sign of winter surrendering to spring. Indeed, winter's still, stark beauty "has its own personality," Meridith marvels. As well, her husband relishes the solitude winter brings to the lake. "It's a neat thing when there are no boats or docks out there; there's hardly anybody here," he muses. They estimate that less than half of the homes ringing Lime Lake are occupied year-round.

....

Meridith anticipates more people coming north, to stay for good, in the near future. "People are going to start moving toward the Great Lakes because of fresh water." She tells me that her mother's thinking is being influenced by climate change, which, she believes, is becoming a more common consideration in people's relocation decisions. "My mom said, 'I think I might take a little money and try and buy a lot in the UP.' She's also thinking for [our family's] future generations, that might be a better place to own property."

Like most Up North relocators, the Mulcahys came for the water aesthetics, as well as to be near the spectacular topography of Sleeping Bear Dunes National Lakeshore, where they hike frequently. They're especially fond of the dramatic views of Lake Michigan, such as seeing the Manitou Islands from Pyramid Point. Says Pat, "What draws me is just the shape of the [Leelanau] peninsula. Even if you don't know anything about the area, you look at a map and say, 'I wonder what that place is like right there. And you can go in any direction, ten or fifteen miles, and be able to drop into Lake Michigan."

My father-in-law once asked me why my wife and I kept returning to northern Michigan year after year rather than travel elsewhere and expand our horizons. Since discovering the region decades ago, our migratory habit commences in the trout fishing and morel hunting days of late April and concludes in mid-October with the blazing fall color signaling winter's approach. Meridith echoes my answer: "Isn't it amazing how you can always find something new up here? Every time we come up, I say to Pat, 'We did something new. Saw a new road, a new restaurant, or this little art gallery, or this hike. There's been something new every time.'"

When it comes to tourism and the increasing numbers of people in the area, Meridith chooses to accentuate the positive by "making a strong mental effort that I'm not going to go down that path. When it's busy, then we say, 'Look how many beautiful people get to come up here and enjoy a little slice of what we get all year-round.' If it means that I have to wait a little longer in line at the grocery store, then you look at the kids in their bathing suits covered with sand and you say to yourself, 'Wow, look how many happy people are up here right now.'" I can see why she entered the teaching profession.

Meridith says they used to effuse about their love of and experiences in northern Michigan to family, friends, and acquaintances, gushing about the "really nice spots" they've discovered. "Now we keep our mouths shut." I laugh in concurrence. "You say 'last one in shut the door,' but that's because we're in, right? This is the rub. Not that the [Leelanau] conservancy doesn't do good work; I know they do; and I know it's a good thing. Yet sometimes I feel it's people with money coming up here saying, 'I want to protect my area and I know how to do it. So I'll try to keep everybody else out.'" The Mulcahys are members of the Leelanau Conservancy and endorse the locally renowned nonprofit's property acquisitions to ensure that large tracts of woodlands, wetlands, and ag land stay undeveloped in perpetuity. Pat candidly states, "I would like very restricted development of just about everything. I don't want to see franchises here in the county. I don't want to see restaurants popping up and 7-Elevens and things of that nature. . . . You'd hate to see that strip mall scenario; good God, that would be just a terrible thing."

He jokingly adds, "Let's keep out the riffraff." We all laugh. But isn't it true. Getting away also means getting away from the never-ending and often-violent crime endemic to America's urban areas. Yet the typically well-educated, moneyed classes owning seasonal/vacation homes need not worry much about their neighborhoods in the Grand Traverse region or the Great Lakes at large or other highly prized outdoor destinations across the country, as access is allowed or prevented based upon one's net worth, a kind of natural selection. The figurative door opens and shuts predicated on means; on affordability. On a seasonable or permanent foothold basis, such highly sought outdoor playgrounds are only open to the upper-middle and upper classes. "Last one in" may, in fact, be a misnomer. Clearly, you can always pay your way in. Yet this is really nothing new: that's always been the ticket to ease of entry to northern Michigan.

....

Before I leave, Meridith mentions their shoreline project. I lean over the balcony railing and look down at their seawall, which they plan to replace with "a more lake-friendly solution" that will entail organic fiber coir logs and perennial grasses for erosion control. A retired high school biology teacher who lives on Lime Lake has been working with property owners to install this environmentally sound structure. Then she points to the beginnings of a large butterfly garden and talks about perennials she'll be planting this fall, a haven for hummingbirds too. I sigh before I turn to go. The four seasons have profoundly entered the Mulcahys' lives. I'm happy for them.

Um, Make Mine Seasonal

Through my Nextdoor online solicitation to folks in the Cedar area, I make contact with several other neighbors of mine, all new to me. One, Carrie Beia, forty-nine, owns a "super cute" post-and-beam constructed chalet, built in the seventies, near Sugar Loaf golf course. With the help of an inheritance from her father, she purchased the home pre-pandemic in 2019, working with her cousin, a real estate agent in Traverse City. An East Lansing native and Michigan State University graduate now a human resources consultant with KPMG, one of the "big four" accountancy firms, Beia wanted a vacation home in northern Michigan, where she has some family, including a relative who lives on Good Harbor Bay in Leelanau County. Then, thanks to the pandemic and no longer traveling four days a week for business and working remotely, she decided to become a year-round resident. Her first-year experience in rural northern Michigan, however, changed her mind.

Up North winters can be brutal. For example, during the winter of 2013–2014, Maple City in Leelanau County recorded 266 inches of snow.[12] That winter, the Manitou Passage froze over. Aside from snow and ice, wintertime daylight is short in northern Michigan, lasting about nine hours in January. Despite the heavenly summers and the delightful shoulder seasons of spring and fall, not everyone is a fan of winter. Beia is one of them.

Moving to Cedar "took a little while to get used to," she confesses. For those accustomed to the incessant background noise of the big city, the quietude in the wooded, rural northern Michigan country can be unsettling, as it was for her. Beia experienced her first winter here in 2021. "I'm a Michigan girl and snow doesn't bother me. What got me with this first winter was the isolation and darkness." Moreover, "I was now a resident and no longer a vacationer. That changes things."

She discovered that it can be challenging to get things done in the hinterlands of Traverse City, which is about a thirty-minute drive from her home on the outskirts of Cedar. She tells me, "I had a simple incident where my car battery died. I could not believe the effort that was required to get it fixed." It was a Friday night, and she couldn't get the battery jumped. Then she called for a tow truck, which took two days before it could get out to Cedar. She ended up renting a car. The price tag for getting the issue resolved reached $1,000. During the weeklong ordeal, she came to the conclusion that "this is hard, and it shouldn't have to be."

During the winter of 2023 she rented in Athens and Marietta, Georgia, each six-week stints, and returned to Cedar in early April. In February 2024 she purchased a home just outside of Atlanta, a more temperate place to overwinter that also offers "a little more suburban convenience." Remote work affords her that opportunity, just as it does in northern Michigan. "I will keep my house here; I love to be here in summer and fall. Then I can spend winter and spring in Georgia."

Housing Inclusivity

I spoke with Tony Lentych, executive director of the Traverse City Housing Commission, by Zoom in March 2022. (Note: In April 2023, Lentych accepted a job with the Michigan State Housing Development Authority as chief housing investment officer, putting him in a position to impact housing policy throughout the state.) I was curious about his leadership role with the commission and his experience providing affordable public housing for older adults and disabled persons in Traverse City since 2015. This segment of the local population is easy to overlook in any city, perhaps even more so for a tourist town. People come here to temporarily escape their cares, to take a timeout from demanding jobs and kick back for a week or two. Understandably, their focus is elsewhere; they're not on the lookout for neediness. Yet the task of meeting the basic human needs of those on the lower end of the economic scale never goes away, no matter the location.

Lentych, fifty-five, has a serious, professorial look about him, suggested by his salt-and-pepper hair, goatee, eyeglasses, and intent concentration when listening. Yet he is disarmingly quick to laugh and an easy conversationalist. No doubt these traits were honed when he first moved to Leelanau County in 2006, relocating from Lansing after a six-year stint as the executive director of the Community Economic Development Association of Michigan, and then as the general manager of Leelanau Cellars winery in Omena. He ended up marrying and relocating to Traverse City in 2008. "I always told myself after visits Up North that if I could figure out a way to make a living in northern Michigan, I was going to do it." Now that he's been living here for the past seventeen years, he says, "It's hard to get me away from this region." As is the case for many northern Michiganders, Lentych comments, "More people come visit me here than any other place I've ever lived."

After our introductory conversation, he asked when I would be Up North again and invited me to "come downtown and we'll get some coffee." I would do that in late May, having breakfast at J&S Hamburg on Front Street, a locals' haunt since 1938 and just a short walk from his office in the Riverview Terrace apartment building on the westside of Traverse City along the Boardman-Ottaway River.

As soon as I arrive, Lentych fetches a bulging keychain, and we take an elevator several floors up in the ten-story building for a quick tour of some empty apartments. On the way up, a petite older woman holding a geriatric teacup chihuahua enters the elevator, smiling broadly and greeting Lentych. He engages her in conversation, jokingly calling her "Grumpy." He knows all the residents by name and nickname. She enjoys their casual interaction, as does he. I comment that the dog is cute. "She's pretty old, but thank you," Grumpy says, bidding us good day as she steps off. "I tell my people here in the building that it's an honor to come into your home every day and work," he says to me once the door closes behind the tenant.

Riverview Terrace, the commission's flagship, as it manages several other public and low-income housing facilities throughout the region, is "a community asset," Lentych says. It serves low-income residents sixty-two and older and those with disabilities. Those fortunate enough to get in—the building is currently on a five-year waiting list, indicative of the affordable housing crisis in the area—"pay approximately one-third of their adjusted gross income for rent and utilities."[13]

As we continue our elevator ride, he tells me, "A lot of people who raised families and worked here don't have a lot of other families that can take care of them multigenerationally. So they move into a one-bedroom unit with us." As well, the commission assists younger disabled adults who can't take care of a home by themselves but can manage the requirements of living in an apartment. Some of the latter are part of the local low-income workforce, he explains, making them vitally important to the tourist-serving industry, given the profound shortage of service workers.

Riverview Terrace has 115 units. A major renovation at a cost of $11 million was completed in September 2023. The building was constructed in 1974 and opened in 1976, when there were eighty-eight units. Part of the renovation targets ten units to be updated to the latest Americans with Disabilities Act standards for universal accessibility.

Each unit is just under six hundred square feet. We enter one that's being prepared for the next tenant. The one-bedroom apartment is cozy—just enough for someone who's downsized and plans to keep it that way. As he shows me the unit's rooms, it triggers a memory of a similar apartment my widowed grandmother Gertie lived in at the end of her days in Scranton, Pennsylvania, more than fifty years ago. It is an unexpected déjà vu-like moment of reconnection.

"Well, here's the view of the lake that everyone's entitled to," Lentych emphasizes as we look out the north window toward Hotel Indigo on Grandview Parkway and West Bay just beyond, under a cloudy sky. Down below, construction is going on for a mixed-use building that will feature high-end apartments, West Ends Lofts. The four-story structure now obstructs part of the bay view for tenants on the lower floors of Riverview Terrace. It strikes me that water wars aren't just about getting water; it's about seeing water too. To protect views as best it can, Traverse City has a controversial building height limitation of sixty feet. This will work against density—which some, like Lentych, are for—while encouraging suburban sprawl. Managing one of the tallest buildings in Traverse City, he's well aware of the need for public housing and a more contemporary approach to metropolitan development. He finds this "old school" retrograde argument embarrassing for the city.

We finish our unit tour and ride the elevator to the tenth floor, then mount a short flight of stairs to access the roof. "I don't know if you're okay with heights," he says belatedly while opening the door to the outside. I'm tentative but fib, "I'm fine, thanks." The panoramic view is breathtaking: Traverse City to the east, Grand Traverse West Bay to the north, the Boardman-Ottaway River curving just south and west of us, neighborhoods extending toward the southern horizon. I take some photos, feigning composure as I clutch the banister near the roof's edge.

Lentych is a fan of the possible. "I've told people many times that this is one of the few regions I've been where I think we could have it all. We could figure this out." So growth must be intentional and inclusive. This means not forgetting about the local workers who staff the tourist-serving industry. With the lack of affordable housing in the area, Lentych says, "We are excluding the people who work in the kitchens and wait staff and small businesses, like wineries. If we can't find a decent place for the workforce to live, we are going to have more and more restaurants open [just] four days a week." As remains the case today.

He also warns that lack of intentionality when it comes to growth will lead to more complicated problems. As Leelanau County is experiencing, many older people with considerable retirement bankrolls are relocating there. "People make all this money and then they move here, and they made that money by being thoughtful and intentional. But when they get here, they turn their brains off and say, 'No, I don't want any of *that* around me. I moved away from *that*.'" Lentych calls this phenomenon "the old tourists turning on the new tourists."

I ask Lentych how welcoming Traverse City is to newcomers. "Not at all," he says flatly. "They're even less welcoming to young people in general." This includes young newlyweds or partners trying to settle down and raise a family and "be productive members of society." However, he asserts that a certain group of people are indeed well received in the Grand Traverse region: those who have ties here. (His wife, Heather, is a native Michigander, from the Detroit suburb of Royal Oak.) "Somebody grows up here, moves away, comes back with a spouse; it's like a caveman, you know. Catch a spouse and drag them back here."

The image he's suggesting immediately forms a Gary Larson *Far Side* comic in my mind's eye. "We've had this so-called trailing spouse syndrome when the trailing spouse can't find meaningful, gainful employment. Although this has been corrected a little bit with the pandemic because remote working is more acceptable. That's a good thing, but it's also a bad thing in that more people are going to want to move here." In an understatement, managing community growth is complicated.

....

A few days after my interview with Lentych, I receive an emailed photo from him. It's a sunny beachfront scene taken five years earlier. One of his young sons is gripping the chains of a swing at Wilderness State Park as he reaches the zenith of his outbound arc, legs extended for greater reach. In front of him is Lake Michigan; below are sand and dune grass. Lentych writes, "I often wonder what it's going to be like for them when they realize the rest of the world doesn't look like this place. They are spoiled [by their surroundings] for sure. I hope there is a place for them here when they grow up."

Homelessness in Heaven

On an unseasonably chilly day in early May 2022, I'm sitting at a table by myself on the second floor of the Traverse Area District Library's main branch on Woodmere Avenue. I'm a card-carrying TADL member, and I retreat here when in need of some semiprivate space to conduct research in the quiet, relatively distant company of others. The window view of the Traverse Area Recreation Trail and Boardman Lake to the west enhance the contemplative ambiance. Opened in 1999, the library is always alive with patrons and visitors, especially during the summer.

At the table next to me sits a young woman. Her short brunette hair is in disarray; she's wearing two coats, both puffer style, one a vest; her clothing could use a wash; and she's been toting a carry-on-sized suitcase that's decorated with Disney characters from *Toy Story*. Her iPhone is plugged into an outlet as she scrolls, humming some indistinct tune. As I glance at her, she looks up at me. She smiles; I reciprocate and continue working.

About ten minutes later she's no longer alone, the chairs now full of friends or acquaintances. They're warming up and recharging their smartphones too. The conversation is mostly about the newcomers living with them at the Pines, the site of a large homeless encampment near the Grand Traverse Commons. Some meet with their general approval; others distinctly don't. There's some cursing, then some shushing. Four-letter words don't bother me; they're part of my own vocabulary. They keep their voices within reason and aren't really disturbing anyone.

Another young woman walks by me to join her peers. She scowls at me and hisses loudly and quite un-library-like, "What are you looking at, motherfucker?" I stifle a laugh. Instead, I smile slightly and turn back to my work. Ten minutes later, the group starts to dissipate, and soon my original neighbor is alone once again. She rises, puts her now charged smartphone in her pocket, and begins walking away, with rolling suitcase in hand. She smiles at me again, saying, "Have a nice day." I do hope the same for her.

Downstairs, I ask one of the librarians about the homeless population's use of the library. He tells me it's an increasing problem and is concerned that I might have been disturbed by them. I tell him not to worry, they don't bother me. I say that I assume not everyone is comfortable with their presence in the library. He's a good soul, sympathetic to their plight, their need to stay warm and to find some safe place to just hang out. He shares that there have been some incidents, and now the library has a security guard to monitor behavior and keep the peace. It's too bad it's come to this, but I understand. After all, it's a library. The sanctity of this communal space should be respected by all who enter. And being a draw for visitors, for tourists, for young families and their children, the library needs to be a safe space.

When I mention my TADL library experience with homeless patrons to Lentych, he suggests a conversation with a close colleague, Ashley Halladay-Schmandt. She's the director of the Northwest Michigan Coalition to End Homelessness, perhaps the most hopefully named organization I've ever encountered. According to its website, "the Northwest Michigan Coalition to End Homelessness works collaboratively to end homelessness by making homelessness RARE, BRIEF, and ONE TIME."[14]

Halladay-Schmandt, thirty-seven, who is married with two young children, ages five and two, grew up in Cadillac, about an hour south of Traverse City. Her husband, Matt, is from the Detroit metro area. Previously, she lived in Chicago, Virginia, and Kalamazoo, Michigan, where she also worked in the community mental health field. Opening small talk reveals a champion of equity.

I ask her if Traverse City is a good place to raise kids. "To an extent. My eyes are being opened to the region's inequity. One of the reasons we were always hesitant about moving back and having kids here was the lack of diversity." Their children attend a private Montessori school. Although she and her husband are quite pleased with the school, she says it doesn't have the diversity she would prefer. This isn't surprising: according to the U.S. Census Bureau, Grand Traverse County is nearly 93 percent white.[15] In hindsight, she adds, "I don't know that I, as a young professional person, would choose this community had I not had ties here."

Her husband's work led her back to the region. "We were on a sailboat when we decided to move here," a view that would entice any young couple to put down roots in the area. Another critical factor in their decision to move back to northern Michigan: her parents and grandparents live in Traverse City and assist with childcare. "That's why we live here."

Halladay-Schmandt echoes the coalition in her belief that homelessness can be overcome. The solution, obviously, is housing. She says, "You support them in housing, and you see their lives dramatically improve the second they get housed." Yet when she started her job with the coalition, she discovered that "there weren't a lot of people around here when we moved back who were really educated around how to end homelessness." To help the homeless, she first had to help the greater community understand the issue. That is no small challenge.

In every one of her public speaking events, the coalition director starts by saying, "We believe healthy, thriving communities have ended homelessness." Traverse City is a thriving community in many ways, she affirms. But for all? "Well, is it really, or just for some? But that's what our work is: to make it inclusive."

How does the general population of the Grand Traverse region perceive homeless folks? "Generally, the perception is negative," she answers. "There's a fear and misunderstanding of people experiencing homelessness." She says that sometimes when there's a bad experience involving a homeless person it gets amplified, and that's how the population gets demonized. On the other hand, she notes, there are those who say, "'We don't have that problem here, that [homelessness] doesn't exist here.'" She points out that there are three homeless persons in the coffeehouse we're sitting in, which she noticed immediately. "If you've been in the downtown area during summer, it's obvious in a community this size." Becoming aware of the homeless around us does not have a shelf life. "When you see it, you can't unsee it."

Halladay-Schmandt further clarifies the coalition's focus on ending homelessness. "When we say an end to homelessness, we don't mean there is never going to be home-lessness." Yet from an individual standpoint, it can indeed be a rare, brief, and one-time experience. With decent housing and the right support, "people get out of it quickly, and for that person, they never fall into homelessness again. It's the functional definition of ending it."

When I share my TADL experience with the homeless, she informs me that the Pines is the largest homeless camp in the area. It's near the site of the former Traverse City State Hospital, which was an asylum, now known as the Grand Traverse Commons, a thriving retail space featuring shops, art galleries, and restaurants. How ironic. The shutting down of psychiatric hospitals throughout the country during the eighties and nineties is "what started homelessness," she reminds me. Traverse City State Hospital closed in 1989.[16] Central State Hospital in Indy shut down in 1994.[17]

I assume that during the warmer months there is something of a homeless migration to the area. "That's a huge misconception for this region," she corrects me. "We studied the data for our shelter stayers last year. Ninety percent of them said they were from this county [Grand Traverse]—where the services are—and for the five-county region, it was nearly 97 percent." She indicates that approximately 250 homeless persons live in the region. She adds, "You'll have one-offs because that population is transient by nature. But it's not this great migration." She explains that there are not enough emergency shelter beds available in Traverse City during the summer; however, there are enough in the winter through Safe Harbor and Goodwill Inn. "In the winter, we have next to no one sleeping outside. But in the summer, there's a lot because Safe Harbor is seasonal" (open from October 15 to April 30).

The area's chronically homeless population's age "is usually between the ages of fifty to sixty-five," she says, "if they make it to sixty-five." Most of them are white and male, and a significant number are veterans. Alcohol abuse is common. And getting sober is nearly impossible when living on the streets. "It's terrible. They're trying to make their existence bearable. If you have mental illness on top of it, you're not getting the care you need. You can't get to your appointments very well; you can't manage your medications very well." She tells me that when she asks the homeless why they stay in the area during the difficult winters, "The reply is always, 'Well, I grew up here; it's familiar to me; it's home.' No matter what point in your life you're at or how dire it is, you're always looking for that [sense of] community. You're always looking for comfort. Being homeless here offers that to them. I hear this all the time."

....

CHAPTER 5

A TASTE OF NORTHERN MICHIGAN

Q: Could you tell us why you're in Michigan today? What is it about Michigan—coming on the eve of Independence Day, what brought you here?

THE PRESIDENT: Cherry pie.

—Joe Biden, White House Briefing Room/
Speeches and Remarks, July 3, 2021

O nce I exit U.S. 31 North in Antrim County, at the northern tip of crystalline Torch Lake, I'm distinctly in farm country. About a mile from King Orchards, my destination, I pass a neighboring farm replete with can't-miss banners declaring support for former President Donald Trump. Farm families in northern Michigan, like much of the rest of the country, are predominantly Republican. Yet King Orchards is something of an anomaly in that regard, having hosted a visit by President Biden in 2021 on the eve of the great American patriotic holiday, the Fourth of July. Democrats welcoming Democrats.

They Say Money Doesn't Grow on Trees

I arrive at King Orchards, located on M-88, the morning of Thursday, May 26, 2022, just before the Memorial Day weekend, which kicks off the beginning of tourist season in northern Michigan. Farm workers are busy topping off fruit trees just behind the King Orchards Market (one of two, the other on U.S. 31, which is also the location of the King Orchards Bakery). My interview will be with Juliette King McAvoy, vice president of sales and marketing. Her mother, Betsy, lets me know that her daughter is running behind due to her four-year-old son being ill. She offers me a cup of coffee while keeping me company for the time being.

As we chat outside, I take in the ambiance of the farm. The air is alive with barn swallows, the steely-blue-backed, tawny-bellied avian acrobats dart just above and around us. I tell Betsy how much I love them. "I love them too," she agrees, "but they are a bit of a problem." Swallows like to eat cherries, as do the black-masked cedar waxwings, several of which she points out to me perched in a nearby tree, another favorite of this amateur birder. Other birds will peck at the apples, not fully eating them, thus destroying the fruit. The pleasures of birding and the practicality of farming are not necessarily compatible.

As we wait for her daughter to report in, Betsy excuses herself for a moment to confab with one of the farm managers about the overnight growth spurt of the asparagus that's already needing to be cut once again. Sounds like the stuff of Jack and the Beanstalk to this city boy; however, this is a very real fairy tale. I keep my surprise to myself.

My interviewee arrives about 9:30 a.m. I feel badly about her chaotic start, but King McAvoy will have none of it, faithful to her commitment. She invites me inside the family's farmhouse, out of the spring chill. Then Betsy has me sit down in a specially designated chair: hers. "It looks out on the orchard," she says, smiling. "You can watch the birds too."

King McAvoy, thirty-seven, has already had a morning, seeing to her sick child. She looks tired as she pulls her dark, shoulder-length tresses back, but she's eager to talk farming.

King Orchard was founded by her father, John King, in 1980. Growing up downstate in Flint, his family mostly worked as autoworkers and teachers—solid middle-class Americans. He earned a degree from Michigan Tech in the UP in mechanical engineering, assuming he was just going to make the auto industry his career. But after a few years, he left to manage a cherry farm. Then at the age of thirty, he purchased the original 80 acres, now part of the 250-acre entirety of King Orchards. The farm was purchased "on 100 percent credit," King McAvoy says, through the United States Department of Agriculture's Farm Service Agency's Beginning Farmer Loan. A bachelor, John soon met his future wife, Betsy, and they began farming together—true first-time farmers. Soon after, his brother, Jim, joined the enterprise, and later, Jim's wife, Rose, the two couples sharing ownership. King McAvoy attended Michigan State University, being the only one of her four siblings—all of whom work at the farm and are college educated—to receive a degree in horticulture.

After a stint in Chicago as a marketing consultant in the fresh food industry, she returned to Antrim County to work for the family business in 2015. Today, King McAvoy handles the administrative end of the enterprise, which includes overseeing food safety, export sales, and regulatory matters such as crop insurance.

"King Orchards is a very diversified and vertically integrated business," she explains. "We grow many different crops and have many different markets. Our primary acreage is apples, sweet cherries, and tart cherries." Of note, the family farms more than 140 acres of Montmorency tart cherries. They also grow apricots, nectarines, peaches, pears, plums, and that sometimes overnight wonder, asparagus. As well, King Orchards attracts agritourism throughout the u-pick seasons. And their two fruit stands offer sundry items for visitors, notably bakery-fresh fruit pies, cookies, and muffins along with jams and jellies and other delectables.

"We make processed, value-added food products, mainly concentrates," King McAvoy explains, including the increasingly popular Montmorency cherry concentrate. She asks if I'm familiar with the concentrate's health benefits. I'm not, but what I learn quickly converts me into a new consumer of the "nutraceutical product." She tells me that "people swear by it for arthritis and gout, and it helps with muscle recovery and inflammation." She adds, "Montmorency cherries are very high in antioxidants—higher than blueberries." When I go for my annual physical a month later, I add cherry concentrate to the ever-growing list of remedies I take as the years pile on. When asked about its ability to reduce arthritic inflammation, my doc says the verdict is still out. He adds, "But with all the other benefits it offers, I say keep taking it, regardless."

King Orchards' export business continues to grow, King McAvoy tells me, with tart cherry concentrate a big seller. International orders are taken through kingorchards.com, with direct shipping to customers in, for example, Great Britain, New Zealand, China, and Taiwan.

They also supply cherry juice to more than six hundred brewers, she says, another growing part of their portfolio, especially over the last decade with the booming craft beer industry. "There's a really good chance that if you see a cherry beer, it came from us." They also ship cider base for hard ciders.

....

King McAvoy is an activist for family farmers. She tells me the Kings have "tried to be apolitical." As for her, "I try to keep my advocacy purely around environmental related things. People are so polarized, especially in this area; it's been hard." The Kings' farming colleagues, who are also contending with the increasingly challenging weather impacts attributed to climate change by most climatologists across the globe, generally are not labeling them as climate change–caused just yet, she says, anticipating a gradual acceptance. At this point, perhaps it's just a matter of semantics.

When President Biden visited King Orchards in 2021, King McAvoy used it as an opportunity to school him on the plight of today's family farmers. As the *Traverse City Record-Eagle* reported, she capitalized on having the president's ear, as well as that of Michigan Gov. Whitmer and both of the state's U.S. Senators, Debbie Stabenow and Gary Peters. She focused on the impacts of climate change: more severe weather and inconsistent weather patterns—such as the spring frost then soaring unseasonable temps in 2021 that led to a loss of 75 percent of the Kings' sweet cherries and 85 percent of their tarts. This was the second crop failure for King Orchards in consecutive years and the fourth in the past twenty.[1] Since 2011, "we've had a crop insurance claim nine out of ten years," she tells me. As well, Turkey has taken a significant share of the U.S. cherry market in recent years, negatively impacting domestic prices of the crop and American cherry farmers' revenue.

"In 2012, when we had that devastating year, many people started importing Turkish cherries to keep their businesses alive," she explains. "That opened the door. The Turkish growers are highly subsidized by their government. They can come in and sell cherry juice concentrate for a fraction of what I can even make it at. The big food companies like Pepsi and Coke (who sell popular cherry-flavored sodas) that don't care—it's all bottom line—they're going to go with the cheapest option no matter what. Imports have grown so much that they are now over 50 percent of the tart cherry products consumed in the United States."

As well, she says, "farmers are going out of business at a crazy rapid pace." Plummeting prices due to import competition and volatile weather from climate change is driving out growers, an almost 50 percent decline in northern Michigan over the past decade, she says. Small cherry farms, hobby farms in particular, have proven to be unsustainable in the current economic and weather climates. "Those people have exited the industry very quickly."

King McAvoy characterized the president's visit to King Orchards as "wild." It came together in a series of steps. First, her youngest brother, Mike, a professional skier and videographer, made a video combining his passions of skiing and agriculture, depicting how climate change was affecting both. The video, called "Feast or Famine," was then viewed by Biden presidential campaign officials in 2020.[2] Later, Jill Biden paid a visit to King Orchards in September 2020. Then Gov. Whitmer's office called in 2021, asking if the Kings would be interested in hosting the president. With just three days to prepare for the once-in-a-lifetime visit, they readily agreed. "What are you supposed to say?" she asks rhetorically. "Yes, of course!"

After the planned thirty-minute walking tour of the farm, President Biden stayed for an unscheduled additional three hours. "It was incredible," King McAvoy recalls. "I talked to him about climate change and the vulnerability of family farms and labeling laws to help the import issue, about infrastructure and reducing our reliability on fossil fuels, but mostly about farming. He was very receptive, and it was a great conversation. He let me tell our whole story. It was just a really great opportunity for him to hear about the struggles we're experiencing."

....

King McAvoy serves on the Michigan Cherry Committee and is a commissioner for the Michigan Department of Agricultural and Natural Resources, both governor-appointed positions. She's also the co-chair of the Great Lakes Business Network, a group of business leaders that advocate for a variety of environmental causes, such as shutting down Line 5. "We depend on the water, we depend on tourism, we depend on a thriving environment for our workers and our visitors. So a spill in the Great Lakes would be detrimental to our businesses. Our position is not anti-pipeline; it's anti-pipeline through the Straits of Mackinac. We're putting this invaluable resource at risk. The fact that it hasn't had a major leak is really unbelievable."

Two anchor strikes on the seventy-year-old crude oil and natural gas pipeline system—which crosses the bottom of the Straits for 4.5 miles and is estimated to have a fifty-year lifespan—during the past several years have amped up Great Lakes environmental groups' sense of urgency, as well as that of Gov. Whitmer's office.[3] (As of February 2024, Enbridge refuses to comply with the state's May 12, 2021, shutdown deadline.)[4] Should the pipeline be compromised during a major storm or when the Straits are ice covered, the release of oil would be catastrophic.

The Kings "have started being vocal about the effects of climate change on our farm because we felt that there hasn't been enough attention paid to it." She adds, "King Orchards, particularly, is a canary in the mine. We are on the northern cusp of the fruit-growing region here in Michigan. We've got colder winters, our summers are shorter, so we don't have as much flexibility with the weather patterns because we're so far north."

Growing fruit trees "is an incredibly long-term process," she explains. It takes two years to get cherry trees from the nursery. Once planted, sweet and tart cherry trees will take another seven years to mature and produce fruit. "So we invest nine years from when I decide I want to plant a tart cherry orchard before I get a single dollar back on my investment," she says. "And then I hope that those trees will provide some kind of income for about thirty years." With that decades-long timeframe in mind, it's difficult, if not impossible, to predict what the climate in northern Michigan will be then. "So I don't know what to plant, I don't know what to plan for." Of course, the Kings are doing what they can, which means more diversification than in previous years. "We're doing a lot more dwarfing root stocks, which is a smaller tree." She points to apples being grown on trellises, which can produce fruit in three years. They also have several orchards with sweet cherries being grown on dwarfing root stock for a quicker return on their investment.

Although rain is becoming less frequent in the region, with intermittent periods of drought, torrential rains are becoming more common, she tells. "These not only cause erosion and flooding, but they are not nourishing to the plants because [the rainfall] doesn't actually seep into the ground"; rather, "it just rushes to the low spots." Mitigation efforts have included digging drainage holes in all low-lying areas throughout their orchards.

Moreover, nearly all their fruit tree acreage is irrigated for sustaining crops through periods of drought.

The region has become more humid, too, which brings more insect pests and ruinous bacteria and fungus. And more warmth means more cycles of insects. So their farm's assets are under attack more frequently now. Since the dreaded spotted wing drosophila was first documented in Antrim County in 2015—at King Orchards—it has added to northern Michigan farmers' distress. The invasive tiny fruit fly originated in Asia. Says King McAvoy, "It pokes a hole into the soft flesh fruit of cherries, strawberries, raspberries, and blueberries and lays its eggs in there." The pest's life cycle is short—approximately seven days—but its ability to lay waste to those fruit crops is rapid as well. "As soon as you see one in your orchard, the next week it will be an explosion."

To combat this devastating invasive, the Kings have been forced to spray once a week. She admits that the insecticides are expensive, an additional burden on the tractor drivers, and "it's terrible for the environment." Spraying is done late at night, her father, brother, and uncle handling the chore. The nighttime application is done to inflict the least amount of damage on the pollinators (chiefly honeybees). Yet not all cherry farmers have successfully contended with this crop-killing critter. The spotted wing drosophila has caused even more cherry farmers to bail out of the business, she says, because the ever-mounting challenges are just too daunting anymore. Or, they're converting to growing apples, because they're less susceptible to such pests.

....

At one time the Grand Traverse region's orchards employed a tremendous number of Hispanic (largely Mexican) migrant farmworkers—more than thirty-five thousand in the fifties alone, according to an article in the September 18, 2003, edition of the *Glen Arbor Sun*. It reported that by the early 2000s, that number had dropped to just over four thousand, mostly thanks to the advent of cherry-harvesting mechanization.[5] The *Michigan Migrant and Seasonal Farmworker Enumeration Profiles Study 2013*, published by the Michigan Interagency Migrant Services Committee, confirms this significant decrease, reporting then that Grand Traverse County had 592 migrant farmworkers and Leelanau County 1,084.[6] Ginger Bardenhagen, a member of a sixth-generation Leelanau County farm family who works for the Michigan Department of Agriculture and Rural Development's

Producer Services Division, adds, "The number of workers for cherries has dropped but probably has been pretty steady since the mid- '80s to early 1990s." Indeed, skilled migrant workers continue to be an essential part of northern Michigan's agricultural landscape.

It's worth noting that since the publication of the *Enumeration Profiles Study* and into the pandemic years, many migrant workers have experienced the same economic challenges as that of the middle and lower classes of the local citizenry, though made more acute by being in a foreign country. H-2A Temporary Agricultural Workers receive free housing per program-participant employer obligations, and farmers are increasingly relying on these documented workers due to the chronic local seasonal labor shortage.[7] However, undocumented migrant farmworkers and those H-2B Temporary Non-Agricultural Workers in the construction and service industries—who are also in high demand—are not guaranteed free housing and struggle with the lack of affordable housing and transportation.

Gladys Munoz, seventy, has been an advocate for Hispanic migrant workers since coming to the Grand Traverse region from Puerto Rico in 1988. She's a co-founder of the Justice and Peace Advocacy Center (JPAC), a Catholic nonprofit organization supporting migrant workers in northern Michigan, and serves on the Northwest Michigan Migrant Resource Council. Munoz tells of a new wrinkle the region is seeing in the migrant worker population: a surge in H-2B workers in the local construction industry. "Construction is exploding here," she observes, "and the majority of migrant people working in it are from Central America, especially Honduras and Guatemala." Most of the H-2B construction workers are young men unaccompanied by their families, which has led to a mental health crisis among this group, including substance abuse and depression, Munoz says. She attributes this to loneliness caused by up to nine months of separation from their families. Munoz and the JPAC is working hard to address this. "We're trying to become a family," though she admits such community-building "takes a long time."

King Orchards employs ninety-five people, about thirty year-round, the rest seasonal. "Seasonal employees are very difficult to find," King McAvoy remarks. The labor force is no longer being replenished as it once was. Perhaps ten years ago, King Orchards had about thirty full-time migrant workers. They were provided housing, which, she says, is not unique to their operation. "In order to keep people here, we diversified and extended our growing season. Instead of only needing them for cherries, which is one month long, we added apples, peaches, and apricots on the back end, and asparagus and strawberries on the front end. We employ those people for about ten months a year and house them for twelve months a year so they can send their kids to local schools and be part of this community and grow with us. We have four people from Guatemala that have been with us for over thirty-eight years. They arrived as teenagers." An American success story, their college-educated children are working in dental hygiene and radiology and as entrepreneurs. Unfortunately, because of the political climate in America during the past decade or so, King Orchards is now down to a permanent field worker crew of twelve.

These days, King Orchards relies upon the H-2A visa program to bring in temporary farmworkers. This is costly and ponderous, owing to the red tape. The expense includes providing transportation from Mexico to Antrim County. Although grateful for these four-month workers, King McAvoy says, "we would much rather see people have the ability to have a pathway to citizenship, because we're investing in these people. It's absolutely a skilled position: they are horticulture professionals."

Most telling, she adds, "In forty-two years, we can count on one hand how many people with an American education have applied for these jobs." And even if local high school students would be interested in the harvesting work, they tend not to pay close attention to the care required. For example, damaging honey crisp apples is easy; they should be handled quite delicately. "If you pick them too roughly, you'll get five-finger bruises on them."

The challenge with securing seasonal fieldworkers also extends to many other positions, including middle managers, store managers, crew leaders, and tractor and forklift drivers, says King McAvoy. The job vacancy problem has a lot to do with where King Orchards is located. "It's becoming increasingly hard to find good labor that can afford to live here." On a personal note, she shares that her family is having a hard time finding an affordable home in the Central Lake area. During the pandemic, housing in Antrim County—just as throughout the Grand Traverse five-county region—was bought up by many out-of-towners with larger incomes who could afford the skyrocketing housing prices while contributing to driving them up.

A *New York Times* article published in June 2021 highlighted the political divide in Antrim County that heightened during the pandemic. It profiled a Democratic grower—the Kings—on one end of the Covid-19 safety spectrum, and a Republican farming family just twelve miles away—the Friskes—who sued Gov. Whitmer in 2020 over her masking mandate. It also showed that even born-and-raised northern Michigan voters, especially in rural communities, on both sides of the aisle are united by their concern about their new neighbors. "The pandemic brought a new breed: younger tech-savvy entrepreneurs from as far away as California who could work from home. They arrived with families and paid for houses in cash, fueling resentments."[8]

Even though she's making "a quarter of what my friends are making in Chicago," after all, she admits, "I can live in northern Michigan." Still, her frustration is obvious. As I listen to her, I begin to feel guilty about owning a seasonal home that could permanently house a middle-class local family, whereas we have effectively removed it from the available housing inventory. "Owning a home has been the primary way that you collect wealth and pass it on to your children," she notes. "And if you don't have access to that anymore, it really changes the game."

King McAvoy's vision of the future of Antrim County is one of uncertainty. "It's pretty scary from a horticulture perspective. But I think the area is going to continue to grow and there is going to be way more people here in the next ten years. That's going to make our job harder because of the rising cost of property to grow fruit on and homes for our employees to live in."

Growing specialty fruit crops in northern Michigan calls for being close to Lake Michigan, within several miles, and on sloping ground. This, of course, also makes for perfect view property. "Our desirable fruit-growing land is getting turned into golf courses and subdivisions and wonderful view mansions that can see Grand Traverse Bay," King McAvoy explains with a tinge of cynicism. "Almost all of our farmland has view property because we need the protection of the lake. The Great Lake cools the summertime highs and warms the winter lows. So it provides a calming effect to the spikes in temperature, which is really important to growing fruit." As well as an increasing demand for high-end residential property here in previously lower-demand Antrim County. As a result, property prices are escalating, and affordable housing is rapidly disappearing.

....

Before I go, I tell her that for years, one of my best friends, a Traverse City native, would invite me to come visit whenever I could while half-kiddingly instructing me to "bring lots of spending money" for local businesses to relieve me of. She concurs, "We make money off tourism. We want people to have access to the wonderful things that we have access to like the lakes and beaches and trails." But they need to appreciate it and to join in the effort to protect it, she states unequivocally. "We're hoping all those people who stop by King Orchards can understand that in ten years we might not be able to grow cherries. Then maybe they'll realize that climate change isn't just a conspiracy thing; it's a lot closer than we realize."

Life, Liberty, Beaches, and Pie

On May Day, 2023, my brother Chris and I visited downtown Traverse City so he could pick up a gift for his girlfriend. We had driven up from Indy the Thursday before to open our family cabin in Cedar for the spring, summer, and fall and for some Opening Day trout fishing on Saturday. The weather, as forecast, turned decidedly colder, as we awakened on Monday to snow showers and windy conditions. So a walkabout on Front Street with stores to duck into as our wandering eyes dictated was as fine a diversion as any.

After stops at booklover's paradise Horizon Books and On the Rocks minerals, fossils, and jewelry store, we crossed Front Street and headed for Cherry Republic. Which is code for Cherry Everything: more than two hundred cherry-based products can be found in the spacious store. Cherry wine, cherry beer, cherry salsa, cherry barbecue sauce, chocolate-covered cherries, dried cherries, cherry-infused maple syrup, and so on. For cherry lovers, it's practically a religious experience. Chris purchases a few items, including a bottle of pinot noir with 2 percent cherry juice. I pick up a bottle of medium-heat cherry salsa. This cornucopia of all things cherry is Bob Sutherland's doing.

Sutherland, sixty-one, Cherry Republic's founder and owner, and I met a year earlier on a warm May morning, on Friday the thirteenth, for a hike near his home on Little Traverse Lake. The day before, the mercury had reached an unseasonably high ninety-plus degrees, and today would be more of the same. Just across the street, Sleeping Bear Dunes National Lakeshore beckons us. Rather than take a hike on an established trail, we roam the woods with his two-year-old greater Swiss mountain dog, Sonny, an imposing yet friendly beast that stands almost three feet high on all fours with tri-colored black, brown, and white fur. Wherever Sonny wants to go, we follow.

Sutherland is basketball tall, thin, and athletic; otherwise, he's thoughtful, engaging, and unconventional. There's a basketball goal in the driveway, which, he tells me, saw some action the evening before from him and his two sons, Colebrook, seventeen, and Hawthorn, fifteen. He greets me in shorts and a T-shirt, ready to go hiking.

Sutherland first came to northern Michigan from Detroit in the early seventies, his parents moving the family to Glen Arbor as an ideal place for kids to grow up. After college he pursued several entrepreneurial efforts. One was selling Cherry Republic T-shirts—out of the trunk of his car—with the still-used motto "Life, Liberty, Beaches, and Pie." A few years later, he sold the Original Cherry Boomchunka gourmet cookies, a product that eventually took off and continues to sell to this day. The iconic northern Michigan company started in 1989, with the flagship store in Glen Arbor opening shortly thereafter.[9]

Since then, the Sutherland success story has resulted in Cherry Republic stores in Glen Arbor, Traverse City, Charlevoix, and downstate in Frankenmuth, Holland, and Ann Arbor. The Glen Arbor store is a "half block of cherry wonderland," he says. Something of a compound, it's comprised of three buildings and surrounding gardens. He tells me that on an average summer day, 2,500 customers will pass through the Glen Arbor store, and 3,500 will visit his Traverse City location. In Glen Arbor, tour busses make stops at Cherry Republic as part of their itinerary.

Although renowned for his cherry-centric business, Sutherland has also earned local legend status for his walking-on-water adventure. He and three other amateur explorers once hiked across the ice-covered Manitou Passage, from Pyramid Point to North Manitou Island, an eight-hour roundtrip. The risky daytrip took place on March 6, 2014. In the 1970s, Sutherland's father and two of his brothers made the attempt as well, though open water a mile from their objective, South Manitou Island, forced their return. Sutherland and his companions, however, managed to complete the journey with no mishaps.[10]

The cherry products magnate prefers the road not taken, as we hike through hilly areas of the parkland near Shalda Creek, across meadows, under trees, and through shin tangle. The dog favors this exploratory route, too, and he soon disappears, showing up on a nearby trail twenty minutes later, obediently awaiting his master. We do some birdwatching, the woods teeming with songbirds such as indigo buntings, rose-breasted grosbeaks, and wood thrushes. Common green darner dragonflies as big as the palm of my hand cruise in wide circles around us. I tell him that identifying the insect order Odonata—which includes both dragonflies and damselflies—is a new hobby of mine, and that Michigan boasts 171 species.[11] He smiles, watching the darners patrol their territory.

An hour later, we return to Sutherland's lakeside home. As we talk inside, he picks five ticks from his legs. This rattles me, as the previous summer I had a tick embedded in my thigh for a full twenty-four hours, discovering it by accident. When I called my doctor's office in Indy, the nurse practitioner said I had little to worry about, as Lyme disease is rarely transferred from ticks to humans in Indiana. "I'm in northern Michigan," I revealed. "Oh," she responded, immediately going into a troubling explanation of symptoms I might experience, but thankfully didn't. Now permanently paranoid about ticks, I ask Sutherland to check my back for the creepy crawlers; he asks me to do the same. Relieved by clean results, I'm able to go on. He just laughs.

....

Why cherries? "Since I was seven years old, I've been selling items to the tourists that come up," he explains. "It was only natural that I would take Michigan's fruit—we're the cherry capital of the world—and start selling it." Back in the eighties, Sutherland recalls, people's taste for cherry pie ground to a halt and shifted to high-end ice cream, with brands like Haagen-Dazs taking market share formerly held by fruit pies. The cherry industry needed to be reimagined, and he took that on. Cherry Republic began churning out numerous creative, tasty products that helped bolster the Grand Traverse region's identity. Then, a weekend spent with Yvon Chouinard, Patagonia's founder, led him to implement a philanthropic mechanism as a central tenet of his business. Like Patagonia, Cherry Republic gives away 1 percent of sales to environmental and community groups. The company also charges customers a 1 percent "tariff," which is donated to select nonprofits. And cashiers round up sales to increase nonprofit donations.

Surprisingly, Cherry Republic keeps a low profile during the National Cherry Festival each July. "Unfortunately, for the cherry industry itself, it's the hardest time to pull away," he notes. "I'm absolutely swamped [then] in my stores." I ask if Cherry Republic uses only Michigan-grown cherries. "Hell yes," he declares. His company processes two million pounds of Michigan cherries annually; three hundred million pounds are harvested nationally, he says. And he wishes he could do more.

Most of Cherry Republic's customers come from out of state, approximately 65 percent. The rest are Michiganders. "They're buying for themselves, but they're also proudly buying the essence of Michigan and sending it to friends and family around the country," he tells me.

As a company intrinsically concerned about the greater good, Cherry Republic takes climate change seriously. So much so that in 2022, Sutherland established a new position: vice president of climate and community impact. The VP oversees the Impact Department, which is responsible for distributing up to 2 percent of gross annual revenue to worthy causes. Since the company's inception, Cherry Republic has donated more than $2 million to local-serving nonprofits, including conservation and environmental protection groups in northern Michigan such as FLOW, Friends of Sleeping Bear Dunes, and Inland Seas Education Association.[12]

Like King McAvoy, Sutherland attributes the inconsistency of Michigan's cherry crop over the past decade or so as a direct consequence of climate change. One year there's a near total loss of cherry crops; the next it's a bumper harvest; the following year it's half of what was projected. This irregularity impacts the processed cherry product pipeline as well. As King McAvoy stated, cherry syrup contracts with Coke and Pepsi go to Turkey as a result. This, remarks Sutherland, who is close to many local cherry growers as both business associates and friends, "is a sad story."

Sutherland mentions Kurt Luedtke, a longtime acquaintance and local and lovable curmudgeon. He suggests I look him up for an interview. I do, but unfortunately, Luedtke died in August 2020. That gets a laugh out of him—not about the deceased, but about him not knowing about it. Luedtke, former executive editor of the *Detroit Free Press*, won an Academy Award for writing the screenplay for the 1985 film *Out of Africa*. Upon his retirement, he lived for many years in a condominium at The Homestead in Glen Arbor. Luedtke wrote a cynically playful essay titled "Please don't come to Leelanau County," discouraging people from visiting or even relocating there.[13] In a "sword-fighting" conversation with Luedtke, Sutherland said, "Bob, do you realize how many people are out there? If you don't, you gotta get out in the world and see. Go to California. And when they discover us, they're coming."

But that's okay with Sutherland. He welcomes the company, of course, as a retailer would. Yet there's more to it than pure capitalistic self-interest. "I know what joy it's brought me [living in northern Michigan]. I want to give the same joy to everybody and share it with everybody."

Feeling welcome here doesn't happen overnight, however. He says it took years for him to feel comfortable in Glen Arbor as a transplant to the area. "It takes a while to be accepted." Seasonal people are eager to get to know their neighbors, the locals, he says. "They're only here for two months. And they're ready to be friends, and then they're gone. So we have like a shoulder distance with these people. You have your local friends, then these summer people. We have people who will earnestly move up here with the intent that they're going to make their stake here. And then they find out it isn't for them. It's not for everybody; it's for maybe 50 percent of the people [who come here]. They're like, 'Wow, this is not what I thought.' They're not connected to building firm relationships, the cultural work." And then there's this: "The winters are way longer. So there are those people who are only here for one or two years. But if you're here for three years, I'll start getting to know you," he says, laughing. As for the pandemic migrants who relocated to the area since the outbreak in the spring of 2020, "A lot of people came during the pandemic; we'll see who stays."

As for those who choose to stay, many are retirees who got a taste of the region years ago and made plans to retire Up North. They tend not to sit back and let the world go by, Sutherland comments. "The active retirement community is a very powerful influencer here." Just about as soon as the moving van drives off, these retirees jump in and get involved, often in environmental causes to keep the land and the water the way they found them: respected and protected. They're well-educated professionals, having had successful careers as, for example, executives, business owners, physicians, and lawyers. They have wealth and know-how to make things happen. Most make positive contributions to the place they now call home. Others, though, fail to connect with the people in the region, not "fully realizing what the area is all about," he says, and fold up their tents.

But if newcomers *get it*—appreciate the magical attributes of this special place—like Sutherland certainly does, then, as he asserts, "I'm absolutely convinced that this area can bring joy to anybody. How can I deny them that?"

Wine Country

As a preliminary to my April 29, 2022, interview with Larry Mawby, retired founder of MAWBY sparkling wines in Leelanau County, I visit the winery's website and come across the intriguing term "MAWBYness." I would be sure to ask Mawby to define it for me.

That Friday afternoon, as I step out of my SUV in Mawby's Suttons Bay home's driveway, his wife, Lois Bahle, intercepts me. She assumes I'm one of her campaign workers pulling up to get some promotional material in support of her candidacy in a special recall election for a seat on the Leelanau County Commission. (Bahle won the election, which took place on May 3, 2022). When I inform her otherwise, she jokingly forgives me and calls for her husband.

Mawby seems surprised by my appearance as well. "What are we going to talk about?" he asks as if teasing—I think—his close-cropped salt-and-pepper beard framing his smiling visage, his collar-length hair covering the top half of his ears, a seventies look. "I mean, why are you here? I don't remember." That may well be true, but his infectious laugh makes everything right. Having formally retired several years earlier and gradually selling off his interest in the business, he confesses to not knowing what's going on from day to day, an enviable position. Then he suggests, "It's such a nice day; why don't we talk outside?"

As we get acquainted while sitting at his patio table in the revivifying spring sunshine and sixty-five-degree temperature, I become slightly distracted by my first sighting of a white-crowned sparrow this season, seed pecking on the ground beneath a feeder. Goldfinches make an appearance, too, most notably the males in their vivid yellow coloring and black-and-white-barred wings. "Oh, they actually turned," Mawby says delightedly, as we pause to watch. Black-capped chickadees and white-breasted nuthatches participate in the pleasant commotion as well. It really is nice here.

Now, about MAWBYness.

"It's not well defined, and that's the beauty of it," he relates, saying he has no idea who came up with the term. It's essentially about the experience one has with a MAWBY sparkling wine, of which there are eighteen offerings. Among them, for example, is their bestselling brut rose named Sex; champagne alternative named Us; and a semi-dry Lambrusco called Redd. All come in distinctive corked bottles. The wines run from $15 to $45 a bottle, "not your everyday drinking wine," he notes. "Whether visiting [the winery] or sharing a bottle in Denver or walking into a Meijer store in Grand Rapids and grabbing a bottle, what separates us? How do you define us? It's *MAWBYness*. It should be hard to define. If it's too simple, it's not complete enough," he explains, as if describing Buddha nature through a Zen lens. "I believe as a marketer that a little mystery, a little uncertainty, is a good thing."

....

A native Michigander born to a Grand Rapids–area farming family, Mawby was three years old when his parents purchased another farm just south of Suttons Bay. They had an interest in diversifying their crops, already growing apples and peaches downstate, and would add Leelanau County–grown cherries to their produce portfolio. For the next ten years Mawby would spend his summers in Leelanau County, returning to their home northeast of Grand Rapids, in Rockford, for the school year. When Mawby was thirteen, his father, who had longed to live in Leelanau County, moved the family there for good. "I've spent a significant chunk of my life here," he says, and not regrettably.

Mawby spent his entire career "growing grapes and making wine" as one of the first winegrowers in Leelanau County, which now boasts more than twenty wineries.[14] "It's the special nature of the soils and climate here that makes this kind of agriculture possible," he explains. "There are very few places on the planet that allow this kind of agriculture. That's really special."

He continues, "Now, a side effect of that is the geography that makes it special also makes it beautiful. Some people approach it from the beauty end or recreation end; I approach it from the food production end. But it's all the same thing. You're still looking at the same jewel; you're just looking at different facets of it."

Mawby founded the Leelanau County winery way back in 1973, planting his first vineyard with the objective of producing table wines. By 1984 he began his sparkling wine production, for which the winery is now renowned. In the early days he did his homework to see if wine grapes would grow well here, which included researching the winegrowing areas in New York and Oregon. His vision was simple: "To grow grapes and make some wine and see if anybody would buy it." Back then, there weren't any wineries in the region. Would the grapes grow adequately, and would they produce decent wine?

And if the wine was worthwhile, would it sell? "The advantage in this area," he says, is "you get a seasonal influx of visitors, and they want to see what the area has got. They're up for new experiences." He says it took nearly a decade for locals to begin supporting locally produced wines. "Visitors figured it out way earlier."

Word-of-mouth is the main promotional vehicle for the region's wines, notes Mawby. "People love to talk about their vacations. That's the way we advertise the wine industry in this area. Get people to try the wine and take it home with them, and they pop a cork with their friends and say, 'I found this funky little winery when I was on vacation in the Traverse City area, and here's this charming little wine.' That's what we want."

Sparkling wine made in northern Michigan complements the regional wine market, he says. It's a very small percentage of that, around 5 percent or so. And they don't have to rely exclusively on local tastes to sell their product. "We have people coming from all over the Midwest and hauling it away." Eventually, Mawby made a complete transition to making sparkling wine. The increasingly fickle weather encouraged it, and the consumer demand was there. "It's what we do; it's all we do."

If sparkling wine is your thing and you're visiting the Grand Traverse region, "MAWBY is one of the places you've gotta go," he suggests, bias gleefully admitted. Even though he's a retired winemaker, he speaks as if he's still at it, viscerally attached to the craft. (Mawby partnered with the current owners, the Laing family, in 2009, working closely with them for years before they acquired the business.)[15] "At the same time, if you've come to the area and you've tried sparkling wine and you don't like it, don't come in my door. You're going to be disappointed. You're going to take my staff's time. We want people to come in and have a good time. If you don't like what we make, it's really difficult. We're not making something for everybody."

According to Mawby, climate change is "upending a lot of things." And northern Michigan winegrowers have taken notice. "It's changing the growing season," he affirms. "Is it warming? Sometimes. Is it cooling? Sometimes. The bad effect of climate change for all tender horticultural crops, which wine grapes and cherries are, and which are grown extensively here, is they don't like rapid swings in temperature. It's really tough on the plant. Some years it wipes out the crop." He says that premature spring warmups will put too-quickly blossoming cherry trees and budding grape vines in a "sensitive position" when followed by dramatic cooldowns, as frost will damage this early critical growth stage. Once rare catastrophic crop-killing frosts affecting cherry trees and grapevines are occurring far more frequently nowadays, directly attributable to climate change. "It's not once in a century anymore," he says. "So it's much more difficult and challenging. We are going to have to look at cultivars that can tolerate that more and different ways of growing the vines and what kind of wines we can make."

Mawby goes on, "When we plant a grapevine, we want it to be economically productive for forty or fifty years—or more." So growers in the region are confronted by a glaring uncertainty. "I would really like to know how much the climate is going to change in the next forty years here, so I have a better sense of what varieties I should be planting so that they'll still work forty years from now." He has posed the question to climatologists. "Nobody knows the answer to that."

....

Although the pandemic contributed significantly to the surge in new residents in the region, remote work had its start here about thirty years earlier, he says. That's when Mawby "first started seeing a lot of professional people who could live anywhere in the world and conduct their business would [decide to] live here. Why not? Bond traders in Chicago don't have to be on the floor there to trade bonds. They can live here and go sit in their office and trade. Intellectual property attorneys can live anywhere. None of them go to the patent and trademark office."

Yet thanks to the pandemic's relocation phenomenon, the cost of housing soon went out of reach for those of lesser means in the region. "It's a huge issue," he remarks. "It's always been a problem, but it's gotten worse." In Mawby's county of residence, Leelanau, known for its opulent lakeside seasonal homes, both inland and on Lake Michigan, the income disparity is profound. As reported by the *Leelanau Ticker* in February 2022, 43 percent of the county's residents are either in poverty (6 percent) or fall into the Asset Limited, Income Constrained, Employed (ALICE) category (37 percent), a term developed by the United Way. The latter are people who hold jobs but are perilously close to going off a financial cliff, unable to afford any emergency expenses, such as home and car repairs or unforeseen healthcare costs.[16]

Mawby says with evident concern, "It's just crazy." Income inequality reduces opportunities for all, he asserts. When people pay a million dollars for an 800-square-foot cottage on Long Island and come across a 1,500-square-foot lakefront cottage in northern

Michigan for less than that, it's considered a bargain to these out-of-staters accustomed to a very high cost of living. This leads to rising real estate prices and the pronounced negative impact on northern Michiganders.

So Mawby decided to do something about it. In 2022, the retired winegrower started Peninsula Housing to help make a dent in the affordable housing challenge in Leelanau County. The nascent 501(c)(3) is deploying the unusual mechanism of a Community Land Trust (CLT). This type of trust owns acquired land in perpetuity, upon which affordable housing can be constructed, bought, and sold. "Most of the affordable housing that's built in this area doesn't stay affordable for very long," he said in a *Leelanau Ticker* article back in January 2022. "It's usually as little as five years." The CLT arrangement will help ensure that it is, however, for decades thereafter.[17]

(As of early 2024, Peninsula Housing acquired and rehabbed its first house in Suttons Bay, readying it for sale. More property acquisitions are underway.)

....

Mawby says that the change in Suttons Bay and the greater Grand Traverse region over the past twenty-five years has been dramatic. "In the fifties and the sixties, tourism in this area was very different than it is today. . . . There wasn't really what I would call tourism; it was summer people who had cottages, often in the family for a couple generations, and they were clustered around the lakeshore." Then came the Interstate Highway System, and the advent of the two-week timeout to longer yet drivable vacation destinations, such as Leelanau County.

Another notable change occurred within the agricultural industry. Though overstated, Mawby says, "Coincidentally, the mechanization of the cherry harvest meant that about a half a million migrant laborers didn't come to this area anymore in the summer. And that changed the feeling of a lot of these communities."

In the sixties, the Mawby farm in Leelanau County housed three hundred migrant workers for the cherry harvest. These foreign agricultural workers went to surrounding area stores, many of them catering to the seasonal Hispanic community. Every weekend they frequented stores in Suttons Bay and Traverse City. Bahle's of Suttons Bay, in business since 1876, sold clothing catering to Hispanic migrants' needs and tastes. The Bay Community Theater played Spanish language films. By the mid-seventies, Mawby says, that subculture started to disappear. Gradually, tourists in larger numbers began to discover the region. "It changed the nature of the retail businesses, the restaurants. It changed the community in a dramatic way that people don't really appreciate. That's true of Leelanau, Benzie, and Antrim counties—all the areas where fruit is grown. It was dramatically different between 1950 and 1980."

Now tourism is shifting once again, he observes. Most visitors get here by car, especially when coming from other Midwestern locations. Another tourist segment flies into Cherry Capital Airport. Then there's the wealthy who travel here by private jet. Used to be, says Mawby, the affluent seasonal visitors came for a quiet summer getaway. "The cottages of the wealthy in Leland and Northport were almost invisible," he recalls. Nowadays, mega-mansions keep appearing on lake frontage, some almost unimaginably well over twenty thousand square feet. "Now, more and more, the wealth that's here is splashy: they want to be seen. That changes the feel of the area in a subtle way." Mawby attributes this to "a phase our country is going through." A hundred years from now, it will be something very different, he predicts.

As we converse, Mawby transitions into an explanation of how grapevines work. "The thing that most people don't appreciate is half of the grapevine is invisible under the ground. You see part of it, and you think that's a grapevine, the part that interacts with the flora and the fauna of the atmosphere." But there's more to the story. "The other half interacts with the flora and the fauna in the soil. They both get nutrients. Some of them get sunlight and use photosynthetic activity to transform some of the other nutrients that the other part of the vine has brought up from the soil, and magic happens in the leaves. The vine is trying to do two things: it's trying to cover the Earth and intercept every photon that strikes the planet, which ideally should hit the grape leaf as far as the vine is concerned; that's what it's all about. That's why it goes up and climbs the trellises."

He leans toward me, holding my gaze, continuing his poetic viticultural exposition. "We thoughtfully provide trellises so they can stay up there. It just wants to get all the sun it possibly can and all the nutrients in the soil and turn it into seeds and cover those seeds with something that will make animals take those seeds away so that it can spread itself—that's the way it moves. We happen to care about the seed coating. We're one of the animals it works with." He leans back, smiling. "It's a very cool process. It's not unlike most other life processes where things come into a living being and they get transformed and they go out again in different ways. The living being thrives or doesn't, lives or dies, reproduces or doesn't."

Our conversation winds down with Mawby educating me on the French word *terroir*. "It's the place on the planet where the thing comes from. The terroir is the birthplace of the wine. It's the soils, it's the slope of the land, it's the rainfall, it's the sun, it's the people who are tending the vine. The cultivation of the wine is also part of the terroir. I hope that the wines that we make are expressive of that terroir."

The retired winegrower has never been a parent. And so, he admits, he romanticizes things like the soil—never blaspheme it as "dirt" around him—and his former role as a shepherd of the entire winegrowing process. Yet to be successful in this climate-dominated enterprise, practicality is an essential ingredient. The winegrower's job is to carefully, mindfully bring the wine to completion, from vine to table. Mawby holds sacred the "annual cycle of pruning, harvesting, and making wine" that extends from two to five years, from the harvest to the actual winemaking itself to maturity of the wine for consumption, an annual repetition which he finds "wonderful."

After my two hours with one of the fathers of the Leelanau winegrowing boom, he ends our conversation with this: "Any farmer who's a real farmer and not just an extractor of resources cares about the soil and hopes to leave it better than he found it. And that's what we would hope we as a species would be doing with this place, with this Leelanau Peninsula, this Grand Traverse Bay. I found it one way. I hope it's better when I leave it." As Mawby suggests, in an area as precious environmentally and scenically as northern Michigan, its people should all be focused on ensuring a sound legacy for tomorrow.

Feeding Foodies on Front Street

Before the foodie craze descended upon Traverse City, there was Amical. The European-style bistro has been serving customers on Front Street in the heart of downtown Traverse City since 1994. When I meet Dave Denison, the founder/owner/operator of Amical, and mention the inelegant term "foodie" early in our conversation, I find him to be likeminded about it. "I wish someone would come up with a different one," he almost pleads. Then he says, "That's your job."

Having spent many years myself in the restaurant-bar industry, mostly behind bars—the alcohol-serving kind—I immediately relate to Denison, sixty-six. He's affable, funny, and a fine storyteller. I get the sense that he can talk to anyone, a talent honed by his food and beverage career and not something acquired through a three-credit hospitality management college course.

We have our conversation at Amical at 1 p.m. on the Thursday following Labor Day. When I arrive, the hundred-seat restaurant is devoid of customers while a handful of employees prepare to open for dinner at 4 p.m. I've never been here before, though the thought has crossed my mind. Before the pandemic when Amical served lunch, on any summer day my wife and I strolled by, the outdoor café's tables would always be full of lively diners, a good sign.

As we sit down at a dining table, he tells me about his roundtrip flight to Portland, Oregon, over the Labor Day weekend. During a layover in Minneapolis, he ran into Trevor Tkach, president and CEO of Traverse City Tourism. Small world. It only got more interesting, as the return flight to Cherry Capital Airport on a large commercial passenger jet was full, and "for the first time, I didn't know anyone on the plane," Denison marvels at this telling sign of the region's growth.

Early in the conversation, he recounts his northern Michigan relocation story. "I migrated here thirty years ago from San Francisco," he says. "My wife and I are from southeastern Michigan." Back then he was a corporate chef with the Mountain Jack's Steakhouse chain; his wife, Nancy, was an early childhood teacher. They had two young children at the time. Aside from living through the Loma Prieta earthquake of 1989 and the tremors that are not that unusual in the bay area, they had other concerns. "We were getting nervous about our kids growing up out there: what they were going to be faced with, and what we were going to be faced with as they grew up, from a cultural and societal standpoint." In other words, life in the big city.

The couple began traveling to prospective relocation areas, such as Bend, Oregon, the Carolina coast, and Traverse City, with the ambition of eventually opening their own restaurant. TC it would be. So in 1990 they quit their jobs, sold their home, and moved to Denison's father's house on Torch Lake in Antrim County, northeast of Traverse City. "We loved the beauty of California; we hated the day-to-day hassle of living there." Part of their rationale for coming Up North was this: "If we move here, we're in a small town and our kids are going to grow up and they're going to leave. And if they ever want to come back, they will probably be able to afford to come back here." As for the cost of living in the San Francisco Bay area, Denison says, "It's crazy expensive there. So fast forward to this, and here I am."

The risk-taking Denisons realized their dream by opening Amical (pronounced ah-MEE-call, which is French for "friendly"). Initially, it opened as a bakery café. The idea was to reproduce the concept and open several regional locations, then sell the business, a plan that appealed to Denison's now-deceased partner, a venture capitalist. "We had multiple honeymoons here to change our game, and this is what it turned into."

Amical has been a fixture of the Traverse City restaurant scene ever since. "We've had this restaurant for twenty-eight years," he says, adding facetiously, "In dog years, that's how we measure restaurants." His corporate restaurant career prepared him well in developing the disciplined financial management approach required for running a successful restaurant, which includes overseeing food and beverage costs, inventory, equipment and maintenance, and labor. Moreover, with restaurants being a distinctly people-centered business, it allowed his relationship skills to flourish. "It's how you treat your people and how you treat your guests. It's all pretty easy, actually, at least that part. Being nice is free." Yet as all restaurant-goers know, not just anyone can pull that off. It takes an aptitude and an intentionality to provide a truly heartfelt service experience.

....

From Denison's standpoint, the pandemic brought about a long overdue adjustment to the restaurant business. "The pandemic was, to me, the exact thing that the industry needed but couldn't do," he states. "All of us in this industry figured there was a reckoning coming somewhere." The labor shortage that became a widespread predicament during the pandemic, especially in the service industry, is, according to Denison, nothing new. "The labor crisis has been going on since way before the pandemic." The pandemic, however, exacerbated the problem.

The career restauranteur says this reckoning was analogous to when smoking was banned in restaurants and bars. "Everybody had to do it. So now, everyone has to go through the labor crisis; everyone has to adjust their salaries; everyone has to adjust how they're doing things—as crazy as it is—and then figure it out. That's what happened, at least here." Nevertheless, Amical was well positioned to ride out the coronavirus-caused economic storm. "We just happened to be fortunate enough to have been in business for a long time and not leveraged," he says. "I feel a lot of empathy for businesses that started right before [the pandemic], or didn't have any history, or didn't have a client base or a brand that they developed. So there's a bunch of reasons why we've been able to stick it out."

The labor shortage is multifaceted, Denison explains. What he witnessed throughout the pandemic were employees in their late twenties and into their forties who tired of the "elevated drama" that occurred with some guests who rejected abiding by Covid-safety protocols. He portrays their experience by saying, "I've been treated like shit in the past; I'm getting treated like shit by people who should know better. I used to give them a pass because they just didn't know better, but now, how could you not know what's happening here with the frontline employees?"

Ever protective of his people, and of those working throughout the industry, Denison says adamantly, "Restaurant people aren't lazy." However, their personal circumstances were compromised during the pandemic, such as having to worry about bringing the illness home due to being "essential" workers, having to find dependable childcare, and having to adjust their schedules with little warning when schools would decide to go virtual. A wave of service workers called it quits, "absorbed by other industries that allowed them to work from home," he says.

The pandemic also gave older diners pause. "A lot of clients were like, 'No, I'm not going out,'" Denison recalls. So Amical took extra care to be cognizant of its customers' safety concerns. And they needed to be—not just for safety's sake but for their own business survival. Restaurants were now being judged by patrons and prospective customers as to whether they were following Centers for Disease Control and Prevention Covid-19 safety protocols. "Are they following the rules? That's how restaurants were reviewed by certain generational people," he says. "It didn't matter if the food was any good. Are they wearing masks? Are they six feet apart? It was this really weird time." A time to do the right thing for the people you serve, which came naturally to Denison and his staff. "We understood it. Our job is to always make sure our guests are safe."

....

Amical's customers are "all over the place" in terms of demographics, says Denison. Young professionals with children are common customers, so a kid's menu is offered. "Mainly, my client is a woman from forty-five to sixty-two or so," he explains. "Face it, they make the dining decisions most of the time." With just one bartender working at any given hour of business, he notes, "We don't have a bar scene." No TVs. No iPads. "You come here to dine."

Denison tells me that Amical's customers marvel at his servers' "remarkable memories" when it comes to remembering their preferred wines, cocktails, appetizers, and entrees. It shows how much they care for delivering an exceptional dining experience by making it personal. "We treat them really well," Denison emphasizes. "They think, 'How does this happen in a tourist town?' That little thing, and we got 'em. But you have to deliver the goods."

In general, he observes about the Grand Traverse region, "people are just kind here." He adds, though, that "we're, of course, worried that we will lose our Midwestern kindness as a town because we're overrun," a concern he has shared with Traverse City Tourism. "One of the main reasons people come here is because we're nice. And all of a sudden, we're not nice? It took us a long time to get 'Fudgies' out of the vocabulary. And now we're dealing with another aspect of a thinly disguised contempt for the people that actually come here." (Although the term "Fudgie" may have diminished in use in Traverse City and in small town destinations that depend upon tourism dollars for their year-round survival, in rural parts of the Grand Traverse region, the somewhat derisive term isn't all that unusual to hear, especially as the summer tourist season wears on.) Typically, Amical's local regulars avoid the bistro during the summer season. Tourists make up nearly 70 percent of his business, Denison estimates.

You wouldn't know it today—judging by all the new construction in Traverse City, especially with the hotels being built to accommodate the ever-rising tourism—yet Denison says that in the early nineties, downtown Traverse City "was dying." With new malls opening well away from the downtown area and large retailers leaving—such as J.C. Penney moving from its prominent Front Street location to the Grand Traverse Mall as an anchor store in the early nineties—"everyone was freaking out." But local retailers such as Horizon Books stepped up, with Horizon moving into the former J.C. Penney space and smaller retail vendors capitalizing on the newly available prime locations, especially for catering to tourists, which reenergized the downtown scene.

....

Over the past decade, says Denison, another stage of change has occurred in Traverse City. "When they started renting kayaks," such as at Clinch Park, "I went whoa, that's for when you go to other places, not here. I should have known. I should have realized long ago when I moved from California that this would get here because of the water." A more specific worry looms regarding the city's collective identity going forward, especially as a popular tourist destination. "Now our concern is that Traverse City just becomes this bar and dining and drinking town." This can drive out a broader, healthier retail mix, Denison says. Of course, that happens of its own accord in a free market system. "You can't legislate the landlords here," he acknowledges. However, even in such an ever-changing business climate, a renowned, long-established local restaurant can stay in demand by continuing to offer a high-quality dining experience, as Amical long has.

With a sense of wistfulness, Denison recalls how quiet and laid-back Traverse City was when his family relocated here thirty-three years ago. Like everyone who comes here, the Denisons were awed by the region's natural beauty. "It's a special, mystical place," he says. Yet they also appreciated the tight sense of community. "When we got here, nothing was happening. I got here at the same time a lot of these other very creative, likeminded people came because they wanted to live in a beautiful area and be part of a small community and practice their craft. They were working hard in their little restaurants creating great food, and the next thing they know, they look up from their cutting boards and look around and go, 'Holy shit, what happened?' They were just working and loved being here. We weren't brilliant. We didn't think about moving here and then in twenty years this place was going to explode."

Denison says that he and other local restauranteurs are also worried about patrons heading elsewhere, to other northern Michigan destination towns such as Glen Arbor, Leland, Petoskey, and Charlevoix, for their dining experiences. "A lot of us are concerned that we are pricing ourselves out of a visitor's market and no one wants to come here." Notably, he's heard this from his contacts at the Traverse City Horse Shows. There is "some pushback from the Horse Show people that they feel they are being taken advantage of financially" due to bringing their stratospheric spending power to the region. "My ears perk up when those people start saying it's getting expensive, because they are not price sensitive."

Nonetheless, Amical's owner believes that despite the many challenges it faces today, the local restaurant scene will persevere, if not thrive. "We're the second-oldest profession, so we're not going anywhere. It might change, but it's not going anywhere. Through good times and bad people have figured out how to dine and entertain." And local and visiting gourmands will ensure that life in the industry goes on.

"The foodies started dining as entertainment," he says. "Most people go to a concert or show and maybe grab something to eat. But now it's 'I'm going to the big-name chef's restaurant that took me a month and a half to get in, and we are going to have ourselves an experience.' And that has helped our industry too. It's allowed people to make better educated judgment calls on what is actually happening in their dining experience, whether it's at Applebee's or here. So it's enabled us to survive and flourish. I think it's going to be fine. Will it be overpopulated? Well, are there enough brewpubs around? It will all take care of itself."

An Up North Ice Cream Institution

To be an official Traverse City area resident or certified Up North visitor, one must pay a visit to Moomers Homemade Ice Cream. The iconic ice cream store, located west of Traverse City near Long Lake, concocts more than 160 flavors of premium ice cream, with more than 20 offered daily. Everyone I know in the Grand Traverse region has been to Moomers; everyone, that is, except me. That changed today.

It's Wednesday morning, August 10, 2022. I pull into the parking lot east of the kitchen area directly behind Moomers, slotting my car between two employees' vehicles. Then I see a much larger parking lot that strikes me as overkill for an ice cream parlor. I later learn that it overflows during busy periods in the summer. This is one serious ice cream enterprise.

Two educational posters filled with photographs affixed to an outside fence explain how the dairy works—"Moomers Farm Creamery"—and the process of making ice cream—"From Cows to Cone." A photo on the ice cream poster shows Holstein dairy cattle surrounding Jon Plummer, his mother, Nancy (holding an ice cream cone), and his middle sister, Becky, all with broad smiles. It promotes what the Moomers experience is really all about: ice cream just makes people happy.

Inside I'm welcomed by Jon—Bob and Nancy's son—who's a co-owner with Becky and his parents. He's busy prepping ice cream in containers for delivery, along with Sommer Deering, who's worked for the family business since its inception in 1998. The two work quickly, scooping as if it's muscle memory, which it is. A radio provides white noise in the background, nobody really listening. Standing in the Moomers kitchen/prep area, I'm reminded of my years working in the food and beverage industry and feel right at home, even enjoying the sounds of the walk-in and reach-in freezer latches opening and closing. Yet it's almost fatiguing to watch the ice cream virtuosos as they fill seemingly endless cardboard containers. Jon, who's a trim, clean-shaven forty-three-year-old with close-cropped hair and a ready smile, meeting well my expectation of the appearance of an ice cream making and serving professional, answers my questions while prepping wholesale orders for delivery, reading from a customer list while never losing his place in the conversation. Workplace psychologists say multitasking is a myth; after watching and interacting with Jon, I beg to differ.

Nancy Plummer taught mostly first grade for twenty-seven years at Long Lake Elementary School (a Traverse City Area Public School). Tiring of the "administrative baloney," as her son puts it, she took a leave of absence and worked at the ice cream shop to help get it off the ground. Jon refers to his father as "a jack of all trades, master of none," having been a brick mason, builder, farmer, school bus driver, as well as a high school wrestling referee for thirty-eight years. He notes, "Without this business, there's no way in hell we could continue to farm, with the economics of a small, eighty-acre dairy farm."

Jon tells me that they're milking eighteen cows today (the herd totals thirty). Some of the ice cream mix is produced by their dairy operation, but the majority is outsourced to keep up with customer demand. Moomers Farm Creamery is a separate business, which features a food and milk plant. There, milk is pasteurized and bottled: whole, 2 percent, and chocolate. Eggnog and ice cream mix round out the dairy's product line.

In 2022, Moomers celebrated its twenty-fifth season. Along with its busy retail operation, the family-owned business has 150 wholesale accounts, supplying grocery stores, restaurants, and convenience stores. About seven hundred gallons will be shipped out tomorrow to some of those accounts. "We sell just shy of 100,000 gallons of ice cream a year," Jon reports. "It's morphed into more than what we ever thought."

That catchy name—Moomers—was Nancy's doing. "She's always called baby calves 'Moomers,'" Jon explains. "In hindsight, it's probably the best decision she ever made. Everyone can say Moomers. A three-year-old kid is the driver of our business." Then he shows me how that works: "Grandma, Grandpa, I want to go get ice cream! I want to go to Moomers!"

The retail store is seasonal, open from March through New Year's Eve; wholesale production is year-round. All their product is sold locally, meaning throughout northern Michigan, as far north as Mackinac Island, which he calls "a big-time account." Meijer is Moomers' largest corporate account.

People come for the "Moomers experience," he says. "It's folks walking into our business with their family, friends, and loved ones and getting an ice cream cone." It's a child's heightened anticipation being realized by the tasting of the frozen dessert—lick after delicious lick—fully surpassing expectations. Their top seller? A scoop-and-a-half serving in a homemade waffle cone. Treat in hand, walk outside on the deck overlooking the Plummer dairy farm, and take it all in. "It's the whole ambiance," says Jon. On a busy ten-hour day, he estimates Moomers will serve nearly two thousand customers. And that's not a typo.

Even though Moomers is a tourist destination—"we wouldn't be near what we are without the tourist economy"—the business still caters to locals. "They are our lifeline," Jon emphasizes, providing a steady stream of year-round support.

Moomers was on the itinerary for President Biden's visit to northern Michigan on July 3, 2021, following his stop at King Orchards in Central Lake. He recounts, "It was cool—and bizarre. There were about sixty Secret Service agents. I knew things were real when there was a German Shepherd here. And there he was in our freezer." Rest assured, most likely checking for explosive devices and not sampling product.

While Grand Traverse County today is "a different place" compared to his childhood experience here—fewer people, less traffic, slower pace—Jon has no qualms about Moomers being a popular local business that's interested in serving as many customers and selling as much ice cream as possible. "As [part of] a for-profit, tourist-driven industry, it's not a bad thing." He refers to himself as "a local citizen who does like TC and thinks it's a cool place," and yes, "it's busy." His father, who just walks in, pointedly begs to differ. "It sucks." Smiling at me, Jon diplomatically remarks, "We look forward to 'Locals' Summer'—it's called September."

Bob stays for a few minutes and joins the conversation. He tells me that when he and his wife bought their dairy farm in 1972, moving here from Flint, their neighbors were miles away. He built the family home himself, which took four years. Soon after, they were no longer alone. Two houses were built next to theirs, which he "thought would never happen." For someone seeking the tranquility farm life can offer, things only got worse. "I look around and it's a subdivision over there, a subdivision over here. It's absolutely nuts. It's a curse more than a blessing, I think, at least for people who have been here." Yet he admits that "we're part of the problem"—as purveyors of to-die-for ice cream. "We can't totally say it's somebody else's fault."

It all started one night twenty-six years ago when Nancy woke him up and told him that "she wanted an ice cream store." And Bob said, "'Are you outta your freakin' mind?' And everybody told us we wouldn't make it." Too far from Traverse City. Their property is on the wrong side of the road. No formal business plan (which, he says, they still don't have). He recalls being informed by one of the two members of SCORE Traverse City (a nonprofit that provides experienced businessmen and -women as volunteers who mentor startups)[18] who visited him that another problem was their business would be located next to "a stinking farm." When asked who owned that farm, Bob answered, "I do." Once they opened against the well-intended advice, their SCORE advisors became "two of our best customers until they died," Bob says. He heads toward the door, waves goodbye, then gets back to farming.

....

The pandemic put a crimp in Moomers part-time workforce, Jon says. "It was tricky finding kids who wanted to work during Covid. And this is the first year of the past three that we can actually say, 'I'm looking for a junior or a sophomore who can work during the school year' and we can be a little more selective." Yet the fast pace at Moomers, combined with being on one's feet for the entire shift and working with the public, isn't for everyone, especially young people who have little workplace experience. The good news is, about

80 percent of their seasonal hires stay the course. The ice cream store has five full-time, year-round adult employees, while employing approximately twenty-five seasonal workers, predominantly high school and college kids.

Moomers provides basic training for young workers, such as explaining how to understand a paystub and how to interact most effectively, as a representative of Moomers, with the public. "We're in the indulgence business," Jon notes. Customers don't have to wait for a table, but they do have to queue up in line and wait to be served, which patrons—especially return customers—expect. According to Jon, customer complaints are rare. There's no sending back a steak for being undercooked or a cocktail for being too weak. And when people are jonesing for ice cream, they typically aren't in a bad mood when they get there. Says Jon, "Sure, there are jerk customers. Everyone has had an interaction with someone who wasn't pleasant. It's called working with the general public. It's working anywhere. Name a place where everyone is always pleasant: it doesn't exist." So the employees get coached on how to best work with the clientele. "We feel like that is a little bit of our duty, to educate our staff about what the real world is."

Given all the change that has come to the Grand Traverse region since Moomers' inception, the ice cream parlor's customers haven't really changed over the years. Visiting Moomers "is still an indulgent, family-friendly outing that isn't like a necessity of life; it's affordable." But one thing has changed post-pandemic: customers have become much more demanding. "Their vacation was earned and deserved, and we were lucky to serve them," he characterizes this occasional bad attitude. As normalcy returns, "we're now coming back into the 'No, we don't act that way'" behavior management mode. "Outside of that, we really haven't had any issues."

Similar to the peacekeeping standard operating procedure for bar customers—no talking about politics and religion—Moomers makes it their business to not get involved in such conversations with their customers. "You'll never see a political sign in our front yard," Jon attests. In today's contentious, extremely tribal political environment, "it's always fifty-fifty and somebody's going to be pissed off." Neutrality is best for ice cream sales, especially in times like these.

Jon refers to his staff as *Flavorologists*. Employee contests are held to come up with new flavors, which is their patrons' ongoing expectation and "the number one question from customers" every spring. Jon's favorite is Pralines & Cream. He's also fond of Buffalo Tracks, an Oleson's Food Stores exclusive. The concoction is put together with caramel, sea salt, chocolate flakes, Oleson's special house-ground peanut butter, and, of course, Moomers' Caramel Sea Salt Ice Cream. "So good," he says dreamily. Grasshopper is his close second: crème de menthe–flavored ice cream with Oreo cookie pieces. I can hardly stand it.

Having restrained myself from begging for samples, as I walk back to my car, I remind myself that I have yet to have the true Moomers experience: feasting on a waffle cone, mine most likely filled with Cow Tracks: vanilla ice cream, Reese's Peanut Butter Cup pieces, and chocolate fudge swirl. That will change later this week, as I text a local friend with an invitation to join me. Not one to answer texts quickly, she responds in seconds: "I'm always up for Moomers."

CHAPTER 6

INVASIVE SPECIES

Maine sucks. Tell your friends.

My youngest brother, Chris, traveled to Bar Harbor, Maine, in September, a bucket-list trip. While there for a week, he texted me photos of the hiking trails he tried out, including several in Acadia National Park, along with pics of majestic Frenchman Bay leading out into the Atlantic Ocean. The most striking image, though, was of a decal in a tourist shop: *Maine sucks. Tell your friends.* I immediately substituted "Northern Michigan" for Maine. Then "Leelanau County." You get the point. Well, if you're a local, you certainly do.

....

Like almost everyone I know (which includes a lot of boomers), I'm a fan of the dramatic series *Yellowstone*, starring Kevin Costner. In season five, Dutton has been elected governor. His election night speech echoes some of the concerns I've heard from locals in northern Michigan, especially from outdoorsmen and -women who have multigenerational claims to the region. Gov. Dutton proclaims: "What will Montana look like in one hundred years? Much of that is dictated by the way the world sees us today. Right now, we are seen as the rich man's plaything. We are New York's novelty and California's toy."[1] Substitute "Chicago," for example, for a more local interpretation.

Dutton's acceptance speech goes even further. In it, he declares that he will propose the Montana Legislature double nonresidents' property taxes and apply a 6 percent sales tax to all goods bought in Big Sky Country by nonresidents, as well as levy a registration fee on all nonresident vehicles. Then he emphasizes, "The message is this: We are not your playground. We are not your haven from the pollution and traffic and mismanagement of your home states. This is our home. Perhaps if you choose to make Montana your home, you will start treating it like a home, and not a vacation rental."[2] Ouch. This scene summarized the feelings of numerous folks I've interacted with in small towns across northern Michigan. Not exclusively, of course. But this sentiment of being invaded is real. *Yellowstone*'s popularity resonates with many Americans' sense of territory, home, and freedom. I do believe Gov. Dutton has struck a nerve in season five with those feeling overrun by "outsiders" throughout the Great Lakes region.

....

Throughout May and the first three weeks of June 2022, walking in my Cedar neighborhood once or twice a day is topmost on my agenda, spring's advance toward summer in northern Michigan being utterly exhilarating. I traipse out of Manor Green, the development where our cottage is located, just east of Sugar Loaf—The Old Course golf course, to Bodus Road. Depending upon my mood, I either head west, uphill toward the golf course, or east, accessing South Good Harbor Bay Trail near the closed Sugar Foot Restaurant, the view replete with hillside cherry and apple orchards. This is a pleasant, relaxing stroll in the off-season, as traffic is light, the locals typically giving me a courteous wide berth as they pass by. And almost every driver waves. That safe-and-sound mood changes dramatically, however, when the last week in June arrives. Then the traffic becomes a new phenomenon to contend with.

While out for a walk that late June weekend, I find the roadways much more heavily trafficked than usual, mostly with late-model SUVs and vans. Granted, it's hardly the bumper-to-bumper, road-rage building congestion endemic to large cities. But now, instead of a vehicle passing me every five to ten minutes, it's often several per minute.

The vacationers zoom by on Good Harbor Trail heading toward M-22, their destination typically Sleeping Bear Dunes National Lake Shore. The speed limit is an unposted but locally known and usually observed fifty-five miles per hour. Many locals tend to drive at a pastoral pace. This more easygoing driving approach is guaranteed to unnerve the vacation driver barreling toward the next diversion on their packed schedule. When it's Wednesday already on a hard-earned seven-day respite from work and you need to start getting ready to go home in the next forty-eight hours, "Sunday drivers" can be a pain in vacationers' posterior.

I walk on Good Harbor Trail's well-marked bike/pedestrian lane facing oncoming traffic, the widely accepted safety practice when sidewalks are lacking. Now that the invasion's vanguard has made landfall, I need to pay even greater attention than usual if I want to continue being among the living. Summer Saturdays are vacationers' shift change, the tourists rushing to their $3,000 (and upward) weekly short-term rentals, largely ignoring the speed limit, showing little concern for the scant pedestrian traffic—which as far as the eye can see happens to be just me. They seldom give me that exaggerated safe distance, as the locals tend to, from their hurtling steel machines—five-thousand-pound-plus pickup trucks included, sometimes towing a boat—rigidly staying in their lane while I step aside as much as I can, the tall roadside weeds and wildflowers preventing me from getting off the shoulder more than a foot or two.

The Leelanau County Sheriff's Office will place a radar speed trailer along Good Harbor Trail for those driving southbound toward Cedar, which does help calm things a bit. What helps even more, though, is to have a county police vehicle, occupied by one of Leelanau's finest, idling along the roadside. Yet deputies can't be everywhere at once. Here in Leelanau County, they have a lot of ground to cover—more than 348 square miles of land to patrol.[3] When the summer rush is on, lawbreaking while driving is likely occurring at any given time on a Leelanau County road. It's just part of the annual tourist migration phenomenon.

Vacationers' vehicles are easy to spot. Luggage carriers, kayaks, and paddleboards are strapped to their rooftops, and a tangle of bicycles are mounted on bike racks in back. Whenever one of them zooms by me in too-close-for-comfort proximity, I try to resist the urge to check the license plate. And I fail. The most frequent out-of-state plate I spot is from Illinois, especially for speeders. (Not to worry, Illinoisians: the rest of the Midwest is well represented in the category of "dangerous while driving" in their mad dash Up North, as well as other visitors from around the country who compete for worst-driving honors.) Many of the Illinois tourists here in northern Michigan hail from Chicagoland. (Of note, Glen Arbor has earned the nickname of "Little Chicago," with many second and third homes owned there, often over generations, by those from the Windy City and its suburbs.) Of course, this doesn't excuse downstaters and even locals who are risktakers when behind the wheel. It's just that these anecdotal trends are obvious to those, like me, making field observations. That unfortunately turn into stereotypes. That tend to stick.

Confession: I used to be one of those stressed-out northern Michigan vacation agenda captives. But I'm seasonal now. And there's nothing more judgmental than a convert.

The Mad Angler

During my research, Dave Dempsey asked if I had spoken with the local writer Michael Delp. I was not familiar with Delp's essay writing and poetry, which I would soon come to find as being deeply reverent in portraying nature. He had been the former director of creative writing at the Interlochen Center for the Arts, where he began working in 1984, and is now retired. He's also the co-editor for Wayne State University Press's Made in Michigan Writers Series.

I picked up Delp's latest collection of poetry to familiarize myself with his work: *Lying in the River's Dark Bed: The Confluence of the Deadman and the Mad Angler*, published in 2016. The layout of the book is quite clever. Two distinct entities—the Deadman and the Mad Angler—are represented by two "front" covers in upside down opposition (one substituting for the back cover), cluing me in that the poet I was trying to reach would make for a most intriguing interview.

Delp and I emailed one another numerous times trying to schedule a phone interview. He had been commuting between Interlochen and Ann Arbor, helping his daughter, who teaches at the University of Michigan, with some family matters. Finally, one evening in September we end up connecting. Early in the conversation, I mention that I had purchased a copy of *Lying in the River's Dark Bed*. "I love good poetry," I say. His warm laugh fills my phone's receiver as he answers, "You best reserve judgment."

Delp, seventy-four, owns a cabin on the Boardman-Ottaway River, which he calls Reeling Waters. He's a long-time fly fisherman. He's also a fierce protector of northern Michigan trout streams—thus his nickname the Mad Angler—which provide optimal habitat for brown, rainbow, and brook trout, and which are attracting more and more use by tourists and new arrivals to the area. With this the focus of our conversation, Delp does not hesitate to be candid.

I share that I like Ann Arbor. "You do? I can't stand the place. It's the only town in Michigan that loves itself more than Traverse City." I nearly spit out the water I'm sipping as we both laugh. "I mean, I like it; it's all right. But everybody's the same age and nobody really makes face contact and not many people are friendly. They're just too wrapped up in themselves." Known in my circle of family and friends for being generous with my opinion, I suspect I may have met my match.

Within minutes we're onto the subject of rivers, and his concern for the ones he spends time on in northern Michigan, especially the Boardman-Ottaway, becomes crystal clear. "There's no question there's more pressure, especially on smaller river systems," he comments. "On the Boardman, I've seen a real uptick in the pressure because it's getting a lot of publicity and the dam's gone" (referring to the Brown Bridge Dam, removed in 2013). It's really being overused right now." Hoping for a Boardman-Ottaway River usage plan but doubting it will come about anytime soon, he adds, "It's a free-for-all down there [in Traverse City], with liveries and kayakers and breweries on the river, which I hope doesn't manifest itself upstream."

Before we get too far into the interview, I diverge for a moment to share a recent trout fishing story. He indulges me, of course, as fellow anglers will, wanting to hear all about it.

....

For the past twenty-five years, most every spring, usually on trout season's Opening Day in northern Michigan—the last Saturday in April—I rendezvous with my friend Greg, who's from a seventh-generation Czech family that originally settled along Good Harbor Bay, and we head to the Jordan River in Antrim County. Sometimes we meet up with one or two of his brothers. This familial ritual has gone on as far back as they can remember, including times spent on and in the river with their great-grandfather, grandfather, and father.

Years ago, their hunting and fishing camp cabin in the Jordan River Valley would be opened by Greg. His brothers, uncles, cousins, and a few select friends (all males, per tradition; it's a break the women of the family look forward to as well) would gradually trickle in and claim one of the bunks or sleep at an uncle's house near East Jordan. The Canadian and domestic whiskey and beer would break out on the eve of the trout opener, as well as a lively poker game that would run into the wee hours. In the morning, though, the business was trout fishing on the Jordan, first light being the goal, sometimes accomplished though not always realistic under the partying circumstances.

On April 29, 2022, a Friday, I receive an out-of-nowhere text from Greg. We'd been out of touch for a while, a multifactored distancing, yet trout season makes for an irresistible urge to reconnect. I respond, "I'm back in Cedar. Chris [my youngest brother] and I are going fishing in the morning." Which just happened to be the Michigan trout opener. "Care to join us?"

"Up early? Boardman or Jordan?" he replies instantly. The Jordan. Fewer fishermen. A good place to lose plenty of tackle and not feel too badly about it. The stretch of the Jordan we typically work, at least for starters, is very technical, with lots of downed timber, and the stream is usually high and running fast from springtime snowmelt. This can make for a very frustrating day for anglers. But for us, not catching a fish isn't a downer at all. We're thankful just to be in the presence of the river, with the migrating songbirds, the early butterflies—mourning cloaks and red admirals—the blue sky, cottony clouds, and occasional refreshing breeze. This is happiness. Fresh-caught trout is a bonus.

After several hours fishing independently, we three reconvene at our pickup trucks. Chris had gone crickin' along a tributary; Greg had worked some beaver ponds; and I went downstream, working about a half-mile leg of the river. All of us had a few hits, but no catches. "I got a spot we should go work," Greg suggests, and we agree to relocate without asking where. He knows the river and his guiding skills have never failed us. This secret location always provided some nice trout for dinner, ensuring that we would never go home empty-handed.

Near a large culvert pouring river water into a pond, we toss in our redworms, allowing them to drift in the churning current. A few minutes later, it feels like I have a snag. I don't: the snag comes to life, pulling my rod tip down with strong tugs then turning in the water near the surface: an orange and silver flash, a huge trout for my four-pound test monofilament and five-foot ultralight rod. "Need a little help, Chris," I say calmly, given the gravity of the moment. He hustles over, helping me land the eye-popping German brown (this highly prized northern Michigan game fish is a non-native species, brought over to the United States from Germany in 1883[4]). We're all amazed, and my companions cheer. A trophy fish for one is a success for all. The brown is over two feet long and has a remarkable, well-fed girth. We laugh giddily as we take stock of the largest Jordan River trout I ever caught, each of us taking turns holding it during the requisite photo op. "That must be seven pounds," Greg says in awe as he works a rope through the gills and mouth, for our undersized stringers aren't up to the task.

Then, not ten minutes later, I have another trophy fish on. The silvery trout, a rainbow, is all fight as it madly thrashes the surface and makes several drag-whining runs. Greg hustles over and expertly nets it with one careful scoop. In just twenty minutes, I've landed two of the largest stream-caught trout in my fishing career, spanning decades, the brown a personal best. Not bad for a guy that only gets out twice a year—in a good year—on a northern Michigan trout stream.

We break for lunch around noon, Greg thoughtfully supplying hot dogs from Buntings Market in Cedar, something of a local delicacy, as the meat is butchered on area farms, with an accompaniment of orange slices and iced-down bottles of Coors Banquet Beer. Once we finish, a Michigan Department of Natural Resources pickup truck pulls in off the two-track. Two female conservation officers—a trainer and her trainee—get out and cheerfully hail us. "Catch any fish?" the senior of the two asks expectantly, smiling.

"Yes, we did," I answer exuberantly, like a little boy that can't contain himself. "I'll be right back." Mysteriously, and apparently presciently, for the first time in my trout fishing history I decided to bring along a large cooler, just in case. I hoist the cooler out of Chris's SUV, swinging it to the ground. It's heavy with stream water—and two lunker trout.

"Holy shit!" the trainee exclaims as she opens the lid and reaches in to lift up the brown. "Sorry, I mean, wow," she laughs.

"No problem," I respond. "You can imagine what I said."

The conservation officers are well schooled in public relations. They kindly offer to weigh the fish on their scales—the brown turned out to be 6.5 pounds, the rainbow 3.5, pose for photos with my trophies, and spend time talking trout with us.

Once our casual conversation ends, as expected, they ask to see our fishing licenses—as a formality. "We know you have them, since you couldn't wait to show us your catch," the senior officer says, grinning. As they say goodbye, I point out the trash strewn about ten yards away. "That's not ours, but we'll be sure to clean it up."

"Don't," the senior officer warns me. "I already checked: it's toilet paper with feces," her face screwing up in disgust. "I won't even touch it."

Although this was quite unexpectedly the trout fishing outing of a lifetime for me, and I will always savor and be grateful for this incredible experience (whether an arbitrary event, fate, or divinely inspired), what we encountered that day was a disrespect for nature I hadn't seen to this degree before in the typically unspoiled Jordan River Valley. We also came upon empty beer and soda cans and other refuse during out outing, a sacrilegious blot on our otherwise spectacular day in nature. Although I'm quick to blame those not familiar with these parts, and Chris echoes that accusingly, saying, "Must be downstaters or out-of-staters," Greg questions our certainty. "Don't be so sure. We have locals who don't give a damn about respecting Mother Nature. You'd be surprised."

I was. No matter who was responsible, I was.

....

As I get deeper into my conversation with Delp, it occurs to me to ask him, "How many fly fishermen are too many fly fishermen?"

"It depends. If I'm a certain mood—I won't say whether it's the right or wrong mood—two is too many," he responds candidly. "To me, fishing is not a social enterprise. I don't go out to socialize, although I do like to fish with my dear friends. I really don't relish running into people. Usually when I see people coming, I fade into the woods until they go by."

Delp is probably doing more fading the past few years, as the pandemic brought out millions of people to explore outdoor pastimes, fishing among them, fly fishing included. In an interview with *UpNorthLive* in April 2021, Matt Hartman, manager of The Northern Angler, a Traverse City fly fishing specialty shop, reported that he had seen "a huge increase in people" stopping by to shop and learn more about the pastime. "Difficult to fathom how many new folks we've had in the doors looking for how to get started, and where to go and what to do in the sport."[5]

Like Delp, for me one of the primary reasons to head to a trout stream is to get away from it all—"all" being code for people. I'm not one to go shoulder to shoulder with salmon fishers on the Boardman-Ottaway or Betsie or Platte rivers during the annual run. Defeats the purpose. A successful fishing day for me is, in this order:

1. Getting to spend the day along an awesome northern Michigan river.
2. Seeing as few people as possible.
3. Catching fish.

Delp is strictly a catch-and-release fly fisherman. But he's okay with those who keep the fish they catch, which I'm glad to hear. "I understand how good it is for your spirit to take a fish from the river and eat it," he says agreeably. "It's one of the best things you can ever do for your spirit."

As Delp understands and I wholly concur, there *is* something to catching and eating a fish. The intention of seeking wild-caught game. The hopeful act itself. The joy of the catch. The animal life taken and the gratitude for the harvest. The preparation of the meal. And the feeding of self, family, friends. This is an ancient connection, a holy process far removed from that of checking the price per pound of the butcher-case-displayed filets of farm-raised, pellet-fed fish sent via container ship from abroad to a grocer near you. Rod-and-reel fishing really is good for the soul.

The increasing numbers of fly-fishing enthusiasts soon discover "that it's the least efficient way to catch a fish," notes Delp. "You could throw stones and probably get more fish than you do when you fly fish. So they get frustrated really fast, and then they stop." Frustration thins the herd. But newcomers just keep on coming, taking their place.

....

In early May 2022, Chris and I drive southeast of Traverse City to the Boardman-Ottaway, near Spider Lake, for an afternoon of trout fishing. We park in the dirt lot near the Brown Bridge Quiet Area Trailhead off Brown Bridge Road, the location of the former dam. On October 6, 2012, the dam removal project's dewatering structure unexpectedly failed, resulting in a sudden emptying of Brown Bridge Pond. Water rushed downstream, flooding sixty-six properties along the way (thankfully, there were no injuries or fatalities).[6] A decade later, the river is running its natural course, and the trout fishery is thriving. We spend the day several miles upriver from the trailhead. As we fish our way back, near the site of the old dam about a dozen fly-fishing novices practice casting and fishing, right on top of one another, their instructors tweaking their inchoate technique. We decide to cut short our outing, not thrilled by the company—who have every right to be there, just like us.

Delp is extremely concerned about *how* the Boardman-Ottaway River should be used, and *by whom*. "There's a large population of kayakers and tubers and less fishermen because of all the people in the river," he observes. "I don't know where the balance point is. There are some mentalities and philosophies that say the most use for the most people, as opposed to the best use for the most people, or the best use for the best people." Indeed, interests are clashing regarding multiuse of the twenty-eight-mile river, with no answer in sight. As for Chris and me, we'll be back to fish in the fall, when the summer season is over, the air is cool, and the kayak rentals are done for the season. Sharing involves knowing when to make your own best use of the rivers when fishing.

"If I had my druthers, all the rivers would be choked with trees so we couldn't get down them," Delp asserts. "So if you wanted to fish, you'd have to risk your life to go fishing. I know that's an extreme position. But to me, rivers exist to fish." Of course, this is a distinctly human-centric point of view. Up until the appearance of *Homo sapiens*, rivers had always done just fine without us, no argument. So if rivers could talk, they might suggest otherwise.

Delp likes a good cigar. And a good drink now and then, whiskey his preference. Which makes sense, as a line of locally distilled whiskeys carries his alter ego's name, the Mad Angler. The three whiskeys in the series, including bourbon and rye, are made by Iron Fish Distillery in Thompsonville, about thirty-four miles southwest of Traverse City. It sounds like he's smoking while we're talking; he may well be sipping too. A capital idea at this time of day. I'm getting thirsty. But I'm working.

His legitimate complaints about shared use of natural resources and how to manage them—and if we can't do so successfully on our own, state and local governments might have to step in to referee the situation—remind me of a fishing outing on Little Traverse Lake a few years ago. It was the third week in June. The smallmouth bass were on their nests. They seek shallower water at that time of year for spawning purposes, so this boatless fisherman could take advantage of the close reach. I waded into the lake, having parked nearby in a small gravel lot for those visitors without the advantage of lakeside property. I was in water up to my crotch, perhaps twenty-five yards from shore, casting my lure out into about ten feet of water.

I had been there about fifteen minutes when a guy about my age pulled up approximately an eighth of a mile down the road from me in a late model black Chevy Suburban, the kind favored by the Secret Service. He towed a paddleboard trailer. His son and daughter, I assumed, appearing to be in their mid-twenties, popped out of the vehicle and then the threesome put in their recreational watercraft about seventy-five yards north of me. Sitting down on the paddleboards, obviously new to the sport, they paddled slowly out into the lake about twenty feet beyond me at an intersecting angle. Of course, I assumed they would move farther out, away from my casting zone. But they didn't. They just kept coming, the two young adults passing by me, idly—and loudly—chatting away. I had reeled in my line, just in case they were, well, oblivious. And they were. Then, a few seconds later, dad brought up the rear.

As I stood in the water holding my rod and reel, annoyed by such rude behavior and staring at him through my sunglasses, he turned to me, said hello, and then, with an almost comical delayed action—though I wasn't in the laughing mood—asked, "Are you fishing here?" In response, I raised my fishing pole a bit higher. "Oh, I'm so sorry," he apologized, genuinely, or so it appeared, and picked up his pace, now trying to be polite but only scaring off the fish.

Delp informs me that his slice of heaven on the Boardman-Ottaway is getting more and more congested by rowdy kayakers during the warm weather months. "There's a little feeder creek that dumps into the river just above the cabin, and there's a little deck that overlooks the creek," he explains. "I sit out there all the time—it's probably the best spot on Earth to me. And I can't tell you how many times I hear people coming down the river with Bluetooth speakers [when they're] a mile up the river. And the other thing people do is they shout a lot. I don't know why." But, right or wrong, he has a suspicion: "Well, they're drunk for one thing."

He says he's been "hit, knocked down, forced out of the river, sworn at, you name it. But I've also had some nice encounters with people too." No doubt usually it's the latter. Though most people are law abiding and tend to follow the golden rule, the less harmonious among us often get more attention due to their inability or lack of desire to coexist. Perhaps the same can be said for users of northern Michigan's rivers.

As the interview winds down, Delp asks if I want to talk about the proposed FishPass for the Boardman-Ottaway River in Traverse City, where the Union Street Dam is currently located. He served on the original dam removal committee and remains a skeptic of the project, calling it a "boondoggle" as a $20 million tourist attraction.

"I'm really passionate about that not happening," he continues. "My real concern is upstream migration of anadromous fish [salmon, notably] into the smaller, colder water.[7] There's a movement afoot to get salmon up there, but the real movement is for steelhead." He calls these the "money fish," with each one having a "calculated value." They're non-native to the river. He's concerned about the wild trout population that thrives in the upper part of the Boardman-Ottaway, which he wants to keep intact and undisturbed by steelhead and salmon. "We already have tons of rivers around us with steelhead and salmon. We don't need another one." He makes his final point rhetorically, saying, "Why ruin a beautiful river for money?"

About 10:30 p.m., Delp begs off. "It's my bedtime," he says unapologetically. Although I'm sorry to stop the lively conversation with the Mad Angler, it was past my bedtime too.

A River Runs through Him

Delp encourages me to talk with Bob Summers, a.k.a. R.W. Summers: Maker of Fine Tonkin Cane Rods. Summers has repaired and built handmade fly rods since 1956. When it comes to the sanctity and preservation of trout streams in northern Michigan, the two Boardman-Ottaway River neighbors are of the same mind. In fact, Summers might even be a madder angler—in an angry, disappointed sense, that is—than his riverine friend.

Summers, eighty-four, is in high demand as a living legend bamboo fly-rod maker, a craft that has brought him customers from all over the United States, and beyond. His rods command prices in the $3,000 range, which doesn't seem to get in the way of sales. (This is an astonishing price to this more typical rod and spinning reel fisherman, who catches trout with a $75 dollar Okuma rod and reel combo. But I must keep in mind that I'm clearly in the category of the uninitiated when it comes to *A River Runs Through It* romance of fly-fishing.) When Summers started out decades ago, he worked for another famous fly-rod maker, Paul H. Young. Summers specializes in repairing and restoring Young's rods as well as those crafted by Lyle Dickerson, a good friend and another renowned fly-rod builder.

I check Summers' website, get an email address, and reach out. Instead of emailing me back, he calls and leaves a message, saying, "We can get together and talk about what's happening to our poor north here. It's quite a disaster, I think, in the overall picture." I call back several times, but with no voicemail, Summers is hard to catch. Eventually I succeed: he answers, thinking I'm the IT specialist calling to help him with his computer issues. He chases me off the line, not peevishly but out of an urgent technical need, telling me to "call back in an hour." *Click.*

Summers echoes Delp about his concern for the changes that are overtaking northern Michigan's trout streams, especially as to how they are used. The man loves his rivers, fly-fishing for trout, and the solitude it brings. He has a hard time comprehending why it all must change. But he certainly recognizes that despite his wishes, indeed it is.

"Well, it's human beings," he plainly summarizes the problem. "You're bringing in all kinds of personalities and cultures from all over the country. A lot of them people think they went to heaven because they got away from where the hell they came from. But what are they doing? They're going to create the same thing here." They already have.

I've seen this for myself, most notably on Spider Lake. The 450-acre all-sports lake was a perfect getaway for us for the five years we co-owned the one-acre waterfront property, which featured one hundred feet of lake frontage and teemed with wildlife (including the living legend common snapping turtle that roamed our cove—perhaps more accurately, *its* cove—its oval-like top shell nearly two feet long). While kayaking the lake after we moved in, we noticed that a few too many lakefront homeowners had put in lawns that ran right down to the waterline. Some of the lush chem-lawned yards almost glowed green and required more frequent cutting, a sign of being well fertilized. Of course, the fertilizer runoff contributes to algal blooming, which lowers oxygen content and blocks sunlight. Phosphorous and nitrogen, common ingredients in grass fertilizer, are the primary culprits polluting lake water. Summers noted other changes as well.

"It used to be that you could go downtown on Front Street, and you couldn't walk from one end to the other and not meet a couple of people you know. Now I do it and I haven't seen anybody I know in a couple years." He goes on to say that the very thing that makes the Traverse City region so desirable—a small town surrounded by miles of woodlands and clean water resources: Lake Michigan, trout streams, and abundant inland lakes—has been compromised by champions of "progress": Realtors, talk show hosts, and other promotional entities enticing people to come north and grow the area. "Wait a minute—in that same mouthful, you're destroying what you're talking about," he protests, noting the contradiction. "This wonderful lifestyle was because there wasn't so many human beings."

Summers has fished on some of the finest trout streams in the country, even worldwide. But those areas, too, are experiencing the same surge of overwhelming interest. "I used to go up to Montana a lot, but it's getting to be bad out there, because a lot of the good water is all bought up by big money-making lodges on them. It's dramatically different than what it was twenty years ago. It all gets down to too many people and too many different personalities and cultures." The Madison River in southwestern Montana, for example, has received so much fly-fishing pressure in recent years that its trout population has declined by 50 percent. One incident there in summer 2021 points to the frustrations of locals, when fifteen out-of-state vehicles parked at a Montana Fish, Wildlife & Parks access point along the river had their tires slashed.[8]

Although he wishes things stayed the way they once were, that nagging human tendency, the flyrod maker is generally resigned to the changes that are occurring in his beloved adopted home, which he came to from Detroit decades ago. "I guess that's the way it's meant to be because that's the way it's happening. But it ain't gonna be like it was." Never is.

....

Summers, who lives along the Boardman-Ottaway "about five bends" from his friend Mike Delp, is concerned about the vacant property in the area, which contributes to space for wildlife to thrive. He fears that in time, "Somebody's going to develop it and pretty soon the road [along the river] is going to get paved. And when that road gets paved, we've just cut up another big chunk of wilderness." As if proof of the discontent among old-time river fishers, he says, "I got two or three friends from around here that sold out and moved to the UP to get away from all this."

I turn our conversation toward fly-fishing in particular. Gradually, he softens, but not entirely. When it comes to understanding the ecological needs to sustain a healthy trout fishery, Summers observes, "There's no damn way that you can have people coming down that river getting out, tipping over, going on the brush. You're screwing up the fishes' habitat. But a lot of the people that do this, they're totally ignorant of the subject. They have no idea what it takes to raise a trout." When something is as sacred as a river to those who frequent them, who listen to them, who cultivate a deeper understanding of them than casual users ever will, every fish matters.

What drives the venerable fisherman's concern for protecting the integrity of trout streams is most evident when he talks about the art of fly-fishing: "I want to have hold of a rod, I want to manipulate it so that cast goes in a nice curve and the fly is going down the river and you're not being dragged by the fly. To a lot of people, that would just be a pain in the butt; they ain't gonna work that hard at it." Not everyone appreciates art.

Summers, who comes by his struggle honestly with change taking place on the rivers he loves, recalls a fly-fishing customer of his from Kentucky who used to tell him, "Bob, you gotta remember: fishing means different things to different people." Now talking one fisherman to another, I'm urged to share my recent Opening Day adventure, the pinnacle of my trout fishing experience, and he immediately discerns that I caught those personal-best trout using live bait. But he doesn't admonish me. And when I tell him that I wanted to release the two lunkers, as I admired how long it took for them to reach their trophy size but was foiled by my fishing buddies who insisted we keep and eat them, he uses my confession as an educational opportunity.

"I prefer we release them without taking them out of the water," he suggests. "You don't have to lift the fish out of the water and show it around for a camera, because it's gonna die. You can reach down in that water and get the hook and wiggle the fish off; I use barbless hooks, and release fish in the water. A lot of people can't totally understand that." But now, this guy does. I tell him that from what I learned from him today, I should probably pick up fly-fishing, something I first and last did in Indiana when I was eighteen. A fellow just-graduated senior from Lawrence Central High School had borrowed his father's fly rod (without his father knowing it, standard operating procedure back in the day), and we went to Delaware Lake at Fort Harrison on the northeast side of Indianapolis one mid-June afternoon. Using dry flies, we caught quite a few largemouth bass and bluegill. Having the fish rise to the surface to suck in the dry flies was action-packed fun.

"Yeah, you should. Plus, you can catch them fish out on the bay there," he says, referencing the story of my recent attempt to catch salmon schooling at the mouth of a creek in Good Harbor Bay just before the upstream run. "You're not gonna get as many, but there can be days if you hit it right, boy. . . ." That joy of fishing.

Toward the end of our conversation, improbably but fittingly, the topic turns to the Amish. His son-in-law, Jeff Smith, wrote a book, *Becoming Amish*, published in 2016. It's the story of a man who worked for General Motors "and became quite successful and said to hell with it and came up to Clare, Michigan, and became Amish," Summers tells me. "He just couldn't take it anymore." I mention my wife's extensive work with Amish settlements in northern Indiana, acting as the project manager for the first dental clinic in the United States to serve such communities. He tells me to get the book for her, and for me to read it too. Witnessing the negative impacts of the increasing popularity of his beloved trout streams for non-fishing entertainment no doubt appeals to the Amish in him. Who isn't Amish, figuratively speaking, at one time or another? Who doesn't need an occasional separation from modernity to seek solace in nature?

Our conversation winding to a close, Summers asks if I'm still in the area and invites me to his home on the Boardman-Ottaway to show me how to cast a fly rod. Like now. I'm almost beside myself, as how many people get an invitation like this from an internationally acclaimed fly-rod maker? I just returned to Indy, I respond disappointedly. "Well, if you get up this way, then come by. I can show you what we're doing." This is an offer I can't refuse. *Click.* And we're done.

It's the Boardman-*Ottaway* River

Carolan Sonderegger, department manager, and Brett Fessell, river restoration ecologist, both working in the GTB's Natural Resources Department, suggest meeting on Wednesday, July 20, at the site of the proposed FishPass at the Union Street Dam. I park nearby at the Central United Methodist Church. There's an ominous warning sign posted in clear view, promising all non-church business visitors who decide to park their vehicles there will be subject to towing. I do a doubletake, from a Christian standpoint, but I get it. Lord knows, parking is in high demand in Traverse City during the summer season. Despite the numerous empty parking spaces, as I step away from my Honda CR-V that's impolitely parked, I think twice about taking a risk, blaming it on my Catholic upbringing. I drive over to the dam parking lot.

There are fishers and kayakers near the dam, and two folks who I'm sure are waiting for me: Sonderegger, thirty-six, a GTB member who is thoughtfully masked, as I learn she's feeling under the weather, and Fessell, fifty-three, who looks prepared to go hiking, dressed comfortably in a flannel shirt, shorts, baseball cap, and hiking boots. We sit on the dormant grass under the shade of an ornamental tree on a hillside overlooking the dam.

The construction of the world-class, one-of-a-kind FishPass had been repeatedly delayed in court due to a citizen's lawsuit. (Groundbreaking was originally set for Saturday, October 24, 2020.) The suit contended that because the dam involves city parkland, the decision to build FishPass should be put to a public vote. But in October 2022, the Michigan Court of Appeals rejected the findings of the Thirteenth Circuit Court, which had decided in favor of the plaintiff.[9]

Its legal hurdles finally surmounted, the FishPass project began construction in June 2024.[10] The replacement of the Union Street Dam with the FishPass will complete the series of removals of all four aging dams along the Boardman-Ottaway River. This will be the missing piece in allowing the river to resume its natural course in its entirety.

The $19.3 million project's in-stream "wet work" was originally quoted in 2020 dollars; a reassessment now estimates costs at more than $23 million, not including expenses for an educational facility and other amenities.[11] Notably, the U.S. Environmental Protection Agency awarded $6.4 million to the project, with additional funding provided by a host of partners in conjunction with the Great Lakes Restoration Initiative.[12]

Functionally, FishPass will permit native fish to pass upriver while selectively preventing invasive species from further access, especially the detrimental lamprey. (Worth noting, nearly sixty native species can already be found in the Boardman-Ottaway, which is designated a Blue-Ribbon trout stream.) As Michael Delp stressed to me, FishPass is a contentious issue. Salmon and steelhead are not native to the Boardman-Ottaway, yet they are highly sought gamefish. Delp and other trout anglers are troubled by the notion of salmon and steelhead being allowed to run upriver, which would play havoc with the native brook trout fishery. According to the *FishPass: Project Overview*, published in October 2019, at present, the fish ladder at the Union Street Dam "is thought to only provide limited passage to fishes such as Pacific salmon, steelhead, and brown trout," all introduced non-native species. Concerns remain that the DNR will permit the introduction of salmon and steelhead once a ten-year testing phase concludes.[13]

Fessell maintains that the Grand Traverse Band is not interested in allowing non-native species to enter further into the river, which includes salmon and steelhead. Native suckers, whitefish, sturgeon, lake trout, walleye and the like would be allowed to pass through a sophisticated fish selection and barrier technology. As for salmon and steelhead getting complete access to the Boardman-Ottaway, Fessell acknowledges that the river would become a major producer, as it is ideal habitat for these fishes. Although brown trout already populate the Boardman-Ottaway and are not native, because they have long thrived in the river, he believes they can continue to coexist with the native species. Besides, they're quite a draw for trout fishers. Selectively passing desired fishes while preventing the entry of invasive species would be "a gamechanger in terms of dam removal in the Great Lakes," he says. "That's never been done before."

The Boardman-Ottaway River, as it is largely known and referred to by the area's non-Native population, is a hot topic from another standpoint—its very name. The river is named after an opportunistic lumber baron, Captain Harry Boardman, who had a short stay in Traverse City in the mid-1800s. Fessell had long been curious about the river's original Indian name, so he did some digging. He viewed maps from the 1700s that showed several different names for the river, including Odawa, Ottawa, and Ottaway. These maps were all generated by colonists, and the river's several Indian names were "interpretations of what they heard," he says. "So I thought, if we're going to restore this river and try and restore [a greater sense of] community, then the ultimate capstone to that would be restoring its original name." Ottaway, the appellation preferred by the GTB, is gaining traction in a wider sense, Fessell maintains. This has been my experience as well. All the environmental groups' representatives I spoke with for this book referred to the waterway that courses through Traverse City as the Boardman-Ottaway River, in respect to both the First Peoples as well as the more recent history of European settlement. Fessell says that getting the name officially changed is a matter for the United States Geological Survey. He believes it's only a matter of time.

He contends that renaming the river would be a way for the community to "get to know the tribe better. Yet, if you walk around and talk to tourists about local tribal communities, they don't know much about it at all." This isn't just a regional issue; it's a matter of general unawareness nationally.

The late outdoor writer Barry Lopez, known best for his National Book Award–winning work *Arctic Dreams*, spent significant time with Indigenous people during his extensive writing career. Lopez admired them for their fundamental and largely misunderstood relationship with nature, reflected in this comment: "In order to serve Progress, it's been necessary for us actively to refute the assertion of Indigenous North American cultures that the land is sentient."[14] To walk in nature with this extraordinary realization is to see the world lucidly and, unfortunately if not sadly, through a mostly unshared lens, at least here in the United States. And yet, that deeper awareness is exactly what people like Fessell and Sonderegger are raising in their vocations in serving the band, in advancing the restoration and protection of the Boardman-Ottaway River, and in so doing, educating the greater community and its many visitors.

I ask about the GTB's Natural Resources Department's Green Committee, which I came across on the band's website. The committee is comprised of tribal council members and any other interested GTB members. It's during this part of our conversation that the ancestral voice of the Anishinaabek speaks through Sonderegger when she declares that a core belief of her people is "taking care of Mother Earth. It is our job to protect her and restore her. In return, she gives back to us: our food, our water, our sustenance." The Green Committee's philosophy echoes that, says Sonderegger, "to do everything that's within our reach and our possibilities, and hopefully beyond, in getting more people involved in valuing that as well, in bringing awareness." This consciousness-raising effort isn't exclusively targeting a certain group, she explains. It includes "not only the non-tribal people but also our own people."

Sonderegger acknowledges the assimilation of Native people into modern culture, once an official and destructive policy the federal government used against tribes across the United States, often runs counter to that of traditional Indigenous culture. Now, an uncritical, passive acceptance of mainstream American culture by some Native Americans continues that eradication process. She explains, "It's very easy to get pulled into that and just live in that way. But it takes a lot more to actually remember, 'Oh, yeah, we're Native, we're Indigenous, let's get back to our roots.'"

From an environmental awareness-raising standpoint, the Green Committee is all about education and works in small yet profound ways to engender greater respect for Mother Earth. For example, the committee makes gifts of reusable drinking bottles and grocery bags. It also provides dining packages with reusable plates and utensils to discourage the use of Styrofoam. "We give them to the people to remind them that we have to start shifting our thoughts from this convenient lifestyle and go back to more of the reduce/reuse/recycle mindset." She adds, "As much as I hate to say this, I've come to see humans as more of a parasite. We're the smartest thing on this planet, yet we're the worst thing for the planet." I nod appreciatively. I've told my own family that my greatest contribution to the welfare of the planet will be my death: the removal of yet one more consumer of its resources. (In response, I get some nervous laughter or stony silence.) Now with Earth's population recently reaching a record eight billion people, as of mid-November 2022, this "contribution" becomes more obvious. Alarmingly, a billion people were born just since 2010.[15]

Are people loving northwest lower Michigan to death? Interest in the Boardman-Ottaway River suggests that possibility. The Conservation Resource Alliance out of Traverse City reports a mindboggling statistic: nearly two million people use the river annually for outdoor recreation.[16] Fessell, who has long been involved with the Boardman-Ottaway River restoration/dam removal project, doesn't seem surprised. "Throughout this project we knew that as awareness grew about the restoration efforts, more people would visit Brown Bridge Quiet Area. That would instigate more and more people visiting this area," he says in reference to the future site of FishPass. Improving the ecological health of the Boardman-Ottaway River, especially the stretch that runs through Traverse City, while drawing even more people to recreate in, on, and around it, and how this gets managed, well, therein lies the rub.

The "FishPass Project Overview" identifies "river-related activities" as "paddling, fishing, wildlife viewing, hiking, and *pub-crawling*, just to name a few." It goes on to acknowledge, "Any deviation from the status quo that concerns the Boardman-Ottaway River elicits considerable interest, both from those who seek and resist change."[17] Namely, the dam removal and FishPass projects. When "pub-crawling" is an activity associated with the nature of a river and the human purposes it serves, perhaps we all really need to pay more attention to riverine ecological health and well-being, as well as tighten up that definition.

Before we part, Sonderegger brings up a personal anecdote that shows her conviction in revering Mother Earth and educating careless members of the greater tribe of us all, which she calls "right thinking." While kayaking recently on the Boardman-Ottaway, she witnessed a group in front of her thoughtlessly dropping their empty Capri Sun juice pouches into the water, a clear example of wrong thinking. She quickly paddled to the floating refuse, scooped it up, and caught up with the litterers. "You guys dropped something" she admonished them, "and I handed it right back to them. I was so mad that they had the audacity. I don't understand it, and I never will."

The Captain and Me

I met Sam Worden, owner of Showtime Xtreme Charter, in 2019 when I booked his charter out of Grand Traverse West Bay. For years, I wanted to try charter fishing. However, my go-to Up North fishing buddy always talked me out of it, saying there's no guaranteed catch (understood, after a lifetime of fishing), the weather could be questionable since you must schedule ahead of time (again, understood, that's fishing), and that it's expensive (what isn't; and if it's worthwhile, who cares). But, despite the well-intended warnings, I decided now that I was in my sixties, I wouldn't deny myself the experience any longer.

Since then, I've been out with Captain Sam, as he's known, every summer, bringing along several local friends from Cedar, my youngest brother, and once, my grandson Brennan, a ten-year-old angler who will drop everything to put a line in the water (runs in the family). When out with Worden, we always catch fish. Always learn excellent fishing tips and about the ecosystem of Grand Traverse Bay and the health of its fishery. And always laugh a lot. I never regret booking a trip with Captain Sam.

I've been trying to arrange an interview with Worden, thirty-nine, given his years of experience not only in the Lake Michigan charter fishing industry, but as an international competitive fisherman who annually travels to Florida, Cabo San Lucas on the Mexican

Baja Peninsula, and Costa Rica to try his luck for cash prizes, and does well. Since the advent of the pandemic his charter fishing business has boomed, the first two Covid-19 outbreak years being the most lucrative since he started in 2002. (Note: 2022 would prove to be another banner year for Showtime Xtreme Charter, with the entire season, which ends in September, booked by early June.)

When I text him on Tuesday morning, June 7, 2022, lamenting not being able to put together a recreational outing for July, having nothing to do with setting up an interview, he responds that his morning charter for Wednesday just canceled and that "we could fish the prime hours in the a.m. if it worked for you. Ultra-light setup and a few trout." And an interview out on the water, where Worden is in his element. I was little-boy thrilled at the prospect. "Just like joining a group," he texted me, "only you get all the action!"

I meet him at 6:15 a.m. at the Elmwood Township Marina. It was daylight all the way from Cedar, a first in my fishing experience with Worden. Up North, June sunlight is reluctant to call it a day and quick to reappear, with daylight materializing well before 5 a.m. I stand on the dock near his boat, a twenty-seven-foot Triton, taking in the sunrise over West Bay. "Doesn't get any better than this, does it?" says the tall, athletic-looking, baseball-capped charter captain as he quickly preps his fishing tackle for the outing. The harbor is still and lifeless, the many impressive sailboats, yachts, and tugs, having recently arrived, are secured in their berths. We seem to be the only boat getting ready to head out. *All these poor bastards have to work,* I think. Although this is "work" for me, it's the kind of work I could take every day with a blissful grin on my face.

The twin Yamaha 150 horsepower engines idle smoothly as I climb aboard. Then Captain Sam slips us from the mooring and we're off, sipping coffee as we enter the bay for a morning of lake trout fishing. Ah, summer in northern Michigan.

....

The increasing changes to Grand Traverse Bay's biodiversity are a real concern of Worden's and give him cause to wonder about the future of the fishery, and in turn, his livelihood, the impact of invasive species the driving force to his unease. (Climate change, not so much, as he notes what he perceives as the cyclical nature of water levels and temperatures, based upon his own observations over the past several decades as a Lake Michigan charter boat operator.) Water clarity continues to improve due to the overwhelming presence of zebra and quagga mussels: we actually see lake trout in fifty feet of water. Lake bottom vegetation is becoming more common, thanks to the increased sunlight penetration; Worden has seen aquatic plants reaching up 140 feet from the lake floor. Mussels have put a considerable dent in the zooplankton, the primary food source of baitfish. Alewives, which came in from the St. Lawrence Seaway, led to the introduction of salmon in the Great Lakes in the sixties in an attempt to eradicate that invasive species as well as create a sports fishery. Worden says up until recently, baitfish numbers had dropped, so the Michigan DNR reduced salmon stocking because of the diminished food source. However, according to the DNR, alewife biomass is on the rise, so a correlated salmon stocking is on the horizon.[18] It's a never-ending balancing act, if not an ongoing experiment.

The population of lake trout, Worden's bread and butter, has struggled to maintain numbers from spawning. "This means that the lake trout are not thriving [on their own], so they have to keep getting restocked." He continues, "So the fish we catch now, I would have to say that most of them are fin-clipped—they're planted, not native."

The invasive round gobies, as pointed out by Ed and Cindi John, have improved the taste of the lake trout. Their reputation as being an oily tasting fish—called "greasers" by old-timers—no longer holds, as the goby has proven to be "like a little protein pill," Worden says, becoming the bait fish that lake trout prefer over the alewives, thus dramatically improving lake trout's appeal with his charter customers. Used to be a ten-pound lake trout would be approximately ten years old. Now, thanks to their improved diet, a six- to eight-pound trout is about two years old, explains Worden.

Besides getting a lesson on Great Lakes ecology and the health of the West Bay fishery—and the threats to it—anyone day-tripping out on the water with Captain Sam will learn that he is a man of his word when it comes to being an ethical and responsible charter boat captain. If we catch a lake trout just above fifteen inches, the legal minimum size for Grand Traverse Bay, it's automatically a keeper with this skipper, even though the limit is just two per person—and everyone, especially the paying customer, wants the biggest fish possible. "There's not really a law that says you can't catch and release, but you've got to know what's right for the fishery," he maintains. Worden explains that the trauma of being hooked and pulled up from the depths and temporarily removed for photo ops is often fatal to caught fish. According to the Michigan DNR, in 2020 "throwback mortality" for lake trout in the 1836 Treaty-ceded waters of the Great Lakes—which includes parts of Superior, Huron, and Michigan and all of Grand Traverse Bay—was 41 percent, a figure Worden believes is even higher.[19] This is pressure for a charter boat captain like Worden, who charges $500 for a half day and $900 for a full day out on the water. But this ecologically sound approach is what I love about him, and no doubt all his return customers do too (which, he estimates, is at least 80 percent of his business).

"I know the actual effects of fighting a fish—if you don't lift the fish out or use a Boga Grip and get the hook out and revive him, he probably has a lot better chance than being netted, bringing him in the boat, and holding him up for pictures." And if you hit your lake trout limit before the booked time is up, Worden will pursue smallmouth bass on light tackle, which is plenty of fun due to the feisty nature of the smallies. "So we can fulfill your charter time and still bend the rod."

As we chat, he interrupts, "Fish on right here," notifying me with calm urgency—there's no better way to explain it—as the rod throbs with life. The line is whining as a lake trout makes a run. When it tires a bit, I lower the rod toward the water and start cranking the reel, then raise it back up, a slow pumping action keeping tension on the fish as it begins to run again. Worden spotted the lake trout in twenty feet of water just after it struck the lure. Because of the ever-improving water clarity, he's moved to fluorocarbon line, which is less detectable to fish.

Perhaps forty-five minutes later, the action suddenly goes from zero to sixty in seconds. A rod he's handling receives a strike before it's placed into the holder as I'm putting another lake trout we just landed in the cooler, on ice. He gives me the rod, remarking, "That was cool; I don't think I've ever had that happen." Simultaneously, another rod becomes animated with tugging from beneath the surface—another fish on. We land three nice lake trout in fifteen minutes, from six to nearly ten pounds, each taken in water twenty to forty feet deep. We now have our limit of four, and it's nearly 11:30 a.m.; time flying as we're preoccupied with fishing.

As Worden slowly motors toward the harbor, before we can retrieve the lines that are still out, two more fish strike. I land one, on the small side, and Worden, true to form, doesn't net it and releases it quickly. After about a five-minute battle on the second rod, I lose what would no doubt have been the biggest catch of the day, as my arms were straining, the rod doubled over, and the fish making the strongest runs yet. "Well, that worked out," Captain Sam says, alleviating my disappointment.

As we cruise back to the Elmwood Township Marina, he shares how he came into this business. "My uncle wrote for the *Detroit News*; he was the outdoor columnist, Dave Richey. So growing up, a handful of times we got to go on a charter with my dad and my brothers, and he would write a newspaper article about it." When Worden was eleven, he caught a salmon on a charter and decided that would be the life for him. He wrote a thank-you note to the captain, and when he was twelve, was invited to help crew the boat. A decade later, he was in business for himself on Grand Traverse Bay.

Our conversation then takes a turn away from fishing. He nods toward the western coast of the bay. The shoreline is lined with houses that weren't there when he began chartering twenty years ago; and many of the ones that were there have been remodeled to three times their original size, he relates. This spring, he helped deliver more than two hundred boats to customers from his father's storage business in Interlochen, and said he occasionally got lost because he "didn't recognize any of these houses."

Then Worden pivots to the future—his children's, should they stay in the region where their father was raised, his childhood spent living on Long Lake just west of Traverse City. "It does scare me that when my kids grow up, they might not be able to afford living in a place where I grew up and cherish so much; that's problematic. When is that ever going to slow down?" he says plaintively, adding, "I'll probably never be able to afford lake property, and that sucks." Yet as the Triton motors purr and the water slices away from the hull in a most agreeable, almost musical swishing, Worden shifts his perspective again, noting how few boats are on the water this morning: we count less than a handful. People will continue to come, but "there's plenty of room," he believes. We both smile. Repeating himself from earlier in the morning, as if conjuring the Old Milwaukee Beer commercial in the eighties, "It doesn't get any better than this."[20]

As I take in the scenery, Worden's voice louder now as he throttles up the engines, he says, "I can't tell you how many of these people on my charters can go for an hour without saying a word. They're just looking at the water and the trees and the fall color." Indeed, words fail when in the thrall of such grandeur. Then, unexpectedly, he says, "You'd be amazed by how many people have asked me if this is salt water." I laugh, but in dismay. I suppose you have to start somewhere with an introduction to the great outdoors. Paying customers make for patient charter captains.

Worden shares another non-fishing tidbit, though Lake Michigan may well indirectly figure into it: "A lot of my [high school] classmates have gone from here to Chicago, for example. Ninety percent of them now have families and have returned. I don't think they were really wired for a faster pace." Captain Sam certainly isn't. He cuts the motors to a no-wake speed as we enter the harbor then takes a hand from the wheel and waves it in a grand sweeping gesture. "Look at this," he says in praise of his water wonderland playground, of his good life. "I have my coffee on my back porch every morning at 5 a.m. and hear the songbirds to kick off my day." And then he drives to the marina, fires up the Triton, and heads out into the blue water. Work? Hmmm.

We lift the cooler full of fish he's about to expertly clean for me and set it on the dock, then we collect the rest of our gear. Worden takes the opportunity to point to the sign on the dashboard of the boat: it shows a banana with a bold red "NO" symbol superimposed on it. He hands me my snack bag, which I never touched, too busy having fun talking with the captain and fishing for lakers. "Man, you made me nervous for the first ten minutes, but I let it go," he reveals, smiling ever so slightly, handing me the bag with my banana sticking out of it. This superstition about bananas being bad luck on a boat dates back hundreds of years.[21] I knew better; I'd seen the sign before; I just forgot. "Oh, man, I won't let it happen again," I promise. Captain Sam glances at me, not severely, not unforgivingly, but in a reinforcing kind of way. Then we make our way toward the cleaning station while resuming the easygoing conversation of fishermen. No bananas. Ever. I've been warned.

Lake Michigan under Siege

I met Jason Smith, fisheries assessment biologist for the Sault Ste. Marie Tribe of Chippewa Indians, during a Fishes of Lake Michigan sailing program conducted by Inland Seas Education Association in Suttons Bay in mid-July 2022. (Note: Smith now works for the Bay Mills Indian Community in Brimley, Michigan, as a Great Lakes fisheries assessment biologist.) He volunteered that day to staff one of the stations that participants—mostly families with young children—rotated through, his being about the impact of invasive mussel species on Lake Michigan's fisheries. As I listened in, I became engrossed by his presentation, not only for its content but for his enthusiastic style of engagement and his obvious reverence for nature, especially through the lens of someone who appreciates Anishinaabek culture. Once we returned to the dock from our morning out on West Bay aboard the seventy-seven-foot Inland Seas schooner, I approached him and we struck up a conversation on our walk back to the parking lot, sharing our Indiana roots (his parents, both Hoosiers, taught at Ball State University in Muncie). We would speak several months later by Zoom, Sault Ste. Marie to Indy.

A late bloomer, Smith, fifty-three, resumed his long-abandoned college studies at the age of thirty-nine, obtaining a bachelor of science degree in Natural Resources (fisheries concentration) from Michigan State University. He then immediately enrolled in graduate school, encouraged by his undergraduate mentor, Daniel Hayes, PhD, an award-winning teacher at MSU's College of Agriculture and Natural Resources. Upon finishing his graduate work, he eventually landed a job as a Great Lakes researcher with the Little Traverse Bay Bands of Odawa Indians in Harbor Springs. Four years later, he hired on with Sault Ste. Marie Tribe of Chippewa Indians. This was a dream come true, as a personal goal of his was to live in the UP, in Sault Ste. Marie.

While working for the Little Traverse Bay Bands, he met his guide into Native American culture, Renee "Wasson" Dillard, an Anishinaabe traditional natural fiber artist and teacher. "For some reason, Renee decided she would invest some time in me and teach me some of the things I would need to know to not say all the stupid shit that white people say when they get in tribal worlds," he fondly recalls. Crediting Dillard's influence, Smith developed a mission statement for his work as a fisheries biologist: "To promote tribal sovereignty and protect treaty rights through respectful relationships with humans, our non-human kin, and our environment."

Smith oversees fisheries assessments for both inland waters and lakes Superior, Michigan, and Huron. His territory stretches from Bay de Noc (near Escanaba in the Upper Peninsula) to Grand Rapids to Alpena and back up around Lake Superior to Marquette. He explains that his area of focus on fish habitat "revolves around Dreissenid mussels (zebras and quaggas) and how they have changed both the water and the bottom of the lake. It is now a quagga-dominated system, probably 95 percent or more. They came in a little bit later, but they definitely outcompeted zebra mussels."

Through an unmanned submersible, Smith has seen for himself the carnage the quaggas have wrought. "We've been doing acoustic receiver recoveries with the robot and videoing the floor. This year we went down to 424 feet on a clay bottom, which should have had very few Dreissenids, and it was a carpet of quagga mussels." He emails me a disturbing digital image taken by the robot. The submersible's light reflects a golden-brown mass of mussels almost completely covering the lakebed.

This proliferation of the mussels is playing havoc with fish nesting. Smith states that many fish eggs drift down into interstitial spaces that occur between rocks. These provide protection from predators while exposing the eggs to enough water flow to keep them oxygenated. "Now every place like that on the Great Lakes is basically a carpet of mussels. There are less places for those eggs to tuck away." Yet adaptation can be a strange and wondrous thing. Some fish species are successful nonetheless due to their ability to adapt to changing conditions and challenges to their survival. Says Smith, "There are some documented places where lake trout are doing a pretty damn good job of spawning and surviving on boulders of Dreissenids instead of boulders themselves. We can never predict with grand precision how those things play out."

Besides the aesthetic appeal the Dreissenids have introduced with their Mediterranean Sea–like, tourist-pleasing transformation of Lake Michigan, he brings up another benefit of their invasion of the lake's floor: "Beyond just being pretty, the water is literally less polluted. On the whole, the Dreissenids have been a huge problem to the ecosystem. But they've also done some good things. Water that is not toxic is a wonderful thing, right?" he says evenhandedly. "The actual water itself is of a high quality, it's just that there isn't very much food." So despite the significant damage being done to spawning habitat and the questionable future of the fishery the invasive mussels have engendered, these unintended consequences for the better soften the blow.

Smith offers his scientific assessment as to the health of the three main commercial fish in Lake Michigan: whitefish, lake trout, and salmon. "Whitefish are having a very hard time—lots of larvae in the spring, but very few fish living to adulthood (or, in fisheries biologist speak, get "recruited to the fishery"). He continues, "Lake trout are not fully restored, but natural reproduction is increasing each year and abundance is also increasing each year, with stocking remaining at about the same level," a somewhat more positive assessment than Captain Sam's observations of the lake trout fishery in West Grand Traverse Bay. "Salmon abundance is tied directly to stocking numbers and alewife population, which goes up and down."

To be sure, the spread of the quaggas is daunting. Yet Smith is hopeful that a solution can be found to the mussel invasion. "The first step in a solution is the *will* to have a solution," he asserts. He believes in America's technological prowess and ability to overcome the odds, suggesting, "Getting rid of Dreissenids is not as far out there as sending a man to the moon." Getting people's attention isn't just educating them to act, he contends, it also has to be an emotive response. "You've got to whack 'em in the lizard brain occasionally to get them to feel something. If you feel it, you're more likely to do something."

Although Smith is an optimist, he's disappointed by, in his experience, the public's level of understanding of place and what that should entail. He illustrates this by telling me about a middle school group on a recent field trip to Petoskey State Park on Little Traverse Bay, where he provided some expert fish biology education. "I started out with a question that I knew they could answer: what lake is this? And out of a busload of students, just one knew the damn lake. They were middle schoolers who lived in Petoskey—*Petoskey is on the shore of Lake Michigan!* More of them knew it was Little Traverse Bay. But they did not know that it was a part of greater Lake Michigan." We are gradually becoming more estranged from nature, as this all too tellingly suggests. Yet the kids, of course, are not to blame. PG—Parental Guidance—strongly suggested. That is, if they're equipped with the proper knowledge themselves, which, generally, is increasingly doubtful.

Smith is also continually surprised about visitors and locals' lack of knowledge regarding invasive species marauding in the Great Lakes, although he keeps in mind that this is *his* career focus, *his* mission to study their impact and to raise awareness. As he admits, "Basically, I spend all my time thinking about invaders. That's what makes the job so hard: the new invader comes along and everything you knew last week is no longer true. There were folks who really knew the Great Lakes before these Dreissinids [came], whose worldview is no longer valid because the whole lake changed."

Prior to getting a crash course in Great Lakes fishery education from Smith, many are unaware that alewives and rainbow smelt, for example, are Great Lakes invasive species (smelt were stocked in Crystal Lake in northwest lower Michigan in 1912, eventually making their way into Lake Michigan).[22] This shouldn't dissuade anyone from smelt-dipping in streams in April during their spawning season nor enjoying a basket of fried smelt at the Bluebird Restaurant in Leland, for example. But it should raise awareness and cultivate an appreciation for the biodiversity puzzle pieces in the ever-changing habitat of the Great Lakes, along with better comprehending human impact and our responsibility as stewards of the environment.

The passionate, ponytailed fish biologist emphasizes what he believes is—or rather, should be—at the heart of human existence, especially when living near or visiting the Great Lakes: "Wonder and awe, man. When I'm talking with folks and it's clear that they don't have wonder and awe, it becomes really hard for me to tell my stories, because that's what they're all about." Smith connects with my own childlike wonder when it comes to fishing, saying, "I have never lifted a net in a boat yet where I wasn't almost unsafely over the side trying to see what's coming up, what the next fish is gonna be—it's such an amazing thing." It's one of the chief reasons why people fish: the joy of discovery, of paradoxically seeing something again for the first time.

Smith brings up Frank Ettawageshik, former chairman of the Little Traverse Bay Bands of Odawa Indians, referring to him as a "culture bearer." Ettawageshik provided an explanation of treaty fishing rights, which Smith maintains is grossly misunderstood, that had a profound and lasting effect on him. "People think that the right is to go out and catch fish and sell them at the dock," Smith says. "Frank Ettawageshik would tell you the treaty-retained right is the right to retain a relationship with the fish, to sing for and with the fish, to dance for and with the fish, and to have ceremony for and with the fish. That includes selling fish at the dockside, but that's not the effing treaty right. It's to maintain this ancestral relationship with these fish. I thought that was one of the most beautiful sentences I ever heard a human speak."

I email Smith some follow-up questions. One asks about the increasing human population gathering around the Great Lakes and the stressors that come with it and what this bodes for the future. His answer resembles a simple mathematic equation in its directness:

- More people = more boats = more chance for invasive introductions.
- More people = more houses and cars = more runoff and pollution.
- More people = more demand for Great Lakes water for drinking/households/etc.

This is clear enough that even this English major gets it.

A few weeks later, I receive another email from Smith. He'd been reflecting on our interview and wanted to be sure that he included his observations on "the mechanisms for climate change to impact fish and fisheries," as follows:

- Ice cover seems to be positively correlated with egg survival for fish whose eggs overwinter.
- Decreased light and UV (ultraviolet radiation)—both light and UV appear to trigger earlier hatching (smaller-size fry).
- Increased water temps likely mean more possible invaders.
- Warmer temps have made some folks predict large [human] population increases in the Great Lakes region (increased stress on the Lakes).

He adds that ice cover on the Great Lakes has been declining for the past decade, "with the exception of the two polar vortex years (2014 and 2015). The downward trend is clear."

When I interviewed him, Smith said without hesitation that climate change is "absolutely" occurring in the Great Lakes, and that the tribes have long recognized its implications. The First Peoples lived through climate change during the Ice Age and the glaciers' retreat, so they are no strangers to what it takes to adapt to such profound long-term shifts in the weather. He says, "The tribes were early adopters [in understanding] that climate change was going to be a problem for their relationship to the fish." A problem for all of us, it appears.

CHAPTER 7

AMERICA'S MOST BEAUTIFUL PLACE

There are 360 million Americans who go to our national parks. It is the big experiment in awe and awe practice in the United States. And we get a lot of benefits from that, and it gives us a sense of common purpose.

—Dacher Keltner, *Awe: The New Science of Everyday Wonder and How It Can Transform Your Life*

My family and I have been to Sleeping Bear Dunes National Lakeshore countless times, in all four seasons. Our visits began well before national interest in the park increased substantially thanks to viewers of *Good Morning America* voting it the "Most Beautiful Place in America" in 2011. Back then, ABC News referred to Sleeping Bear Dunes as "one of the nation's best-kept secrets."[1] No more, as attendance is closing in on nearly two million visits annually.

We began frequenting the park in the mid-nineties, even before the National Park Service (NPS) charged for admission. I believe it was in August 1995 when a park ranger apologized to me, driving a van full of rambunctious youngsters, for requesting the then-new nominal entrance fee. "About time," I responded, as I more than willingly pulled out my wallet. What better cause to support than our national parks? That day—and many times before and after—we did Sleeping Bear Dunes' heart-pounding Dune Climb with the kids. Over the years, we would revisit the Pierce Stocking Scenic Drive and *ooh* and *ahh* at the stunning view from the observation deck overlooking Lake Michigan. Hike all thirteen mainland trails in the park, many repeatedly. Luxuriate on its sublime Lake Michigan beaches. Fish in its crystalline streams and lakes; kayak them too. Sail across the Manitou Passage to the islands (including an unforgettable night sail on a nineteen-foot Flying Scot while watching Zeus bolts ripping from a massive thunderstorm about fifteen miles north of our wee vessel) and camp on South Manitou. Explore. Marvel. Sigh in utter contentment. So many special days spent and memories made at the National Lakeshore. Yet one park feature we had never taken in was the restored farmsteads along M-22. That is, until one June day in 2015.

Janet and I were driving on M-22 toward Glen Arbor. We had an agenda-free vacation day. No pressure to be anywhere in particular, our curiosity taking the lead. We decided to turn on Port Oneida Road and check out some of the abandoned farms in the area, part of the park's Port Oneida Historic Farm District. It was just time.

I slowed the car to a crawl when we came upon a former farm field now blanketed with invasive yet arguably beautiful orange hawkweed, as if a Claude Monet Impressionist painting come to life. Behind the blaze of wildflowers stood a white farmhouse and an assortment of outbuildings. The long unoccupied farmstead now preserved by the NPS spoke of a bygone era. I pulled into a small, empty, grassy parking lot. We exited the car and followed an asphalt walkway to the Carston Burfiend farmhouse. The modest wood-sided house and its several outbuildings quietly beckoned us to visit, an opportunity to pay our respects to a hardy people who left their mark upon the land, now conserved in perpetuity as part of the park, honoring their ways, their time.

The Port Oneida settlement was established in the 1870s and farmed for more than one hundred years.[2] The Burfiends were the first settlers, their farmhouse built in 1893.[3] I decided to sit on the back porch for a while, my feet on the grass, and ponder the farm's past. It was easy to imagine children running about, clothesline-hung laundry stirred by a gentle breeze while slowly drying in the sunshine, men working the fields with the equipment of the day, the farmstead alive again. Despite my modern tendency to romanticize aspects of the past, theirs was not an easy life. Farming then (and yet today) required extensive hours of physically demanding labor to earn their daily bread, which the womenfolk literally baked themselves. Left to her own thoughts, Janet milled about. We could hear the muffled roar of Lake Michigan just beyond the tree-lined backyard, the tall maples obscuring the view of the lake. An opening in the trees revealed a stairstep path down to the beach, constructed of timbers inset in the hillside, the considerable riser height designed for heartier stock back then. We retraced the Burfiend family's steps, something of a spiritual exercise, imagining their similar delight. A short, narrow path through dune grass and the beach was ours, not another soul in sight. It might as well have been a summer day in the year 1900, the setting just as it was then. This is what the park is for.

One (Very) Popular Park

On Wednesday, June 29, 2022, I'm to meet with Scott Tucker, Sleeping Bear Dunes National Lakeshore superintendent, at his office at the Philip A. Hart Visitor Center in Empire. As I cruise along the rolling hills of M-72 within five miles of my destination, the piling tourist traffic plays havoc with my attempt to arrive on time. Three vehicles ahead of me are traveling at the speed of retirement, their drivers most likely mesmerized by their surroundings. Who can blame them. Well, me, as I'm now running five minutes behind and counting. I decide to lower my blood pressure and just grin and bear it. Minutes later, our slow-moving convoy makes it to Empire intact. Have a nice day.

At the park's administrative office, I'm escorted by a polite ranger through a small cubicle farm to the big kahuna's office. Scott Tucker arises from his desk chair, a red-and-touch-of-gray-goateed Paul Bunyan–like fellow, a gentle giant with a broad smile who looks perfectly suited for his national park superintendent role.

Tucker transferred to Sleeping Bear Dunes in 2017 from Colorado, his native state; his wife is a downstate Michigander. His twenty-five-year NPS career has taken him to Alaska, Washington, D.C., Oregon, and now Michigan. His immediate connections to the park are considerable. His wife's family vacationed in the region during the thirties, forties, and fifties. And his stepfather-in-law, who recently passed away, served as a maintenance worker at the former D.H. Day State Park—now D.H. Day Campground in the National Lakeshore—during the late fifties.

The park is staffed by 153 employees. This includes wildlife, plant, and water biologists, carpenters, cultural/interpretive rangers, law enforcement rangers, fee collectors, custodians, and education staff. "We run a little city here," Tucker comments. This "city" is surrounded by 72,000 acres of National Parkland, 32,557 acres of it designated as wilderness by President Barack Obama in 2014.[4] Tucker notes that between the mainland property and North and South Manitou Islands, the park boasts nearly seventy miles of Lake Michigan shoreline.

Of course, I'm especially curious about the huge volume of tourists that visit Sleeping Bear Dunes each year. "People get really excited about visitor numbers at Sleeping Bear," he responds, expecting my question, as he gets it each year from newspaper reporters. Then he puts it into proper perspective. "Our numbers are *recreational visits* to the Lakeshore; they are not individual visitors. So it's not 1.7 million individuals; it's 1.7 million *visits*, via a very complex algorithm." They tally this by trail and parking lot counters.

Is the park seeing a mounting number of visitors each year? In 2016, the number of visits was 1.6 million; in 2021, it was 1.7 million. "So we're talking about [an increase of] one hundred thousand more visits over a six-year period," he explains. In sum, more visitors are coming here. Trailheads are busier, campgrounds are full, parking lots maxed out on a busy Sunday afternoon. The first year of the Covid-19 pandemic, the park saw 192,000 visits in June and had to close some areas due to unsafe social distancing behavior. In June 2021, there were 278,000 visits. In 2022, the month of June dropped to pre-Covid numbers. As Tucker says about the visitation count, "It's a tricky number to grasp." Whatever the actual numbers, clearly, the park hosts a heck of a lot of people each year.

He mentions that the shoulder seasons—fall and spring—are trending upward in the number of park visitations. "We were busier in September of last year [2021] than we were in the first year of Covid. Go figure. Same thing in October." Tucker suggests this new attendance phenomenon would make for an intriguing academic research project to unlock the mystery of it all.

In the book *Sixties Sandstorm: The Fight Over Establishment of a Sleeping Bear Dunes National Lakeshore, 1961–1970*, author and Michigan State University law professor Brian Kalt wrote that a 1961 report from the National Park Service on the proposed park estimated that it would "attract 1.2 million visitors a year."[5] Obviously, that estimate has been vastly surpassed. And as Kalt later notes in *Sixties Sandstorm*, in 1967 park attendance projections were adjusted upward, predicting "three million visitor-days" annually.[6] That, thankfully, has not yet happened. Nonetheless, nearly two million visitors per year is a lot of pressure for two low-populated, largely rural counties—Leelanau and Benzie (coming in at 22,301 and 17,970 residents per the 2020 Decennial Census[7])—to manage during the summer tourist run. Of course, who knew then what influence *Good Morning America* would have in 2011—contributing to a nearly 30 percent increase in attendance over the following decade—or could have predicted the surge of Americans and international visitors coming to our National Parks.

For those who complain about the annual Up North tourist invasion, it shouldn't be overlooked that there's a significant inflow of cash that comes with it. This influx of dollars helps many tourist-dependent businesses of small and considerable sizes (such as M-22, the locally branded clothier, and Cherry Republic) stay solvent for the year. In 2021, the NPS reported that total visitor spending reached $206 million. This encompasses the following categories: camping, gas, groceries, hotels, recreation industries, restaurants, retail, and transportation. Hotels/lodging, the largest category, accounted for nearly $92 million alone, followed by restaurants at almost $42 million.[8]

When the pandemic struck the United States in March of 2020, we did not yet understand how the virus spread. The National Park Service, like every other federal government agency, played it safe, taking the necessary precautions. People were encouraged to recreate outdoors, so they came to the park. Tucker recalls, "One of our first moves was shutting down restrooms." Then some people started doing "stupid things," he says. "We found the public doing the exact opposite of what was coming out as [safety] recommendations. We had overcrowded hiking trails." As a result of the general misbehavior, the parking lots and trails were closed temporarily, as were the campgrounds. The public safety decisions mirrored that of the state of Michigan per Gov. Gretchen Whitmer's office. Then just prior to Memorial Day weekend 2020, the governor opened the zone that included the National Lakeshore. This led to a "very busy, very successful summer," he says. Remarkably, Tucker's staff did not record a positive case of Covid until December of that year, a fact he is "super proud of."

When I followed up with Tucker in late October 2022, he reported that Sleeping Bear Dunes attendance had "dipped this summer." By year-end, the park tallied just over 1.5 million visits, its lowest number in eight years.[9] The reasons were multifold: inflation ravaging potential visitors' vacation budgets, soaring gas prices, more diversions available in the region, and the state being completely open as the pandemic waned. The park superintendent also noted the natural alewife die-off that occurred in several waves, the decaying biomass discouraging beachgoers. "There are a lot of factors, and I am not sure we will ever know the [entire] reason." (Tucker says that nearly 1.6 million visits were recorded in 2023.)

Because Sleeping Bear Dunes staff is accustomed to hosting a deluge of visitors, their concern isn't so much how to manage people as it is how to protect the resources. For example, the popular Pyramid Point and Empire Bluffs hiking trails' parking lots will predictably overflow with vehicles during the summer season. When all the spots are taken, visitors tend to park beyond the lots' barriers, damaging the terrain, including plant life—which should not be disturbed per the park's dictates. Parking lot expansion is now under consideration, with Pyramid Point already slated for that visitor improvement.

Yet there are even greater potential impacts to monitor. The National Park Service, as well as Sleeping Bear Dunes superintendent, take climate change seriously. The climate model projections for the park indicate "more intense storms, less winter ice, and shoreline erosion" due to a lack of winter ice, Tucker says. These factors are "causing havoc along the shorelines." As of 2022, he's been at the National Lakeshore for six years and has yet to see Lake Michigan freeze over. He mentions some of the lake's highest water levels on record occurred in the last decade, most notably in 2019, when the lake level rose two feet from January to July that year alone.[10] The climate models being tracked by the NPS indicate oscillations of extreme high and low water levels to come, with "a shorter bandwidth in between." He adds, "Talk about climate refugees! You have almost every climate model saying that northern Michigan is the place to be in twenty years." He thinks that the "silver tsunami" of retirees coming to the area—a migration that's long been underway in the region—will only become more profound in the next several decades due to the influence of climate change.

The historic windstorm of 2015 decimated thousands of acres of woodlands throughout Leelanau County. The park experienced significant damage, with the areas in and around Glen Arbor being ground zero.

Janet and I revisited Alligator Hill Trail in the spring of 2016 to see the storm's wake for ourselves. The evidence of the 110-mph straight-line winds made it look as if the Creator had taken a ginormous bowling ball and rolled it through the woods. All along the mostly uphill trail toward the Glen Lake lookout stories-high trees lay scattered, giant root balls unearthed from their mooring. "This is so depressing," Janet said to me. "It will take years for the woods to recover." That it will. But it was a natural catastrophe, though perhaps climate change induced. We had our birding binoculars with us. And on that fine late May Day, the birding was fantastic. Indigo buntings flew about, too many to even attempt to count. We spotted several male eastern towhees, their striking black, white, and rust colors popping against the emerging green of spring on the hillside below the Lake Michigan overlook, with its panoramic view of the Manitou Passage and the Manitou Islands. South Fox Island even made an appearance. Perhaps a dozen different warbler species hopscotched through the tattered woodlands as we hiked, ever on the move, some continuing to their nesting grounds farther north. The plethora of prized songbird sightings helped alleviate Janet's trauma. Clearly, the birds were fine with the disrupted terrain.

Tucker would arrive in 2016, a year after the catastrophic windstorm. This rare weather event followed the type predicted by the NPS climate models: short, furious storms that can leave considerable destruction in their wake. When I told him my Alligator Hill birding story, he said that birders love the hill now, perhaps more than ever, due to the storm's aftermath. He also tells me that the park continues to receive queries about selling the fallen timber. "There are two ways to look at a downed tree," he explains. "In a national forest, that tree is a commodity, and it's an agricultural product that gets cut and sold. In a national park, our core mission is to preserve and protect and allow natural processes to take place. So when a tree falls in the forest in a national park, we sit back and watch nature run its course." Timber harvesters, understandably, see things differently—through a lens of dollar signs. Yet, as Tucker notes, the park is in an "ecological bubble for scientific study," making it an invaluable living laboratory.

Sleeping Bear Dunes National Lakeshore today looks much as it did when the park was established in October 1970. And, Tucker says, "Sleeping Bear in 2080 is going to look pretty similar to what it looks like in 2020. We'll have some storms, and we'll have some activities that change some of the dynamics." He emphasizes, "If your great-great grandkids can visit Sleeping Bear in the year 2100 and they can actually stand in the same spot that you stood in this afternoon and take a picture, and it's going to be pretty similar, that's success."

....

The superintendent tells me there are very few visitor behavior incidents at the park. He says that most people are just nice, which is nice to hear. But there's one problem that won't be going away anytime soon: canines on the loose. "Our biggest issue is dogs off leash. Honestly, the biggest visitor conflict is with a visitor that doesn't have a pet or doesn't have their dog off leash." They're not crazy about those who think someone else's dog should be given the run of the beach and won't hesitate to report them. I've seen this transgression, willful or accidental, myself many times over the years at County Road 651 Beach on Good Harbor Bay. At the trailhead, a very prominent sign directs dog owners to go east, where dogs are welcome. That regularly gets ignored. Moreover, some dog owners decide to let their four-legged friends off the leash. They can't seem to comprehend that some adults don't care for canines as much as they do, and that some young children are afraid of them. What's more, wildlife can be negatively affected. At the nesting site of the piping plovers, off-the-leash dogs have chased and even killed the protected birds. Domesticated animals and wildlife don't mix well.

There are other behavioral issues that get policed by NPS rangers. Take, for example, the somewhat notorious Platte River party flotillas. Large groups comprised of a typically younger crowd congregate in the river, floating in heavy-duty river tubes, while drinking away the day to their hearts' content. In the process, they disrupt the tranquility others are seeking in their more naturally inclined river outings. Cross-purposes collide. Consequently, non-imbibing outdoorsmen and -women as well as children must navigate their way through these blockades.

One Labor Day weekend a few years ago, we made the mistake of kayaking the Platte with another couple, high school friends of Janet. At several stretches, we paddled through swaths of tubers. They were friendly enough, even sharing beers with our more outgoing friends, lazing in their tubes as they meandered downriver. One group even kindly offered us Jell-O shots. Had to pass; we had kayaking—*safe and sober kayaking*—on our minds. Some even had waterproof music players, cranked-up rock and roll and country and western songs eviscerating the tranquility we came for. "Patience, honey," Janet suggested. It's all I could do.

My own introduction to northern Michigan involved some partying, admittedly. Younger days. My initial connection to the region was through my compadre who was a native of Traverse City, a Steve Martin–like wild and crazy guy. Most of our diversions in those early visits not only revolved around being outside, no matter the time of year, but often included libations. At deer camp (yet never during the hunt). While trout fishing (but only a ceremonial lunchtime beer, concentration being essential to detect and respond to the bite). When sailing on Lake Michigan (only to toast the liberating thrill of being under wind power while gliding across the lake surface, and never overindulging). My friend came from six generations of robust northern Michiganders who had grown up learning how to respect nature and how to be courteous in the field. You gave other people space. When partying, you made sure that loud voices and carrying on didn't intrude upon others. We saved our wilding for late nights out at bars, a venue where we well understood the rules of engagement. When in shared spaces, etiquette matters.

Tucker says that the presence and use of alcohol and drugs has "really squashed down over the past few years after we put a bigger presence on the Platte in the summer. For the most part, visitors behave." He did say that during the first summer of the pandemic, in 2020, they experienced problems with "some visitors who either didn't know how to behave in a national park or were just stressed beyond all belief and were doing what they needed to do to get through the day." Patience is truly a National Park Service virtue.

Hosting such throngs of visitors will inevitably lead to emergency runs. When Tucker arrived in 2016, the park averaged more than one hundred 911 calls for assistance annually. Most involve heat exhaustion and dehydration. Then there's "heart-attack hill," as my wife calls it, below the Number Nine Overlook at the Pierce Stocking Scenic Drive. Some excitable people tend to make a spur-of-the-moment bad decision to descend the 450-foot dune to the shore of Lake Michigan. "It's public land; you can climb," Tucker concedes. "Now, we can encourage you not to because of the stress." But what goes down at the overlook must come up, and it's a steep, all-fours, sand-trudging, sweat-pouring climb back to the top. This is the location that was previously responsible for the bulk of the park's emergency runs.

The Dune Climb also commanded plenty of 911 attention prior to Tucker's arrival. Once people make it up the first hill, a strenuous workout many don't expect, they think the Lake Michigan shoreline lies just beyond it. That's nearly two miles later, as my family and I learned our first time out in the mid-nineties. Yet we were in good shape, wore hiking shoes to protect us from the sunbaked 120-degree sand, and brought along plenty of water to stay hydrated. The hike out to the water for the unprepared quickly "turns into

Groundhog Day," says Tucker, referring to the 1993 Bill Murray comedy in which the day keeps repeating itself, as does hill after sandy hill until Lake Michigan finally appears.

Just before Tucker arrived, a Preventative Search and Rescue (PSAR) program was being developed by the park's law enforcement team. Now these emergency hotspots are staffed by volunteers who engage visitors in preemptive safety conversations at strategic locations at both the top of the Dune Climb and the Number Nine Overlook. Do they realize the degree of difficulty ahead of them? Did they bring water, and if so, enough for the trek? What about snacks? Are they wearing shoes? Do they have sunscreen? Are they making a good decision to continue? Some of the unprepared wisely turn back. As a result of this innovative public safety program emergency calls have dropped sharply, to approximately ten per year. And for those who decide to take on the Number Nine Overlook despite the warning and cannot make it back up, there's a cost. The Glen Lake Fire Department will respond, and they can bill those rescued up to $3,000 for the effort—just as the sign warns at the top of the overlook. Dune climb, then, at your and your pocketbook's own risk.

The biggest challenge in operating the park, Tucker maintains, is seeing to visitors' core needs, such as having enough restrooms and trashcans. It's a big task to manage the expectations of locals, tourists, staff, volunteers, and government officials, he relates. "I don't look for work to do." Yet it's clearly all worth the effort. And the perks of being assigned to Sleeping Bear Dunes National Lakeshore are beyond compare. "I get to work where people go to get away," he says, smiling broadly. I couldn't be more envious.

Plight of the Plover

I ask Scott Tucker about interviewing one of his biologists. He doesn't hesitate, asking if I'd like to meet with a wildlife or plant biologist. Tough call. But since I have my druthers, I decide on wildlife. Vince Cavalieri is my guy.

I reach the Sleeping Bear Dunes Maritime Museum in Glen Haven on a blue-sky mid-July morning at 9 a.m. I'm meeting Cavalieri, a forty-year-old NPS wildlife biologist. As suggested in my email to arrange the interview, I'm happy to tag along with him in the field, though I neglected to ask what he might have in mind so as to dress appropriately. Having had my tick scare the previous year—finding one embedded in my thigh twenty-four hours after hiking, forgetting to check and knowing better making the event that much more stressful—and now carrying a heightened state of tick awareness (a.k.a. paranoia), I decide to err on the side of caution and put on some long pants and a long-sleeved shirt, summer though it may be.

When I show up at the sparsely populated lot, the NPS biologist is just emerging from his Jeep Cherokee. He's attired in his field-ready uniform: gray short-sleeved tactical shirt, fatigue-green pants, and baseball cap. Predictably, binoculars are strapped around his neck. Cavalieri bears the mien of an outdoorsman: burly, thickly bearded, happy to be in his element. After we shake hands, he suggests a short hike along the beach to the piping plover nesting area about a quarter of a mile southwest of the Maritime Museum. His wildlife specialty is ornithology, which I'm delighted to hear, me being an avid amateur birder. He unloads his spotting scope and tripod from the Jeep and off we go.

As we walk and talk, we pass terribly obvious human artifacts on the beach, including an upright half-empty plastic water bottle, a poorly managed campfire's wind-scattered charcoal embers, and three approximately seven- to eight-foot limbs that have been jammed into the sand. Must have been an interesting night. "These need to come down," Cavalieri says firmly as he sets aside his equipment. "Predatory birds might perch on them and watch the plovers." I push over one of the limbs as he quickly dislodges the rest. Then we trudge along the beach and make our way toward the roped-off nesting area, a wide expanse of sand and scattered stones that lies between the shoreline and below a tall sand dune.

As we approach the nesting site, I learn about another problem associated with the invasive species in Lake Michigan as it negatively impacts the bird population. "We have an avian botulism monitoring program," Cavalieri mentions. Zebra and quagga mussels contribute to the botulism problem by their filtering and clarifying the water, allowing more sunlight to penetrate and encourage the growth of *Cladophora* algae, a native species in which botulism grows. This is the unsightly brownish algae that collects along the shoreline at times throughout the summer. Biologists also believe there's an association with warming lake water. Cavalieri says that the lake's water temperature has been increasing over the past fifty years. Several mass waterbird die-offs have occurred in recent years caused by botulism. The park's biologists are monitoring the die-offs, counting dead waterbirds discovered each year to determine the involvement of botulism. In partnership with university researchers, experiments are ongoing at Sleeping Bear Dunes to develop a method of reducing the *Cladophora*.

We arrive. Another NPS wildlife specialist is already on the scene observing the piping plover activity, gazing into his tripod-mounted optics. It's quiet here; nature is doing its thing. Moderate waves break on the shore, the air is full of birdsong, an onshore breeze wafts through the trees. Cavalieri and I talk in hushed tones so as not to bother the plovers. Several plover young are skittering throughout the nesting area. If it wasn't for their movement, they would be well camouflaged, their gray-brown and white feathers blending into the surroundings.

"This is our biggest concentration of breeding plovers on the mainland," he explains. "We have a bigger colony on North Manitou. But in this area, we have six pairs [of breeding birds]." This is an average number for the park. Among the many avian wonders to be found here, piping plovers, who can live up to fifteen years, return to the same nesting area year after year. Half of the plovers that migrate to Sleeping Bear Dunes overwinter in Florida, along with other plover species. The rest migrate from coastal Georgia, South Carolina, and the Bahamas.

Cavalieri kindly invites me to look through his spotting scope, pointing to a chick that's left its nest. It's a Swarovski—premium non-park-issued equipment. "This one is mine," he says. Such fine optics aren't within the park's budget. We're perhaps thirty-five yards from the fledged chicks, yet the sharp optics draw me in for a more intimate view while not disturbing the youngsters as they begin to acclimate themselves to being mobile and explore their brave new world. Cavalieri says the first plover arrived at the park in 2022 on April 12, indicating the close monitoring of the species by its wildlife biologists. "I get out here as much as I can; my crew gets out here every day."

I ask the biologist about problems with dogs, which I broached with Tucker earlier. He says that pet dogs bothering the birds is "an everyday struggle." Owners thoughtlessly let them off the leash, and dogs being dogs, will chase the plovers and sometimes trample the nests, and even kill young birds. "The rangers give out a lot of warnings," Cavalieri says. Incomprehensibly, there are repeat offenders, and they get cited by the enforcement rangers. He points out a small cage set above a nest. The plovers can easily go in and out of this protective enclosure. Dogs and predators such as racoons and foxes cannot. The plover protection effort is extreme, and well worth the trouble, as the endangered species continues to rebound.

Cavalieri informs me that climate change has affected the nesting site. Several years ago, the sustained high-water level played havoc with the plovers. They prefer wide beaches away from tree lines, such as the roughly one hundred meters of open beach found here, which is relatively uncommon terrain throughout the Great Lakes, he says. "Three or four years ago, when our water levels were extremely high, the water was up to the dune edges," he recounts. "So every plover was nesting on a little tip of beach, with water behind them and water in front of them." At least thirteen nests washed out during storms.

Any long-term rise in Lake Michigan water levels is a threat to the National Lakeshore's piping plover nesting area. Cavalieri says the climate models are thus far inconclusive regarding long-term increases, decreases, or staying within the historical average of water levels. But they have already seen what high water can do to the fragile nesting population of the plovers. Risk remains. "There are all kinds of potential wildlife issues that are tied into climate change," warns Cavalieri. "Are we going to have the habitat necessary for some of these species fifty years from now? Difficult to say."

Cavalieri's colleague approaches us. He reports that he feared the plover chicks were going to get eaten by five great blue herons who were nearby this morning when he arrived. "There's a weird concentration of wildlife on the shoreline because of the alewives," he remarks. This includes the countless unidentified small brown moths underfoot and those attracted to the outside of our clothing. Harmless, yet everywhere.

The piping plovers are rare because of habitat loss, meaning, people pressure. Cavalieri says recreational pressure is also contributing to the birds' nesting predicament in a big way. "I almost consider that a form of habitat loss. If this area wasn't closed, we'd get people out here all summer long." While most park visitors keep a respectful—and lawful—distance from the nesting site, the dog issue continues to be vexing. And some people decide to ignore the barrier and enter the sensitive area anyway.

The recovery goal for the Great Lakes piping plovers here at Sleeping Bear Dunes, which includes the nesting sites on North Manitou Island, is to "get to 150 nesting pairs," says Cavalieri. In 2022, the number is approximately seventy. At one point, the population had dipped to twelve. "Every year we shoot for 1.5 chicks per pair to keep them going in the right direction. We're going to do better than that this year." And they did. In following up with Cavalieri in February 2023, he happily reported "a record-setting year for the Great Lakes piping plover." One hundred and fifty chicks fledged across the region, the highest number since the Great Lakes piping plovers went on the Endangered Species List in 1985.[11] Sixty-six chicks fledged at Sleeping Bear Dunes.

Since I'm with a federal wildlife expert, I ask about cougar sightings in the park, a topic of endless speculation. Cavalieri laughs then disappoints me: "There has been no direct evidence of them." He has about eighty game cameras set up throughout the park's seventy-two thousand acres, most for a deer study (or perhaps to record a stray cougar). The Upper Peninsula is a different story, however, when it comes to cougar sightings, with more than forty verified, and counting. He says, "So you figure if they were here—everyone's got game cams up now and are carrying cell phone cameras—we would have better evidence of them." Yet he doesn't discount the possibility of the big cats making an appearance: "It could happen someday."

Sleeping Bear Dunes is truly a living laboratory for science. The NPS is partnering with the University of Minnesota on a piping plover longitudinal study. It's also involved with the University of Wisconsin regarding deer population impacts research on North Manitou Island. As well, the state of Michigan is working with NPS plant biologists in studying beech bark disease as it impacts the pollinator community (insects such as bees and butterflies, as well as bats and birds).

Aside from the piping plovers, there are other federally endangered species, and candidates for that unfortunate distinction, in the park. This includes the northern long-eared bats and Indiana bats. These bat populations are now afflicted by white-nose syndrome, which attacks them during hibernation. The disease doesn't kill the bats directly; it causes them to awaken during the winter, which depletes their energy, leading to death by starvation. Acoustic monitors are employed to track the bat populations; this technology is also used to monitor frog species throughout the park. As well, a declining species of shorebirds, red knots, can be seen at the National Lakeshore in the spring. In May 2022, I happened to spot one at the Arcadia Marsh Nature Preserve. The remarkable bird, with its short bill and legs and striking silvery wings and salmon-colored breeding plumage, was on a mission on that rainy, windswept day. It scrambled along the marsh's shoreline, particularly drawn to exposed roots of small trees and bushes, hunting for invertebrates while waves of migrating warblers passed through the area.

Candidate species for the federal endangered list include Blanding's turtles and wood turtles. Cavalieri says the eastern massasauga rattlesnake, on the federally threatened list, is not on record as existing within park boundaries, although there have been confirmed sightings of them just outside the park, "so it's quite possible they are here," he says. "They're definitely in Traverse City." He adds that the massasauga is a "pretty snake, but you don't want to pick one up," then laughs, as only a wildlife biologist would.

....

We hike back to the Maritime Museum. At Cavalieri's invitation, we climb the back porch stairs and sit on a bench overlooking Lake Michigan. Red-winged blackbirds flit among the foliage. We're serenaded by the sweet trilling of song sparrows. Two male blue jays noisily spar in the trees next to the porch. Birdland.

I'm not an animal rights activist. Admittedly, though, in the cosmic scheme of things, we should probably all be vegetarians. However, as an everyday American, I like a hamburger every now and then. Pork on occasion. Chicken perhaps weekly. We have a dog; we've had cats. I love birds. I'm not all bad when it comes to regard for our brother and sister animals. Here on the porch of the Maritime Museum, the shadow Buddhist in me, who will remove spiders from inside our home whenever urgently summoned by my arachnophobic wife, emerges, prompting me to ask this question of Cavalieri: Do animals have rights?

"I'm interested in this question too," he answers. Cavalieri discloses that he's read quite a few books about animal rights. During his ten years working for the U.S. Fish and Wildlife Service, he would frequently be asked why certain species are worth saving, species that really don't have a discernible impact on the greater ecosystem. "The argument is that it's so rare. Even the piping plover: does it really have an ecosystem impact? No, it doesn't. So you can make the argument about the umbrella species, which is what I often use for the piping plover: by protecting the habitat of the plover, you're protecting the [wildlife of the] dunes in general, and that is an umbrella that helps other species."

He continues, paraphrasing a particular argument he read, and agrees with, by an unidentified philosopher: "If you are interested in conserving a species, you have to believe the message that the species has a right to exist and has its own intrinsic value. If you accept that, then yes, this species has a right to exist and humans have a responsibility to protect it," especially from human impacts, which is most often the case.

The NPS wildlife biologist references world-renowned naturalist E.O. Wilson and his book *The Creation: An Appeal to Save Life on Earth*. Cavalieri says it was written as if a letter to a Christian pastor who believes in the Biblical tradition of God giving mankind dominion over the Earth, which includes all living things. This outlook has led to exploitation and the extermination of thousands upon thousands of non-human species. Cavalieri paraphrases Wilson, saying the renowned scientist argues that if people take such tenets of their faith seriously, then they are actually called to protect the Earth and exercise sustainable management for all its living things.

"So, do animals have rights?" Cavalieri, who grew up in Iron Mountain in the UP hunting and fishing and admits to being an omnivore, returns to my original query to summarize his answer. "I think that's a complicated question. But I feel that they certainly have the right to exist."

Do those visiting Sleeping Bear Dunes have a good understanding of the outdoors and wildlife? "It's very mixed," he answers. "A lot of people have very rudimentary knowledge of wildlife and the environment, especially folks who come from cities. Sometimes they just haven't been exposed to the outdoors." He gives credence to the premise of Richard Louv's seminal work published in 2008, *Last Child in the Woods: Saving Our Children from Nature-Deficit Disorder*, in that "there's a bit of a disconnect between the youth and the outdoors. Not all of them are trained."

Training begins at home. When it comes to teaching children to appreciate the outdoors and realize one's place as part of nature and not apart from nature, that is a parental obligation, one which should not be taken lightly. Yet not all children receive this essential perspective in their upbringing. I saw this firsthand sixteen years ago when I began working in a public charter school in urban Indianapolis. It wasn't just the kids, however, who were generally estranged from nature; many of the young teachers were as well. I tried to influence this for the better.

In mid-May 2007 during the first year of my public-school administrator experience, I noticed an unusually high number of ruby-throated hummingbirds zipping about our elementary school campus, which was next to pockets of wooded areas. I purchased several hummingbird feeders, filled them with nectar, and placed them in the too-seldom-used "outdoor classroom" directly behind the school. Soon the hummers were coming to the feeders positioned near windows of adjacent classrooms. During passing periods to art and physical education classes, as well as during lunch, children would pause at the windowed outdoor classroom exit doors and excitedly point at the hovering birds, shrieking in delight. Kindergarteners or sixth graders, it didn't matter—wonder occurred. This tended to disrupt the martially managed lines, but the teachers and aides indulged in the distraction: for they, too, stopped in their tracks to admire these amazing creatures.

Later that month after the last student pickup, as I returned from the parking lot to the school, I heard male tree frogs calling for mates. One was abnormally loud. I tracked it down to its suction-cup-toed perch on the side of a downspout, where its call reverberated against the aluminum. I called over a group of young children who had been oblivious to the tree frog song. They gathered around as I held the tiny frog in my hand. Their reaction was as expected: excited fascination. This teaching moment was something they would long remember and, I suspected, would be shared that evening with parents and grandparents, most of them having never seen nor actively listened to a tree frog. Sleeping Bear Dunes park rangers and educators facilitate such life-changing awakenings all day long.

....

A Yooper (nickname for a UP resident), Cavalieri grew up in an outdoor-oriented family. His grandfather was a lead forester with a paper company who taught him all about trees. As a boy he loved dinosaurs, and that love converted to birds, a natural evolutionary interest, as birds are descendants of the long-extinct reptiles. Then, on his seventh birthday, his grandmother gifted him with a pair of binoculars and a birding field guide. A birder he would become, developing such an affinity for the pastime that as a teenager he volunteered to participate in bird-breeding surveys in the Hiawatha National Forest. Then later, he was paid as a graduate student while at Michigan Tech for participating in bird count–related studies.

Cavalieri has been delighted by the pandemic's influence on coaxing people outside. Yet the impact of people pressure on wildlife remains a constant concern. "So many of our bird species are migratory," he relates. "The plovers are going down to Florida every year, so they're experiencing that recreational pressure down there, too, in the wintertime." Songbirds spending the winter in South America are impacted negatively by the deforestation underway in the rainforests. Making room for coffee plantations in the Yucatan destroys prime birding habitat.

"So it's really all of these kinds of pressures throughout the hemisphere, not just here." And yet, the pressures there impact the birds that migrate here, Up North. There is no getting away from the fact that nature is a deeply connected planetary-wide web.

Before I drive off, I think what a wonderful way to make a living—as a wildlife biologist. I share the daydream that persisted with me as I navigated our schools through the great unknown of the pandemic: if only I had paid attention in biology and pursued an environmental science career. Cavalieri confirms what I missed out on. "Being able to protect wildlife in parks and get to show it off to the American public, it's a powerful thing," he says in parting. Yet being on the receiving end of that passion for nature education, looking through an NPS wildlife biologist's birding scope to see piping plover chicks up close, was indeed a moving experience for this child at heart.

Even National Parks Need Friends

Hal LaLonde revels in his solitude when spending time on Good Harbor Bay. However, he's not recreating; rather, he's policing the beach for trash. While performing his duty as an Adopt-a-Beach volunteer for the Friends of Sleeping Beard Dunes, he prefers to keep his distance from people. Or so he says.

LaLonde's weekly four-hour routine covers an east-west stretch along Lake Michigan Road within the National Lakeshore. I met him on the morning of September 8, 2022, at Bohemian Road Beach on Good Harbor Bay to learn more about his volunteer work. We sat on the tailgate of his red Nissan Frontier pickup truck (with its hard-to-miss black and yellow Batman "Bat Signal" mudflaps and "U.S. Navy Retired" decal on the back window) getting acquainted, which was also an opportunity to take in the post–Labor Day weekend/summer tourist season–ending quiet. You could almost feel Lake Michigan exhale.

"What I want for Christmas is an orange set of coveralls," he announces. "I'm gonna stencil on the back: Leelanau County Correctional Facility. Then I'm gonna get a sandwich board that says, 'Correction personnel at work: do not engage.'" We both laugh. His joke proves to be even funnier after I spend a few hours with him. For LaLonde is indeed a very likable fellow.

We begin our trek at Shalda Creek, heading westward along Lake Michigan's shoreline, the stunning panoramic view of the Manitou Passage to the north of us. As we talk, LaLonde veers away from me to knock down a manmade driftwood and tree limb structure that serves no practical nor aesthetic purpose. Inexplicably, these have been appearing on Lakeshore beaches for the past several years.

"Some people have taken it upon themselves to build these things on the beach," LaLonde says as he assesses the best way to bring down the unauthorized—and potentially dangerous—construction. "They don't seem to realize that this is a national park, meaning, leave nothing but footprints. And this is like a magnet to little kids." He pulls on one limb, and like a Jenga game mistake—*thunk!*—the crudely engineered conglomeration collapses into a pile.

As I shadow the tanned and fit sixty-two-year-old on his trash-picking detail, we soon pass a retirement-aged couple relaxing on the beach. Surprisingly, LaLonde greets them first. "What a day, huh?" he declares, smiling, on this cloudless late summer morning. As they engage in some friendly banter, for the record, it must be noted that LaLonde never stops walking.

Small talk and sharing personal histories are the perfect accompaniment for a long beach walk, even while undertaking a cleaning detail—"picking," he calls it—at the Lakeshore. LaLonde, born in St. Ignace, is a member of the Sault Ste. Marie Tribe of Chippewa Indians. His European North American roots were established by a French soldier, Jean LaLonde, who arrived in New France (which included the Great Lakes region) in 1665 and was eventually killed by the Iroquois.

His earliest forebearers became voyageurs, a hardy lot who plied the Great Lakes in canoes transporting furs for eventual shipment to France. LaLonde, who stands five foot six, says that men in his family back then were typically his height, an advantage for voyageurs hauling bulky fur packs by land and lake.

LaLonde is no doubt attracted to his volunteer duty along Lake Michigan due to his U.S. Navy surface warfare officer past, having piloted humongous vessels such as the U.S.S. Abraham Lincoln, a Nimitz-class nuclear-powered aircraft carrier. He retired from the Navy as a lieutenant commander in 2002.

An uncle who lived in Traverse City lobbied for LaLonde to relocate to the Grand Traverse region. "When I retired, my uncle was adamant that this was the best place in the state to live," he recalls. So LaLonde and his wife, Kelly, got out a Michigan roadmap to plot their next move. He drew a line on it, a demarcation indicating his refusal to live below a certain point.

"My wife then drew a line and said, 'Well, I'm not living above here.'" They settled on Traverse City, where he became a high school math and physics teacher for Traverse City Area Public Schools and taught for the next eighteen years. Then the Covid-19 pandemic arrived in northern Michigan in spring 2020. "We left the building in March, and I never went back in."

Upon his military service retirement, he realized he wasn't spending enough time at the glorious local beaches. He put a stop to that personal neglect by enlisting as a volunteer with the Friends of Sleeping Bear Dunes in 2008.

....

The Friends' mission statement is succinct: "Protecting resources and heightening visitor experiences in partnership with Sleeping Bear Dunes National Lakeshore."[12] The nonprofit has a twenty-five-year agreement in place with the park, reflected by "a very close working relationship at all levels," says Board Chairman Kerry Kelly. This arrangement allows the Friends to raise funds for the park while preventing them from influencing decisions made by park administration. Although members are volunteers for the organization, they are, in effect, park volunteers.

The organization was founded in 1994, starting out as about a dozen people who were interested in supporting the park. Today, the Friends boasts more than eight hundred members—those who volunteer their time, donate dollars, or both. More than three hundred members provide volunteer services, which they can do on their own time, says Kelly. Like LaLonde, some monitor assigned stretches of the park, ensuring that it never becomes an eyesore, combing their coverage areas for litter. Some help to maintain trails, including the Heritage Trail, a nearly twenty-two-mile multi-use pathway in Leelanau County that courses through the National Lakeshore.[13] And some serve in the Preventive Search and Rescue program, assisting visitors with making sound decisions about hiking miles of dunes and being properly prepared.

Member demographics are dominated by retirees, most of which are "now locals" like Kelly, who moved to Grand Traverse County in 2004 after retiring from his thirty-year career at Dow in Midland, Michigan. "A lot of them move here and want to get involved."

And involved they are. Kelly says, "We put in somewhere around forty thousand to fifty thousand volunteer hours for the park every year."

....

LaLonde has an acute eye for what doesn't belong in this nearly pristine setting. He explains that sunny days are ideal for sighting plastic, the glare making it more readily detectable. His overall methodology is simple: walk the shoreline looking for what gets washed up and what gets left behind by careless visitors, then return along the upper part of the beach to collect whatever the wind blows there.

As we walk along the beach, as is my habit that cannot be broken, I pick up some Petoskey stones and shards of beach glass. I assumed that the beach glass I found along Good Harbor Bay ever so slowly made its way across the bottom of the lake from the Manitou Islands, refuse tossed into the water by the settlers there more than one hundred years ago. Maybe. But certainly not entirely, as LaLonde reveals. Before the establishment of the park, locals practiced target shooting by tossing bottles in the air above Lake Michigan as well as stacking them up on the winter ice and blasting away. Special thanks to the lake's glass-polishing hydraulics for the finishing artistic touches.

Over the years, he's made some unusual finds while patrolling his beach beat. This includes discovering the washed-ashore remains of two National Weather Service balloons, each with "a Styrofoam box containing data-gathering electronics." (Instructions are provided for returning them to the NWS.) The day after a storm in late October 2022, LaLonde recovered a float and transmitter from the Great Lakes Fishery Commission, which he reported to the Canadian-American fisheries protection organization. He also picked up more than one hundred plastic water bottle caps mysteriously distributed over a half-mile of beach. "You just have to wonder how they got concentrated like that."

One day when his wife accompanied him on his beach patrol, she found an attractive stainless-steel urn with an open lid. The urn was sitting on the beach at the foot of a dune. When they returned to their truck, LaLonde banged the urn on the side of a tire to clean out the residue inside. Then it occurred to him that "it could be somebody's grandpa in there" and emptying "corpse powder" is considered "really bad medicine," at least in the Navaho tradition. (Of note, he's a big fan of Tony Hillerman's Navaho-influenced mystery novels, having read them all.) Even though Navaho afterlife beliefs differ from those of the Anishinaabek, he says it's universal among Indigenous Peoples to be "respectful of the remains of all creatures." As well, "It would be totally inappropriate to keep them, or worse yet, repurpose them." So he took the urn to a park ranger and left it with him, making it "his problem."

The Adopt-a-Beach program keeps meticulous records of items removed from the beach each year, as reported by all Adopt-a-Beach volunteers. Kerry Kelly provided a 2022 Beach Patrol Summary Report compiled by one hundred volunteers who submitted a combined 632 individual reports throughout the year. They collectively worked 1,440 hours and gathered 1,023 pounds of trash. Here are their findings:

- *Most Likely to Find Items:* beverage bottles—includes plastic and glass, both returnable and non-returnable (409), beverage cans (249), plastic grocery bags (114), other plastic bags (207), paper bags (18), cigarette butts (2,138), food wrappers (1,547), take-out containers—both plastic (128) and Styrofoam (34), bottle caps—both plastic (1,318) and metal (191), plastic lids (345), straws/stirrers (1,235), forks/knives/spoons (83), plastic, paper, and Styrofoam cups/plates (137)
- *Fishing Gear:* buoys (16), line (33), nets (13), rope (one yard = one piece: 78)
- *Packaging Materials:* six-pack holders (12), other plastic bottles—oil, bleach, etc. (21), tobacco packaging/wrappers (147), other plastic or foam packaging (230), strapping bands (75)
- *Other Trash:* appliances (refrigerators, washers, etc.: 0), balloons (623), cigarette lighters (18), fireworks (173), discarded food (167), charcoal (55 pounds), cigar tips (500), construction materials (59), tires (1), shotgun wadding (215)
- *Personal Hygiene:* diapers (24), tampons/tampon applicators (21), condoms (7), syringes (1)
- *Tiny Trash (less than 1-inch in diameter):* foam pieces (1,489), plastic pieces (4,578), glass pieces (125)[14]

LaLonde isn't judgmental when it comes to all the trash he recovers. "In my experience, people don't pollute, but they forget." I wish I had the same forgiving attitude.

"There's less glamour in litter picking than you would think," he laughs. For example, sometimes tourists will hand him their trash to dispose of as he passes by. Although that seems almost insulting to me—and definitely lazy—LaLonde sees it differently: "It's okay, that's why I'm here." After reviewing the Friends' annual Beach Patrol Summary Report, I'm glad they do.

Not only do we literally cover a lot of ground at Good Harbor Bay, but our conversation does too. This includes sharing the reasons why I'm a northern Michigan lifestyle migrant and my early-stage recovery from my urban public school administrator duties I recently left behind. I mention the celebrations of life for murder victims in urban Indianapolis. The conclusion of these sad ceremonies often involves the releasing of balloons into the air. I understand the hopeful sendoff symbolism, but it's really bad for the birds. Taking it further, he says, "It's bad for everybody. You know, people complain about the paper balloon with the candle in it [sky lanterns]. But it's like, hey, the paper broke down and the candle went out on the way down. I've never heard of a fire getting started by one of them." Nor birds afire as a result.

LaLonde's handheld trash picker is his go-to tool, though he carries a knife as well, often to sever balloon string that gets snarled around driftwood. His father's hunting knife is his blade of choice, which he uses to cut away a boating cord that became entangled around a twenty-foot limb half buried in the sand by the surf. Less enthusiastic volunteers would likely pass on this arduous task, but LaLonde is committed to keeping the beach shipshape, as is his Navy nature.

While we trudge back through the sand under the bright sunshine in our sweat-stained shirts, he mentions looking forward to winter weather. "It will be even more magical when that first snow starts to fall out here and there will be no one around." This true friend of Sleeping Bear Dunes isn't kidding—on both counts.

An Inholding Outcome at Sleeping Bear

When I accompanied LaLonde in policing Good Harbor Bay Beach, he mentioned a still-inhabited house within the National Lakeshore boundaries, farther west, which we didn't reach during our outing. One day he met the woman who owns it. "Which leads to the question, how do you still have a house here? There's gotta be a story there. I believe her name is Sue."

About a week later, I took West Lake Michigan Road, a graded secondary dirt road that parallels the Lake Michigan shoreline, and managed to find the cabin. I drove up the two-track driveway to the small house, which sits in a heavily wooded lot. The lake murmured a slight distance beyond. Tentatively, I entered the screened-in porch. On a table near the house entryway was an impressive collection of insect repellants, indicating that the property is a fine dining area for mosquitoes. I knocked; no one answered. So I scribbled a note, included my contact information, and left it on the floor of the porch just in front of the door, hoping for the best. Before I left, I paused for a moment outside the house and marveled at the privacy and serenity of the property. Then I backed down the driveway and wondered if I would ever hear from the owner.

About ten days later I received a voicemail from Susan Patton, who, with her husband, Will, co-owns the property along with another family. Via email, we arranged a phone conversation to take place in early October 2022.

Patton and I start off small-talking as we get acquainted. She tells me that she and Will "just saw the original *Breaking Away* movie, which was filmed in Bloomington." The annual Indiana University Little 500 bicycle race is depicted in the 1979 coming-of-age film.[15] The Pattons live in Ann Arbor; like Bloomington, a college town, home of the University of Michigan. As we begin focusing on the interview, I soon learn that their out-of-the-way digs in Sleeping Bear Dunes has an intriguing story behind it.

Patton's parents lived in Jackson, Michigan. They purchased the northern Michigan property in what is now Sleeping Bear Dunes National Lakeshore in 1963, when Susan was twelve years old, with another couple, the Abbotts, and a local dentist, Dr. Adams, she recalls, of which both families were his patients. (Adams purchased the land in 1959. Sensing the park was inevitable, he sold his share to the Pattons and Abbotts in 1963.) They obtained the parcel, boasting three hundred feet of Lake Michigan frontage, and the cottage for $28,000. Back then, though it's hard to imagine today, vacation homes crowded the shore of Good Harbor Bay, with properties subdivided east and west of County Road 669. Property owners often had primary residences in Chicago and Fort Wayne, she says.

"The property was bought as a co-tenancy and still is," Patton tells me. "I am the owner in conjunction with John Abbott, who is the son of the Abbotts. We're the second-generation owners." In a simple usage arrangement that has never changed, the Pattons alternate months with the Abbotts. "We do January, and our last month is November." The Pattons get to stay at the cabin in July, a beloved Up North month for Susan, seventy-one, who's a fan of the July Fourth celebrations in Leland and Glen Arbor.

Although Sleeping Bear Dunes visitors can't tell, Patton remarks, "It's been a really volatile bay geographically. We've lost big chunks of Pyramid Point that have slid into Lake Michigan and created huge sand spits that have changed the nature of the beach." When they bought the property, there were several levels of dunes on it, she says. Two switchback trails zigzagged through them. "The waterline was way, way, way out," she recalls. "The beach was so wide that Jeeps and cars would come from the end of 669 and drive down the beach. My dad would get so pissed off at that. He would get a folding chair and his shotgun and go down in his swim trunks and sit on the beach, and that kind of ended that."

The original location of the Patton-Abbott cottage was approximately eighty feet from the shoreline of Lake Michigan. In 2016, the house had to be moved 140 feet back into the woods due to rising water levels. She reports that the high-water levels and the natural geologic progression that continue to carve out Good Harbor Bay "have just been immensely dynamic. Since we brought the cabin back six years ago, we've lost fifty more feet." A shipwreck located below Pyramid Point—the 133-foot steamship Rising Sun, which ran aground during a snowstorm on October 29, 1917[16]—can sometimes be easily seen from above by boat, or even from atop the point itself. "You didn't even need to snorkel it to see the boiler and the ribs of the shipwreck; but that's all covered in sand now," says Patton. Park Superintendent Scott Tucker said that "sand movements cover and uncover shipwrecks in the Manitou Passage on a regular basis." So at any given time, the Rising Sun may be visible or completely covered over, storms being the main factor.

....

Patton recalls the "sociological phenomenon of the day" back in the sixties: men worked outside the home and women largely didn't, seeing to the homemaking and much of the childrearing. "So there were kids and women all over the place during the summer, and they would stay all summer," she says. The menfolk would come up on weekends and vacation there with their families. She calls the kids back then "vibrantly feral," and not derogatorily, either, but with a fondness for those idyllic summers when free-range childhoods were the norm. She also notes that the middle and high school kids were a flirtatious lot, "and everybody was falling in love."

She continues to reminisce. "Nobody was driving. I didn't get my first car until I was twenty-three." However, she did have a horse, which her family kept at a Port Oneida farm. The kids, often in packs, roamed on foot and by bicycle, when the only expectation besides not getting injured—or worse—was to return on time, per parents' instructions, for lunch and supper. Then her recollective stream of consciousness leads to a memory of a nearby dilapidated house that had a basement with a "dungeon" of sorts. Patton and her friends would break in and "scare ourselves silly." Young imaginations run wild or, perhaps, a crime scene from days long passed? A forever mystery.

And then came the park, she says, and "whoa—everything changed incredibly fast."

Patton's father, Eugene "Pete" Hedges, was an executive with Consumers Energy. He specialized in pipeline distribution and transmission and led the utility's gas division. This expertise came in quite handy in the effort to keep their Shangri-la intact. "The thing about pipelines is that they involve right of ways, right of ways involve eminent domain, and my dad was really experienced with eminent domain issues." The national park was imminent, and so Hedges knowingly assumed the risk when purchasing the property, just wanting to enjoy it for as long as he could. Yet "he wasn't going to be frightened by the [park] superintendent" (Julius Martinek), Patton says. As Sleeping Bear Dunes began to take shape through real estate deals initiated by the federal government once the park was established in 1970 (and dedicated in 1977), many property owners sold immediately to the government, she says. Others negotiated a sale with cash up front and up to a twenty-five-year lease. Vacation homes acquired after 1964 could be leased up to five years, giving their owners time to enjoy their seasonal property while making arrangements to move on.[17]

With so many property sales occurring, the sense of community eroded, Patton remembers. There would be no more new people moving in. Families disappeared from the area. Once homeowners sold to the park, their homes were soon dismantled, and the land allowed to revert to its natural state.

Patton proudly declares, "My dad never sold out." Because of his professional background and having access to the Consumer's Energy legal department as a resource, "he was able to mount the legally convincing argument that [the federal government] didn't have the ability to take that property." Yet her father did play nice with the incoming park, selling one hundred feet of frontage adjacent to the current property. Today, "We're the only ones left in the whole Good Harbor Bay lakeshore." That may be true, but in a greater sense, they're certainly not alone. Superintendent Tucker says there are at least eighty inholding properties still within the park's legislative boundary. "All of the properties have deed restriction[s] placed upon them, but can be sold, inherited, or given away to anyone." As noted by Professor Kalt in *Sixties Sandstorm*, these inholding properties "are immune from condemnation, and their owners have been modernizing and expanding the cottages and houses."[18]

The Pattons and Abbotts possess their Sleeping Bear Dunes property as long as they so choose. Should any legal issues associated with their property crop up, they're well equipped to handle them: John Abbott is an environmental lawyer and Susan Patton practiced law as well, with experience in the environmental sector. Because of this, the two families have been able to work effectively as landowners in and partners with the park. When they moved the house back further into the woods to retreat from the rising water levels, they did so in an "environmentally responsible" manner, notes Patton, keeping to the park's guidelines. They collaborated with the park's botanist regarding tree cutting, for example, even though they had the ability to do whatever they saw fit with the property. "We could have put one of these monster homes in if we wanted, but we didn't; we kept it the same," she explains. Instead, they occupy the original 1959 cabin, built from a mail-order kit. Other than the bathroom that was remodeled in 2021, it remains "exactly as it was built." The only significant change to the property was the installation of a new septic field.

The Pattons are decidedly old school when it comes to the traditional lakeside or woodland cottage. But their view is rapidly becoming a thing of the past. "The demographic of the people that bought the cottages on Good Harbor Bay were all the Greatest Generation: they were veterans of World War II. And they didn't buy a second home: they were buying a cottage. They had all-summer occupancy in mind. It was a different time, a different value system. You wanted a cottage; you didn't want a lawn to mow. You just wanted a beach and a place to enjoy a sunset over a beer."

Patton can't imagine how much they could sell their property for in today's soaring real estate market. But it's a moot point: they intend to pass their share of the property to one of their two sons, or they would like to donate it to the park, which, she says, their partners have no interest in doing. Ultimately, she says, "I would be happy for it to revert to its original state."

Long ago, when the park's existence was being debated, the Pattons were not supporters of the idea. "We were so resistant," she recalls. When she was a freshman at the University of Michigan, she and her father would testify against the establishment of the park. But they soon understood that it was fait accompli. Not too many years after the park's inception, she "could really see the wisdom and benefit of it." As millions have since.

We end our phone call with an invitation from her for me to stop by when they're at the cabin this summer for a glass of wine and, I anticipate and look forward to, more stories of the way things were before Sleeping Bear Dunes National Lakeshore came into being. Meanwhile, I'll keep their cottage's location to myself. Some places deserve to stay largely unknown and their people undisturbed.

CHAPTER 8

PROTECTING PARADISE

Surrounded by 100 miles of Lake Michigan shoreline, four
islands north of the mainland, 341 square miles of surface area
and 28 square miles of inland lakes provides a real challenge
with respect to public safety endeavors! Leelanau County is
well known for being a "tourist destination," rural in character
with 40% of our land wooded, making Leelanau's hilly terrain
some of the most picturesque in the entire state.

—Leelanau County Sheriff's Office (LCSO) website

For the past several years, I've noticed impossible-to-miss yard signs prominently displayed throughout Leelanau County yards and fields saying, "Thank You, Sheriff Borkovich." I wondered about the cryptic public declaration of thanks for the sheriff of this rural, highly agricultural, incredibly scenic northwest lower Michigan county. The answer was easy enough to uncover.

Leelanau County's Constitutional Sheriff

On April 15, 2020, Leelanau County Sheriff Mike Borkovich, along with the sheriffs of nearby Benzie, Manistee, and Mason counties, issued a joint news release stating they would defy the executive order of Gov. Gretchen Whitmer to enforce social distancing during the Covid-19 pandemic. Borkovich, who became Leelanau County's sheriff in 2012, was quoted in the *Glen Arbor Sun*: "The governor doesn't wear a badge. The governor doesn't carry a gun. It's just an [executive] order."[1] This "constitutional sheriff"—who declares he has the final say on law enforcement matters in Leelanau County and not the governor—has long been strongly supported by many residents in his jurisdiction, especially those of a conservative bent.[2] His stance against Whitmer, who many locals in Leelanau county—as well as many rural Michiganders—are not fans of, to put it mildly (with yard signs disparaging the governor almost as common as those supporting the sheriff), only endeared his supporters to him more, and thus the yard sign expressions of gratitude. As he would later tell me, "I'm a sheriff. I don't have to answer to a governor."

The very mention of the name "Borkovich" in the region always seems to get a strong reaction, one way or the other. When I told several of my more liberal acquaintances that I would be meeting with the Leelanau County sheriff as part of my research, they greeted the news dismissively, eyes rolling, heads shaking from side to side. Yet my more conservative friends commended me for reaching out to the county's chief law enforcement officer, collectively giving him plaudits. With such extreme polarities being openly shared, I was eager to meet the man responsible for "protecting paradise." Indeed, Sheriff Borkovich did not disappoint.

....

Thursday, June 9, 2022, is a Rodgers & Hammerstein "June Is Bustin' Out All Over" kind of day. Just a few miles east of the village of Lake Leelanau, I turn north off M-204 and drive up a hill to the Leelanau County Government Center, where the sheriff's office is located. The center moved from Leland to this more central county location near Suttons Bay in 2008.

I walk into the sheriff's office. In the go-no-further foyer I'm greeted by an older female receptionist who smilingly says Borkovich is expecting me and will be right out. Across the way two officers talk quietly, laughing frequently, perhaps swapping war stories from a recent shift, their police-issue sidearms and tasers obvious on their belts. I've clearly entered the world of law enforcement.

In a few minutes, out strides the towering sheriff. Borkovich is six foot five; at six foot three myself, I'm unaccustomed to being the shorter guy in the room. (I would soon learn that he played basketball at Michigan State University, and nearly played for legendary Coach Bobby Knight at Indiana University.) He escorts me back to his spacious office, which features a bank of windows on two sides, with a wraparound desk whose surface is covered by stacks of folders and papers, reflecting the weight of his responsibility.

On the way in, I notice a famous Norman Rockwell framed print displayed near his doorway, "The Runaway." It's a touching depiction of a Massachusetts State Trooper sitting next to a boy at a lunch counter who appears to be considering going AWOL. The print was a gift to Borkovich and the Leelanau County Sheriff's Office (LCSO) from one of his constituents. As suggested in the Rockwell painting, one should understand that Leelanau County is very much Small Town USA, and this is very much this sheriff's approach to policing.

I bring up the tagline on the LCSO vehicles and how much I like it: "Protecting Paradise Since 1863." He shares its origin story, telling me that his predecessor, Mike Oltersdorf, originally displayed it on the department's vehicles, rather than the more traditional "In God We Trust" seen on most county sheriffs' road units. Borkovich left it on the vehicles upon Oltersdorf's retirement, honoring the former sheriff. He mentions that some people find "In God We Trust" controversial. And here I begin to see the steadfast resolve of this sheriff. "I don't, and I really don't care what other people think about that," he says without any reservation or hint of arrogance. "It's on our bills, it's in our constitution. That said, paradise does have a religious connotation to it. It *is* paradise up here: low crime, beautiful weather, nice people. We're lucky to have a good budget because of the tax base." (As reported by the *Northern Express*, in June 2023, SmartAsset, an online financial information firm serving consumers nationally, ranked Leelanau County as the wealthiest county in the state of Michigan. The ranking's "wealth index" factored in median household income and home values as well as investment income.)[3] Then back to the tagline: "We get a lot of positive comments from people who say, 'That is so cool.'"

Early on, Borkovich compares himself "a little bit" to "Andy of Mayberry," the North Carolina sheriff character played by Andy Griffith in the program of his name, *The Andy Griffith Show* (which ran from 1960 to 1968).[4] "I wouldn't have a computer or cell phone in my life, but I'm forced to," he says, alluding to his Mayberry side. "I don't have any form of social media whatsoever that I'm engaged with," although his office does have a Facebook page, which is a necessary part of today's law enforcement public relations efforts.

The sheriff makes it clear to me what he stands for, what he appreciates, and what he doesn't. He detests "woke-ism," which comes up repeatedly during our several-hours-long conversation. Yet he maintains the country is best when liberal and conservative thought thrives in a state of respectful disagreement. He thinks children spend too much time on the Internet. And kids need strong fathers. This all comes up in reference to the elementary school shooting in Uvalde, Texas, on May 24, just weeks before our interview. This is raw for him, and for all law enforcement officers, who train to respond to such incomprehensible incidents.

Borkovich, who is in his forty-fifth year as a law enforcement officer, studied biology and deer management at MSU, a precursor to his thirty-two years of working as a conservation officer for the Michigan Department of Natural Resources. I share that my maternal grandfather was a police officer in Paterson, New Jersey, who walked a beat in an organized crime-ridden neighborhood and cleaned it up. I'm a friendly. I like cops, meaning, good cops—which are the vast majority—having worked with them on and off throughout my career, especially during my three years in emergency management in the nineties.

We briefly discuss what I characterize as a parenting crisis afflicting the United States, a conclusion I quickly came to while working in urban education, with incidents of disrespectful, misbehaving kids continuing to rise. This prompts him to provide a tidbit about discipline from a white-tailed deer behavior standpoint: "A doe swats her own fawn when they go near a predator or if they don't listen. Animals have figured this out." The analogy has a distinctly old-school ring to it. He continues, "What's happened, which has leaked up here and is starting to ruin this area, is that we are lessening the value of correcting things at a lower level," strongly hinting at the responsibility of parents to school their children in civility. "The whole thing has spiraled out of control. We've lost it."

Our get-acquainted discussion winds down as we transition to the topic at hand: the effect of the inpouring of newcomers to Leelanau, most notably pandemic migrants and tourists, and how this affects the work of his office.

I explain my history in the area and my unrealistic concern for keeping things the way I found them so many years ago—my own Norman Rockwell type of allusion—which he shares, especially from a small-town, rural county perspective. "So people like you, who feel like you have roots here and come here and appreciate the area, you are very respectful," he says complimentarily. On the other hand, he discloses, there are "the wokies": the liberals, many affluent retirees, from Democratic bastions like Detroit and Chicago, who, he says, are becoming increasingly common to the area. As we converse, I keep my politics to myself.

"No one is moving here to be a cherry orchardist," the sheriff explains. "You can't afford land here anymore. Who moves here? People who make money in Chicago, Cincinnati, Indianapolis, New York, and California." But according to the sheriff, that's not all. Some are moving here for other reasons: as if regional political refugees. "Ever since the Pure Michigan program came out, it's brought a lot of people from the East Coast here because they're fleeing woke-ism, they're fleeing liberalism, they're fleeing crime, they're fleeing high taxes, they're fleeing civil anarchy—like in New York and New Jersey—so they're moving up here."

Taking into account the phenomenon of human migration to the Grand Traverse region, assimilation is a sensitive subject. The sheriff has some tips to consider as a preferred way of being when relocating to Leelanau County: be nice, engage the outdoors (especially in hunting and fishing), and volunteer in the community—in other words, be like the locals. Conversely, he asks, "Why do you have to get on our school boards, get on our county commissions? Why do you come here and bring your woke philosophy? So that's kinda the way I think, and I think that's kinda what's hurting this area."

Sheriff Borkovich says that many locals tell him that crime is increasing in Leelanau County due to out-of-staters and downstaters. He disagrees. "And I will tell you that it's half of us and half of them. More people, more problems. I would not blame it on out-of-staters, I would not blame it on any demographic."

He notes that it's easy to tell if someone is not from the area: "You walk by them, and they don't even look at you. Or if they look at you and if you wave, they don't even wave." I've experienced this revelation myself in Leelanau County. Whenever I walk along the county's roads, I wave. When I drive these same roads, I wave. When the drivers of the vehicles I pass don't, I immediately assume that they're either not from around these parts or are having a very bad day (or both). He adds, "People are very friendly here because they have a lower stress level. In New York, if you wave at somebody, they think you're going to rob them." The foundations of regionalism are often built upon definitions of what a region is not compared to elsewhere, which may well include negative perceptions and stereotypes that are often reinforced by poor behavior.

Sheriff Borkovich continues expounding on the "type of people that has moved up here in droves," and in the same breath refers to "the People's Republic of Traverse City." I find the appellation clever, telling, and amusing, failing to stifle my laugh, which doesn't seem to bother him. In my own observations on roads, at beaches, in restaurants, in party and grocery stores, there is some undeniable accuracy to what he's suggesting through his nickname for Traverse City, that of entitlement and alien presence, which is especially apparent during the height of the summer tourism season. The four-abreast cyclists on country roads who block vehicular traffic and float through stop signs. The self-consumed people who blithely—and recklessly—enter crosswalks in front of oncoming traffic while on their smartphones and yell at drivers, when Michigan state law says that traffic should yield to pedestrians who have *already* entered the roadway. The almighty-like air which restaurant servers sometimes must endure. "These are the things that we never saw before the wokies came here," he maintains, signs of the times of the cultural changes now underway.

On a personal level, Borkovich understands the desire to relocate to Leelanau County. "Probably 80 percent of the people who live in this county aren't from here," he relates. "I'm not from here. My grandparents emigrated from Serbia and Scotland and landed in the Flint area." He became familiar with Leelanau County as a teenager, when he used to come up to hunt. And, like most, became enchanted with the region. "Leelanau is where I always wanted to be." Who can blame him. Who can blame anyone, that is, unless you don't behave yourself. Then, blaming is easy, and completely understandable.

Borkovich tells me about a woman who recently approached him in Glen Arbor to complain about "all of the hillbillies around this place." He asked what she meant—and where she was from: Tinley Park, a suburb of Chicago. "It's all these pickup trucks and NRA [National Rifle Association] stickers and these toothless people driving around here in their loud trucks," she answered. He took the opportunity to explain that those driving such loud trucks don't like it, either, as they can't afford the repairs, and they can't just whip out a credit card to cover the costs. They can't afford a new vehicle. They can't afford dental insurance or dental care. But if your car slides off the road some snowy evening, "it's one of those hillbillies in a pickup truck—not somebody in a Prius—that's gonna pull over," he emphasizes. "They don't carry chains in Priuses, they don't carry ropes. They will simply pull you out because they're good people up here."

....

On Saturday of the 2022 Memorial Day weekend, I stop by Bunting's Cedar Market around 2 p.m. to pick up some salad fixings, a quart of milk, a package of savory locally made beef jerky, and some Michigan craft beer. As I enter, there's a can't-miss sign taped to the glass door:

VALUED CUSTOMERS:
All businesses are experiencing a lack of workers.
Please treat our staff that <u>did show up</u> to serve you
with PATIENCE.
Thank you for your support and business.

I see the manager behind the deli counter and remark how unfortunate it is that the sign was posted. It was only the start of the long weekend and the summer season kickoff. He tells me that a new employee, a college student of Asian descent, was the target of racial discrimination by a customer, and that enough was enough. As business increases, bad manners can become more common and harder to endure, eroding patience.

The sheriff, an astute observer of culture, says of the people working the cash registers, bars, and dining tables in Leelanau County, "In any of the local stores, they talk one way to the locals and another way to people who are from downstate or out-of-state." To the discerning, it's noticeable. It's almost as if a confidential code of interaction, of how to play the game, is in place. I enjoy engaging the locals in small talk. When you show an interest in people, in their way of life, in the place they call home, in the history of the area, they tend to warm to you, stranger though you may be. Through my countless casual interactions with northern Michiganders, they have shared many "secrets" that have enhanced our experiences here, especially outdoors. I've learned of outstanding quiet spots to hike, kayak, and fish. One June morning, a local hardware store cashier asked me if I had grandchildren as I purchased a plastic container of red worms and a dozen "Walt's Crawlers" for some brook trout fishing in a nearby creek. She then told me about a nearby pond I wasn't familiar with, where my young grandsons could catch panfish all day long. She didn't have to mention it; she was just being nice.

I mention that the busy season is getting ready to launch, and Borkovich says it's already started for the LCSO's twenty commissioned road officers. "We're geared up all the time. What you think isn't busy yet is busy for us. We have approximately twenty-four thousand people who live in this county: people who reside here, have a Michigan residence, and vote here. Then we have a lot of people from Grand Traverse County who recreate up here because of the [national] park, the trails, the scenery." Yet during the bustling summer months, visitors do much more than hit the park. They also stop by the irresistibly timeless villages of Glen Arbor, Leland, Empire, Northport, and Suttons Bay. Which means crowds. And with them, coexistence gets stressed.

"So how many people do we really have here in the summer, knowing a lot of the people are transient like you are? You live and reside in Indianapolis, but you have a place up here. So you are a part-time resident who lives here. We have the part-timers with second homes here, family cottages, or at the RV park on Lake Leelanau." Not so much a case of the more the merrier. For a rural county sheriff's office, he notes, "The pressure is here."

Of course, Leelanau County is far from being alone in northern Michigan in hosting a major influx of people each summer. The ten counties that constitute northwest lower Michigan all contend with a marked annual surge. According to the *Seasonal Population Study for Northwest Lower Michigan*, published by Networks Northwest, there was a collective 78 percent increase in population in the area from winter to summer during 2022.[5]

Borkovich asks me if I'm familiar with a country-and-western song with the refrain, "God is great, beer is good, and people are crazy." I am not. I look it up. The tune, titled, "People Are Crazy," was written and is performed by singer-songwriter Billy Currington.[6] His lyrical general assessment of the human race is hard to argue with, whether cop or civilian. It certainly explains things. Maybe I've overlooked C&W for too long.

After several hours in his company, it's easy to tell—and he tells me anyway—that he feels "blessed and privileged" to serve as Leelanau County's sheriff. "I'm honored that the people would trust me as their sheriff," he says gratefully. "There are eighty-three counties in Michigan; I would argue, geographically, this is the best one." He adds, "The best part of my job is that I can still talk to people here," unlike counties with large cities, in which, he maintains, he wouldn't be able to have such a close working relationship with the people he serves. Mayberry indeed.

I drive off thinking if I have an issue in Leelanau County that requires a police response, this is the guy, these are the deputies, I want to see. I love Leelanau County. He does too. This is something those of us who visit and live here should all agree on in a common practice of affection, and all that entails.

A Word on Crime

The Grand Traverse region, and Traverse City in particular, doesn't escape the crimes that are prevalent in much larger jurisdictions. What differs is the scale and frequency. Traverse City Police Department Chief Matthew Richmond states, "We're not a crime-ridden city. We have every kind of crime a big city has, but the volume of it is miniscule compared [to larger metropolitan areas]." He adds, "We're a safe community."

From 2019 to 2023, the Traverse City Police Department (TCPD) fielded eighty-three thousand calls for service (this includes self-initiated police responses). Not all calls are criminal in nature, as they include, for example, public relations interactions, such as walk-throughs at the public library, as well as traffic crashes. The number of calls for service has remained consistent from year to year, Richmond says. Notably, violent crime, compared to larger cities where police responding to shootings is "second nature" to them, is not a common occurrence here, he attests.

Traverse City covers just 8.6 square miles and is home to approximately fifteen thousand residents. Its business and civic leaders do not want it to develop a reputation as a party mecca. To prevent this from happening, the City of Traverse City, in partnership with the Downtown Development Corporation and TCPD, established the Healthier Drinking Culture project in 2020. The endeavor seeks to forge a strong, cooperative relationship among the players in the alcohol-serving industries—bars, restaurants, breweries, wineries, and distilleries—to curb heavy drinking and the accompanying misbehaviors, such as disorderly conduct/public intoxication and OWIs (Operating While Intoxicated).

Traverse City has a daytime population that doubles during the workweek with incoming workers. On the weekends, especially during the summer months, it can swell to more than one hundred thousand people. Because the region caters to tourists, consumption of alcoholic beverages comes with the territory. In Traverse City alone, there are 225 liquor licenses distributed among 119 serving locations within the city limits.[7] Promoting moderation in such an overwhelmingly alcohol-rich environment is indeed a balancing act.

Another problem common to tourist towns is no stranger here: retail fraud—i.e., merchandise theft, largely shoplifting. Captain Chris Clark of the Grand Traverse County Sheriff's Office says that overall, calls for sheriff's department responses to retail fraud incidents continue to decrease due to stores determining their own policies for when to summon police assistance.

Illicit drug use and traffic, which have been a national scourge for decades, are also present in the region. According to Leelanau County Sheriff Mike Borkovich, as quoted in the *Leelanau Enterprise* upon the release of the Sheriff's Office 2022 Annual Report, "There's [*sic*] hard drugs coming in . . . fentanyl, methamphetamine and cocaine," an observation seconded by Chief Richmond, who adds heroin to the list. Burglaries in Leelanau County rose from six in 2021 to eighteen in 2022. Borkovich correlates this increase with drug enforcement challenges, saying, "You can't go into a bank and ask for money to buy meth. You go into someone's house and steal their safe."[8]

Index crimes—a term coined by the FBI representing a uniform list for tracking and comparing crime data across the country—include "robbery, assault, breaking and entering, larceny, arson, and criminal sexual conduct." In Leelanau County in 2021, index crimes collectively rose 16 percent from the previous year, the highest total in the rural county since 2013.[9]

Of course, these are all serious law enforcement issues. Yet a quick glance at the LCSO police blotter over a weeklong period from Tuesday, December 12, to Monday, December 18, 2023, tells a story of a relatively peaceful community: a citizen misusing the 911 line, a loose dog, two lost dogs (separate reports), a car full of speeding teenagers, a trespassing complaint, a vandalized home (broken window), a suspicious person in a field, downed powerlines on M-22, and a "vape found."[10] Non-headline-making everyday police work—the way communities in the region hope to keep it.

Semper Paratus—Always Ready

Whenever you visit Traverse City, seeing an airborne United States Coast Guard (USCG) helicopter sometime during your stay is almost a sure thing. The air station is adjacent to Cherry Capital Airport, from which its MH-60T Jayhawk helicopters go on patrol, training, and emergency runs. And whenever I hear one of the Coast Guard choppers overhead—and the distinct *womp-womp* of its powerful twin-engine-driven rotors beating the air—I always stop what I'm doing and try to locate it in the sky. My wife finds it amusing, but she, too, will look upward when the white, orange, and black oversized dragonfly-like rescue helicopter is whizzing overhead above our cabin in Cedar, headed toward Lake Michigan.

Used to be, the USCG helicopters would go on training runs out to The Old Course at Sugar Loaf just a half-mile west of us, doing repeat touchdowns and takeoffs on an unused field near a dilapidated barn silo. They no longer use the golf course for training, instead flying up to Northport on the tip of the Leelanau Peninsula, where, I learn, they prefer landing on a dirt surface there to simulate whiteout conditions, as the rotors kick up the dust. We see them head out to the Manitou Islands on routine patrols and to conduct search-and-rescue (SAR) missions over Lake Michigan, especially during the summer when there's more recreational boating traffic, when more people take more chances with Mother Nature. Per the USCG motto, *semper paratus*, their helicopter crews stand ready 24/7, and can be airborne within thirty minutes of an emergency call.

....

On the afternoon of Tuesday, May 24, 2022, I visit Air Station Traverse City. It's a brilliant spring day, in the high fifties with a brisk wind. It's been a long spring this year, on the cool side, the season unwilling to turn over the reins to warmer weather. Winter comes early in these parts, and it can overstay its welcome as the sun climbs noticeably higher, northward, with the passing of the equinox.

For some illogical reason, I thought I could drive right into the air station, but *hel-lo!*—this is a military facility. I stop at the gate and call in to state my business with Lt. Brandon Skelly, thirty-six, a Jayhawk pilot (one of eighteen at the air station) who covers the station's public affairs duties. After a few long seconds, a metallic voice cracks, "Welcome aboard, sir" and the gate opens. A minute or two later, a Coastie walking by who can tell that I'm a visitor and quite unsure of where I need to be is happy to get me squared away, directing me to the hangar and showing me where to park. The parking lot seems to reflect the adrenalized nature of the rescue service, noticeably populated with pickup trucks, several souped-up Jeeps, some Toyota 4Runners, and a few cars that appear to be street-racing ready, along with the occasional almost out-of-place sedan.

Outside, Lt. Skelly awaits. He bears a military-grade physique, wears glasses, and turns out to be a fine public relations representative for the Coast Guard, answering questions with enthusiastic detail and much-appreciated translation from military jargon to civilian speak. We enter the hangar. One of the air station's helicopters is in for major service—what Skelly refers to as "heavy maintenance"—in which all the helicopter's major components get stripped down and put back together. Four mechanics attend to the aircraft. Contemporary dance music thumps throughout the hangar, a beat to work by. I've never heard the tunes before, the distance between me and popular contemporary music an ever-widening chasm. It's their hangar, so whatever works for them. Besides, I kind of like it. We jump into the interview, entirely conducted while walking and standing.

Skelly, like many of the air station's nearly 120 officers and enlisted men and women, arrived here during the pandemic. He came in January 2020 from South Carolina, on a three- to four-year rotation. Preparations for the air station's participation in the National Cherry Festival are well underway, as the air show had been canceled in both 2020 and 2021 due to the pandemic. This includes getting ready for the "Open Ramp" open house, hosted by the Coast Guard, that would take place on Friday, July 1, the evening before the start of the weeklong festival, running July 2–9. During the Open Ramp, visitors get an up-close view of the high-performance aircraft. This year would feature the U.S. Navy Blue Angels flight demonstration team (which alternates every other year with the U.S. Air Force Thunderbirds), the Coast Guard's Jayhawk helicopters, AV-8B Marine Corps Harriers, A-10 Thunderbolts ("Warthogs"), and high-performance stunt planes. Skelly is also involved in coordinating the Coast Guard water rescue demonstration in Grand Traverse West Bay during the air show on Saturday and Sunday, July 8 and 9. He tells me the air show draws nearly four hundred thousand attendees each year. The closest I've come to being amidst this huge crowd was from the safety of a friend's apartment on Front Street several decades ago, where we watched the event from the roof.

....

Air Station Traverse City is considered a small Coast Guard station, says Skelly. In 2017, the station had five MH-65 Dolphin helicopters, but now operates three MH-60T Jayhawks. Skelly calls the replacement Jayhawks "a more capable aircraft." They are larger and can carry more weight, meaning more people, and have a much longer range than the Dolphins, able to stay airborne for five-plus hours. They can also cruise at 180 knots with a light load. "We can go all the way up to Lake Superior and prosecute a SAR case before we have to refuel," he says. Air Station Traverse City covers the entirety of Lake Michigan and Lake Superior (the two largest Great Lakes) and part of Lake Huron (another USCG air station is in Detroit). At least two of the helicopters are in service at all times—one standing by to launch within thirty minutes notice, a flight crew always on base 24/7—while the third aircraft is often offline in routine maintenance.

I'm surprised to learn that many of the Jayhawks are repurposed aircraft handed down (purchased) from the U.S. Navy, essentially derivatives of the Blackhawk helicopter family. The Coast Guard versions, valued at $30 million each, according to Skelly, are specially outfitted with forward-looking infrared radar (that picks up heat signatures), and the tail wheel is situated farther up the fuselage to allow for shipboard landings. Smaller service, smaller budget.

On the way into work today, Skelly observed a male paddleboarder on Grand Traverse Bay without a wet suit, shirtless, wearing shorts, and no personal flotation device (PFD)—a recipe for disaster. At this time of year, the air temperature and water temperature are vastly different. "It may feel great outside," Skelly says, "but you have to dress for the water temperature, not the air temperature, because it's still forty-seven degrees." And with summer comes the Coast Guard's busy season. "When things heat up people are out on the water more, and that's when we start seeing our cases actually increase," he explains. Unfortunately, all too often, people underestimate Lake Michigan. "Not being familiar with the lake water temperatures up here affects a lot of people."

People can make understandable mistakes when it comes to the weather, and some people make awful and regrettable decisions. They don't get outside enough; don't comprehend nor respect Mother Nature's fickleness and power, especially when it comes to the temperament of the Great Lakes. And they don't want their vacation agenda disrupted and think they're in control. I ask the lieutenant about rescuing those in the latter category.

They not only put themselves in harm's way; they also put rescuers' lives in jeopardy. I wonder aloud if the flight crew debriefs the victims of their own making and explains the gross error of their ways. "When we go out on a case, that's not something we ask them," he reveals. "Our job is not to scold them. We don't do any post-mission analysis information gathering."

I blurt, "Well, you should! And you should charge them too!" We both laugh.

The USCG does not invoice for their rescue services—unless a hoax has been determined. Anyone guilty of committing a prank call to the Coast Guard "can face up to six years in prison, a $250,000 criminal fine, a $5,000 civil fine, and reimbursement to the Coast Guard for the cost of performing the search."[11] As of this writing, the direct hourly cost of operating an MH-60T Jayhawk helicopter is $8,822, Skelly reports, which includes employee compensation, maintenance, and fuel. Rescues don't come cheap.

Skelly is unable to provide data on the number of locals compared to visitors who benefit from their rescue services. And I can tell that doesn't really matter to him. It's the overall success rate of the SARs that counts.

Skelly served in the Army for fifteen years, flying Apache helicopters in combat theaters in Iraq and Afghanistan. Now in the Coast Guard, and with his wife and four children ages one to eight, he gets to see his family daily while tending to his passion for flying, "helping people in their community." The outpouring of public support for the Coast Guard in Traverse City is another plus, he notes. Traverse City loves its Coasties. However, there are complaints and concerns voiced from time to time.

The Jayhawks do their water rescue hoist training over Grand Traverse Bay, utilizing both East and West bays. In the summer, Skelly says they tend to get calls asking why the helicopters are hovering over the bays and if "everything is okay." The lieutenant tells me—with no hint of jealousy—that his boss takes the "noise management calls." I chuckle, as "noise management" strikes me as a double entendre. So while out training over Grand Traverse Bay, the Jayhawk pilots "try to stay in the middle of the bay as much as possible, try not to go over to the side as much as possible, maybe go a little further up the bay." He's understanding—to a point: "We're not just out there turning fossils into noise for no reason."

Positioning a Jayhawk in midair for a hoisting maneuver carries a significant degree of difficulty, as Skelly explains: "Learning how to hover over a boat and match the airspeed with the speed of the boat with the weather, while listening to the flight mechanic in back give you directions on how he wants you to position the aircraft so that he can get the basket on deck safely, while you're only looking at a small reference on the boat, while you can't even see the rescue device that you're using, it takes a lot of coordination." I can only imagine, and I'm dizzy at the thought of it. Being hauled upward several stories in a small metal basket suspended above the water is no doubt a welcome salvatory yet fraught experience.

....

Outside the hangar, Skelly points out two of the air station's helicopters in the distance returning from separate runs, noting that the on-duty crew responded to a mayday call near Charlevoix. I feel the urge to take some photos, smartphone ever at the ready, but I resist the addictive reaction, instead surrendering to the moment to appreciate the helicopters as they approach the tarmac in their steadily growing loudness, in their gradually slowing magnificence, announcing their return and daring those nearby to try and turn away from the show. As we watch the landings, Lt. Skelly, not looking away from the just-touched-down Jayhawks, shares that he absolutely loves his office in the sky. Randomly, I happen to mention my affection for *Coast Guard Alaska*, and he laughs. He, too, enjoyed the program—so much so that it inspired him to join the Coast Guard. I'm well past my prime, so the Coasties won't have me. But standing on the tarmac with a veteran combat pilot now flying Coast Guard SAR missions out of Air Station Traverse City is close enough; I'm honored to be here.

....

Lt. Skelly suggests that if I'd like more information about the work of the Coast Guard in the Great Lakes region overall that I get in touch with Karl Willis, the SAR program manager for the Great Lakes. A few days later I call Willis, who is also a retired USCG commander. As befitting his former rank, he's articulate, polished, and precise in responding to questions. When we begin talking, he says about the Grand Traverse region, "That is some gorgeous country up there." He's working out of the USCG's Atlantic Area 9 District Headquarters in Cleveland, Ohio.

Counter to my assumption, he informs me that emergency runs involving the Coast Guard have been trending downward over the past decade. Better boat designs and mechanical systems continue to improve nautical safety. An additional factor: due to a policy change, the Coast Guard is no longer involved in commercial work that marine towing companies now handle exclusively, such as BoatUS and Sea Tow, which has resulted in a drop in USCG case numbers. Willis says that these towing companies work with the Coast Guard "to differentiate between real search-and-rescue distress cases and non-distress, such as getting underway and breaking down on a beautiful day with no emergencies."

As with all military services in the United States, the Coast Guard is a data-driven organization. "We did an informal study years ago called Boatable Days," Willis explains. "We came up with this formula in the Great Lakes to determine what the workload was going to be. We did that based on the price of gas, sea conditions less than two feet, and winds less than fifteen knots. And we were able to project what our workload was going to be [based upon] how many boatable days."

Weather, of course, is a "huge impact" on the USCG's work, he says, referring to "the curse of seasonality." In the winter, the Coast Guard pulls its standard boats that work the Great Lakes—the forty-five- and twenty-nine-foot response boats—from service and shift to ice rescue mode. Once the spring thaw comes, the Coast Guard transitions back to getting ready for its busiest season as the waters warm, what Willis calls "'Mr. Toad's Wild Ride' between Memorial Day and Labor Day," when 70 percent of SAR operations take place. "It's just crazy." The gorgeous Memorial Day weekend weather in 2022 resulted in "ninety response cases, forty of them on May 30 alone" across the Great Lakes, he notes. Owing to the fine boating weather, that was a third higher demand than the previous Memorial Day weekend.

Even though the Coast Guard's Great Lakes caseload is down, Willis comments that they are seeing "an uptick in body recoveries." He adds without being crass, "The Coast guard is not in the body recovery business." District 9 averages about one hundred deaths per year on the Great Lakes that they respond to, and more yet in support of local law enforcement agencies. Bridge-jumping suicides, drownings off pier heads involving rip currents, and boat sinkings and fires included. He mentions a "terrible boat fire" on the Illinois River in Seneca, Illinois, weeks earlier that forced fifteen people to jump in the water when the boat was being refueled and exploded; one boater was critically injured. Incredibly, sometimes sinkings are attributed to boaters forgetting to put their boat plugs back in.

I ask him one of my primary questions concerning the Coast Guard's responsibilities in the Great Lakes: is the increasing number of people in the region—both visiting and relocating—particularly those inexperienced with outdoor recreation, leading to more work for the Coast Guard? Chuckling, Willis, a thirty-seven-year active duty Coastie who is now in his tenth year of working as a civilian employee for the maritime service, gives me an off-the-record response. I find myself nodding in wholehearted agreement, keeping his sentiment between the two of us.

The 9th District responds to about 2,500 SAR cases per year, involving, as previously noted, approximately one hundred deaths: a 4 percent mortality rate. So those saved vastly outnumber those lost. As with breaking the law, ignorance is no excuse for endangering oneself and the lives of others while out on these inland seas. Willis shares that he "still gets very upset with the tragic loss of life. These cases can be pretty traumatic." As the USCG is keenly aware, Mother Nature always deserves our utmost respect.

I mention a neighbor of ours in Indy who told my wife several years ago that she and a friend were going to kayak from Leland to South Manitou Island—on their brand-new sea kayaks, a first venture of this kind for them. Janet politely suggested that they might want to rethink that to avoid the possibility of becoming statistics. Willis well knows how treacherous the Manitou Passage can be: "We have lost several people there. We had a tragic case there five or six years ago where a father and son were coming back, and the boat capsized and both of them died. That's a cold, tough stretch there, fourteen miles on a sea kayak. I'm glad your wife was asking some questions, because apparently that person doesn't know that area of water very well." I listen raptly to several more tragic stories involving extreme weather, disastrous mechanical failure, and/or human error. All fascinating; and some decisions, sadly, unforgiving.

I heard that the Coast Guard's official position on ice fishing is that it shouldn't be done. Willis clarifies that once upon a time the Coast Guard used to say, "No ice is safe ice." Not anymore. He tells me of ice roads to and from Madeline Island, located in the Apostle Islands in Lake Superior's Chequamegon Bay, where people live year-round. Ice roads there are lined with Christmas trees and even school busses will use them. Local public works departments routinely check ice thickness throughout the cold weather months to ensure safety. I shudder at the thought of walking on ice, let alone driving over it. Years ago, driving along Torch Lake while following a local friend, he suddenly veered onto the lake's frozen surface, doing doughnuts, his driver's side window rolled down as he laughed hysterically, trying to coax me to follow. No way.

Willis says that predicting an increase in SAR missions for the 9th District is "a tough read." The numbers have been consistent for the past five-plus years. "It really depends on the economy," he explains. "The economy drives all new boaters. There's a lot of cabin fever from Covid and people saying, 'Damn the torpedoes: we're going boating anyway,' disregarding the price of gas. We're seeing paddleboards and Jet Skis and a lot of kayaks and canoes and, as you said, many inexperienced people trying to get out in some of this extreme sports stuff, and that is probably the most burgeoning industry on the Great Lakes for us."

Technology is, of course, also a great boon to the Coast Guard, especially its computerized SAR operations program. Weather information from the National Oceanic and Atmospheric Administration (NOAA) and other weather monitoring agencies allows for a twenty-four- to forty-eight-hour lookback on weather data on any given geographic area, so the prevailing winds and seas then can be checked for directional flow. The system can run a model to project where a missing person out on the water might be located. Willis gives me a recent example of how this worked to perfection.

"Last year, we had two older gentlemen, who built a sailing vessel, out on Lake Ontario, getting underway about 10:30 in the morning. At some point during the day the boat capsized." They were unable to issue an alert. The Coast Guard was notified. So they ran the recent historic weather data and computed projections to determine where the victims most likely might be located. Bingo. Willis recounted, "As we approached the search area at dusk from one of our stations with our boat, they looked ahead and there they were. There was no search involved because they went right to where the search started. They found the men clinging to the hull. If they were gone another hour or two, they probably wouldn't have been there. That was a great rescue."

Oh, that they all would be. That locals and newcomers to the Great Lakes region would avail themselves of the wisdom to be acquired about the outdoors, its geography, weather and climate, its animal and plant life, the "behavior" of the world that exists outside of our smart homes and TVs, beyond our electronic fascinations and addictions. Alas, this is just wishful thinking. Much as the cartoon character Popeye the Sailor Man boasts unapologetically of his fundamental understanding of himself—"I yam what I yam"—we is what we is. Thank God that United States Coast Guard Air Station Traverse City is here, where the action is. And that they withhold rendering public judgment on some of our more reckless, life-threatening, often water-involved recreational behavior.

Every Day Is a Great Day to Be a Game Warden

Every February, on a non-appointed day when winter's stay begins to wear thin, a bright, promising, grayness-dissipating thought occurs to me regarding the trout opener in April, and a childlike anticipation consumes me for a moment, a reminder to circle the calendar and begin the good-for-morale preparations to head north. Then, that unburdening spring day, while I stand in a pristine northern Michigan river spin casting for browns, rainbows, and brookies, inevitably one of my accompanying fishing buddies will make an unflattering remark about the "fish cops"—Michigan DNR conservation officers. But to an angler like me who's lived in the big city—with its neglected, polluted, murky bodies of water—most of my adult life, I have a much different view. I don't take for granted the critical work of Michigan's DNR enforcement officers in protecting these precious resources. For me, like most who have been Up North, we come, and stay, for the water wonderland it is.

In the summer of 2022, I reached out to the DNR about interviewing one of its conservation officers. Several months went by, with some email exchanges between me and the District 4 office. I was about to give up when one afternoon the phone rang while I was writing: Conservation Officer Rich Stowe was on the line.

Well prepared for our conversation, Stowe tells me that he and his six fellow conservation officers working in District 4, Area 1—comprising Leelanau, Grand Traverse, Benzie, and Wexford counties—protect 2,383 square miles of land. Add in the Manitou Islands, Fox Islands, and Power Island in West Grand Traverse Bay, and their responsibility expands to 4,568 square miles. This includes 159 inland lakes and 257 miles of Lake Michigan shoreline. Because I had roamed three of the four counties in his jurisdiction (not including Wexford) on fishing, hiking, kayaking, and sailing outings, including the Manitou Islands and Power Island, and because I was curious about a day in the life of a Michigan conservation officer, I asked if he'd be game for me to ride along with him in the field sometime soon. "I think I can arrange that," he said receptively. It was mid-September, and Fridays were out because he'd be "spending the night on the river"—which could be the Betsie, the Platte, the Manistee, or the Boardman-Ottaway—making sure that the salmon fishers obeyed the law. So we made arrangements to go out on Wednesday, September 21, at 11 a.m. We would rendezvous at the DNR Customer Service Center/Field Office on M-37 on the southside of Traverse City.

Stowe, fifty-seven, is a big, burly guy, his hair closely cropped. He's a former Grand Traverse County Sheriff's Office deputy—"a road officer for eight years," he notes—and has served as a conservation officer since 2002. He's dressed in his olive-green tactical uniform that clearly distinguishes him as a conservation officer, or game warden, the old-school title he tends to use.

As I fill out the requisite paperwork that states my identity and holds the DNR harmless for my participation in the ride-along, he shares that his wife just bought him several nonfiction outdoor books, including the latest essay collection by northern Michigan author Jerry Dennis entitled *Up North in Michigan: A Portrait of Place in Four Seasons.* I'm impressed with his wife's selection, as I consider Dennis one of Michigan's finest outdoor writers. "You're going to love that book," I predict. "I look forward to it, sir," he answers politely. Not only is Stowe a gentleman, but, as I would soon learn, he is indeed a scholar of the natural world.

Before we head out, I mention my surprise at the unusual number of hawks I spotted on my way over: red-tailed, red-shouldered, and broad-winged. "It's migration season," Stowe reminds me, smiling. "I love birds of prey too." I tell him about identifying my first northern harriers a week earlier at the Arcadia Marsh Nature Preserve in Manistee County. "They're called marsh hawks around here," he explains. My master class in the great northern Michigan outdoors is underway.

"It's always a great day to be a game warden," he tells me as he leaves the field office conference room to file my paperwork. No wonder I've been assigned to Stowe. This is not what anyone expects to hear from a law enforcement officer about their line of work in the year 2022.

About twenty minutes later we're sitting in his service vehicle, a forest-green Chevy Silverado pickup truck, with its distinct black grille guard, searchlights on each side of the windshield, and cages in the bed for varmints he may have to remove. A large laptop dominates the dashboard; a set of binoculars is within easy reach. The cab is snug but neat, every square inch of space optimized. Behind the front console in an upright gun rack rest a twelve-gauge shotgun and police-issued automatic rifle. Although certainly law enforcement weapons, they're typically used for putting down mortally injured or diseased animals, including deer, black bears, and elk.

A significant part of conservation officer work is responding to citizen complaints. First thing, he investigates one involving "dispersed camping"—backpack or car camping—in Benzie County. We turn onto a two-track, bouncing along the rutted trail as he maneuvers us through narrow corridors of underbrush, the branches scratching the sides of the truck a nails-on-chalkboard sensation for me; no bother for him.

We come across a campsite in a clearing along the scenic Platte River. Next to a kayak/canoe launch is a collapsed two-person tent adjacent to remnants of a large campfire. Empty food packages and cans of bug repellant litter the area. Oddly, a seen-better-days dresser stands next to the tattered tent, several drawers missing. Stowe finds a camping permit stuck in between two lower branches of a sugar maple. In the address information section, scrawled in bright green highlighter ink, it reads, "My fucking car."

"If I should make contact with this individual, I expect it will be the same attitude as this," Stowe predicts.

About an eighth of a mile further into the woods appears a parked U-Haul truck and a road-weary Chrysler van. Four children, elementary to middle-school aged, bolt from the van. Their mother, who is very pregnant, politely greets the conservation officer as he gets out of the truck and introduces himself. She's wearing a pink maxi dress, a maroon beanie, pink socks, and sandals, not the everyday outdoorswoman attire. I watch from the cab. The conversation appears friendly enough, with some polite laughter and occasional hand gestures. Several dogs bark relentlessly. He gives her his business card, returns to the truck, and we drive off.

I'm used to seeing homeless people in cities but quite unaccustomed to coming across them in such a setting as along the Platte River, I verbalize. "There are a lot of weird things happening anymore," Stowe comments. Such as an increasing homeless population in the woods of northern Michigan.

"Those kids should be in school," I observe.

"Yes. Among other things."

"How old do you think she is, in her thirties?" I ask, estimating.

"Not yet."

"Is she married?"

"Yes. He's working."

"That's strange."

"We see a lot of that anymore. People getting off the grid for a variety of reasons." From a dispersed camping standpoint, the family has two weeks to stay in this specific location, then they need to move on, to relocate to another spot. A nomadic life.

As we drive away, he says, "Makes you want to go home and hug your grandkids."

....

The influx of people in northern Michigan means an increase in participants in hunting and fishing, and with it, a corresponding rise in misconduct and violations. "I think we're just in a different world from twenty years ago," Stowe comments regarding the violators he encounters in the field. "There are a lot of people out right now that didn't grow up [experiencing] a lot of outdoor activities, and they're attempting to learn." He adds, "A lot of it comes down to lack of knowledge. On the flip side, there are always those that know the rules and still need to bend or break them, just like breaking the speed limit."

To get a taste of the variety of investigations Stowe and his fellow officers get involved in, he suggests I take a gander at the DNR's Biweekly CO (Conservation Officer) Reports posted online. For September 18–October 1, 2022, the top violation in District 4 was snagging salmon. Several offenders were caught in the act of illegally netting them too. Other transgressions for that period involved fishing in closed waters, fishing without a license, keeping quantities of fish over the legal limit, smoking marijuana in public on federal land, shooting protected species (e.g., a dead blue heron was discovered in the trunk of a violator's car), trespassing, putting out bait piles for deer below tree stands, and processing illegally taken deer. Aside from addressing criminal activity, conservation officers rescued an older couple stranded in the woods for two days. A surprising number of offenders had warrants out for their arrest.[12]

The reports are short stories focused on the facts of officers' reports. But they do contain some dry humor in the matter-of-fact reportage. For example, in the reports filed during the end of September, a perpetrator directly netted a salmon and put it on a stringer, the illegal act witnessed by a conservation officer. Upon contact, "The subject denied netting the fish and stated he had just caught it. When it was pointed out that his fishing pole was not assembled, he admitted to netting the fish." The subject was cited, and the salmon returned to the water.[13]

Another report told of a conservation officer observing a man with a large two-piece spear who was trying to impale migrating salmon and was intercepted by the officer. "The man informed CO Hintze that he had warrants and that this just wasn't his day. The man was charged with possession of a spear on a trout stream, fishing a closed trout stream, fishing without a license, and was lodged on two misdemeanor warrants."[14]

Notably, the majority of these offenders call Michigan their home.

....

Stowe wants to check out several prized fishing spots during the salmon run on two famous local rivers: the first on the Platte, near Honor, and later, the Betsie. We hike along a heavily boots- and waders-footprinted riverside path, and he observes how downtrodden the groundcover is due to the many anglers at this time of year. He characterizes salmon fishing on northern Michigan rivers as "a spectacle." But not just yet. The salmon run is just getting started, it's a weekday, and so the fishing activity on the Platte is low.

Several times during the day Stowe mentions the "neutrality" of his profession. "Not taking things personal" is essential, in his mind, to doing his job well. He sees his work as helping outdoorsmen and -women to coexist with the resources he's charged to protect. Despite the many and increasing challenges of his work—more people in the field, more seasons to manage (e.g., there used to be one deer season; now there are bow, rifle, muzzleloader, youth, antlerless early and late seasons, etc.)—he is clearly in his element and especially fond of educating people on the "wise use of the resource," his shorthand for his agency's mission statement: "The Michigan Department of Natural Resources (DNR) is committed to the conservation, protection, management, use and enjoyment of the state's natural and cultural resources for current and future generations."[15]

Inside the truck, our conversation ranges widely. Stowe tells me that someone recently reported a "black panther" sighting. "Seriously?" I respond, disbelieving. As it turns out, it was a fisher, a member of the weasel family. "Mystery solved," he says, smiling. Then I broach the subject of marine rescues. He has never recovered a drowning victim wearing a personal flotation device, other than once: the body of an older man in a worn-out PFD.

Although tempted, I refrain from bringing up Bigfoot. I do, however, inquire about the eastern massasauga rattlesnake. I mention a guy at Good Harbor Bay in July who claimed he just saw a rattler on the short, sandy path leading from the parking lot to the County Road 651 Beach. Not discounting the alleged sighting, Officer Stowe explains that the nonvenomous eastern hognose snake is often mistaken for the massasauga. "But you never know," he says, encouraging my imagination.

....

With the onset of the pandemic, "shots fired" complaints became more common for the DNR in District 4. In Stowe's former assignment in rural northeast lower Michigan, "that never happened." Locals are used to hearing gunshots from hunting, target practice, or farmers eliminating pests. Pandemic migrants living in rural areas Up North sometimes reactively associate gunshots with criminal activities, a phenomenon Stowe finds curious. And with more human incursion into woodlands comes changes in animal behavior.

He explains that owing to human pressure, animals will expand their territory and show up where they previously haven't been seen. Newcomers who are unaccustomed to the great outdoors and living in the woods will report "nuisance" animals to the DNR. "You mix the influence of wildlife with an ever-growing population of people who didn't grow up with that particular species, and it creates a lot of problems that people don't understand." Take black bears, for example. "Everybody is bear crazy right now," Stowe relates. "Someone who has never seen a bear in the wild before now has one living in the woods behind their house. Now he's in your garbage and he's knocking at your door, and he's torn apart your bird feeders. He's still a wild animal—he's a bear—not cute and cuddly," he laughs. Rural northern Michiganders are accustomed to bears. And they typically don't feed them, as more unaware folks might. "You can't feed a bear one day and expect it not to come back," he says. Black bears have become more prominent now in Grand Traverse and Leelanau counties. "Some of these bears are almost urban bears," he adds—not laughing.

Sharing outdoor resources among humans is also an increasing challenge for the DNR to manage, which he brings up. "With the huge movement to get outdoors there's a lot of user conflict. When you used to sit in the woods say, twenty years ago, bowhunting for deer, you probably wouldn't have ever seen a mountain bike or someone walking their dog or someone geocaching. When you're fishing there wouldn't have been wake boats out there. Every time there's a new activity, there are rules and laws that don't necessarily apply. So there are challenges trying to keep everybody happy."

Etiquette matters in the field. Yet unfortunately, breaches of etiquette in fishing and hunting environments are occurring more frequently. And a few too many newcomers in the woods and on the water are clueless about it. For example, Stowe says, "There's early waterfowl season, which is a challenge within itself, because it starts before the Labor Day holiday, and people are kayaking up to and hanging out among hunters' decoys. We even have people fishing adjacent to someone's decoy spread. Of course, it's their right; it's a shared resource. But it's etiquette that sometimes turns into safety issues."

....

Before I know it, we've arrived at the Homestead Dam on the Betsie River. A smattering of fishermen cast hopefully, patiently, while standing in the river in their chest and hip waders. Meanwhile, several hundred feet away, where they can't fish, trophy-sized king salmon hurtle out of the water, going airborne as they try to leap up the dam. Some succeed. An older couple leans against the railing, marveling at the piscatorial power on display. Stowe chats with them. A friendly educator, he expounds on the river, the dam, the fish, the run. Then we take the well-worn path along the river's edge.

Minutes later, we happen upon four Indiana conservation officers who crossed the border for some salmon fishing. Stowe confabs with them collegially for about fifteen minutes. He mentions that things can sometimes get a bit "western" during the run, and they all laugh knowingly. Then he checks fishing licenses on three different groups of anglers: from Illinois, Georgia, and Washington. As we walk back toward his truck, he marvels, "Did you notice that we didn't talk to one fisherman from the state of Michigan?" The day before, he chatted with a fly fisherman who flew in from Germany specifically to salmon fish on the Betsie. Sadly, this growing pressure from downstate, out-of-state, and overseas anglers has dissuaded many locals from salmon fishing here in their own backyard, he remarks. "They've given up and no longer want to be part of the show." He adds that he continues to be amazed by the number of people he talks to in the woods and on the rivers and lakes who are new to the area.

Suddenly, a series of violent splashes alert us to a fly fisherman battling a just-hooked king charging upriver. "Can you imagine what that would be like if there are five hundred or more fishermen standing side by side right here when a fish like that gets hooked and makes a run?" he poses. "That will happen on Saturday." Western indeed.

We watch for several minutes as the angler and a friend try to finesse the salmon out of the hole it's retreated into, a complicated maneuver due to the submerged branches covering it. Smart fish. They keep glancing our way, cognizant of the watchful presence of the game warden. "Let's move on; I think I'm making them nervous," Stowe says considerately, an understanding soul, a fisherman himself. Although he's sensitive to fishermen's need for space in such an engaged circumstance, asserting himself on the river as a conservation officer is no problem for him. "I'm way past whether I'm welcome or not."

As we walk along the Betsie, he says that earlier in the week he spoke with one angler who openly told him he had lost more than forty hooks already that day. "Just think how much hardware gets left in our rivers," Stowe suggests. It's a disturbing thought. I think of my own lost tackle in northern Michigan's trout streams. I've become a more skilled angler as I've gotten older and lose far fewer rigs these days. If I snag a limb or some other underwater obstacle, I always try to retrieve my tackle, especially lures—an environmentally sound move and an economic one as well, as the price of lures is almost obscene. But sometimes they're just irrecoverable. Now multiply that by others who try their luck on any frequently fished stretch of river, especially such an unskilled caster as Stowe crossed paths with, and the image is startling—and very troubling. Monofilament can dangerously entangle waterfowl, and loose hooks can be deadly to them as well. So it seems that northern Michigan trout streams, if not every heavily fished river in the country, are like abandoned battlefields with their unused yet live ordnance awaiting the unsuspecting creature that comes upon it. This blatant sloppiness by people who should absolutely know better—outdoorsmen and -women—and who should take the lead in modeling environmental propriety, is bewildering.

....

As we head back to Traverse City, our conversation travels as well, though on a more meandering path. It's no surprise to learn that Stowe was brought up hunting and fishing, a childhood that revolved around outdoor activities. "That's just what you did where I grew up in those days," he recalls. He met his first conservation officer when he was ten years old, an occasion that would leave a lasting impression that became a career ambition. "I thought he was *the guy*. Big guy in a green uniform. He was an older gentleman that lived out in the woods in our area. I was absolutely intrigued with that man. So I always wanted to do it, and it took me a long time to get there; I just never gave up."

When he was young and growing up in the village of Northport, located on the northern tip of the Leelanau Peninsula (as of the 2020 Decennial Census, having a year-round population of 496),[16] Stowe wondered about the behavior of tourists when they visited his northern Michigan harbor town. They would do things like go fishing on a lake when the water was rough and all the locals "knew better than to be out on a boat." His father, whom he regards as a "wise man," provided an insightful explanation. "He told me, 'You know, they work all year somewhere just to come here for a week. We have this every day.' I think that puts it into perspective." He adds, and I envy him for it, "Since long ago I've been thankful that I don't have to run from wherever I live."

When the pandemic struck, people were urged to get outside and recreate outdoors. In northern Michigan, they did so in droves. Stowe believes that the amount of outdoor gear sold during the pandemic must have been "unprecedented." And it was. During the summer of 2020, I spoke with the owner of the Indianapolis bicycle shop I patronize. All his bikes were sold out—like auto dealers back then, his expansive showroom empty—and he expected his next shipments of new inventory would take at least six months to a year, a problem felt by outdoor equipment retailers throughout the country.[17] According to Stowe, for Michigan's conservation officers during the height of the pandemic, "every weekday was like a weekend, and every weekend was like a holiday," as far as the swelling number of people who were engaging the outdoors. "There were lots of first-time people trying stuff that they had never done before."

The increased people pressure on the area is advancing well into the shoulder seasons, and Stowe has taken notice. "Color tours didn't used to be a thing," he says. But now, in villages that cater to tourists, like Glen Arbor, during the fall "there are days as if it's mid-July. It's incredible. I don't know if it's all pandemic caused, but it has changed."

I ask him what he would like the public to take away from their field interactions with the DNR. "I just rarely have anything but great experiences with people," he says. "The reality is, we're working for the people of the state of Michigan. I hope their experiences are good. I think most of them are, even if a person is in violation. I've always lived by the premise that if you're doing something wrong and get caught doing it, the person who's enforcing those laws or regulations is getting paid by the rest of the people to ensure that these resources are here for our kids and grandkids. I think most people are understanding, whether [their lawbreaking is] an oversight or intentional." But he does acknowledge that "most people don't like to be told they're wrong, and they don't like to get a ticket."

Although we didn't run into anyone breaking the law on my DNR field trip, watching Stowe engage people throughout the day strongly hinted that it would take a lot to try his patience. When it comes to the "touristy areas," he remarks, "I think that everybody is just figuring out that everybody has to get along." Coexistence stands the best chance when peacekeepers skillfully wield diplomacy before exerting police power. If you could pick the Michigan conservation officer who warns, cites, or arrests you, Stowe would be your man.

I ask what he thinks about climate change, a topic he doesn't seem to want to delve into. But he does, in his own abbreviated, downplaying way. "I'm more of a go-with-the-flow guy. What's the winter going to be? I'll know when it gets here." He reinforces his point: "For all the forecasted rain this summer, not that much of it has washed the dust off my truck." He says it in a non-confrontational, easygoing manner. I decide there's nothing further to clarify or pursue here.

Back at the DNR field office, Stowe says in parting that whenever he's around younger conservation officers, especially during training classes he conducts such as trapping enforcement, he tells them—and I'm ready for it—"It's always a great day to be a game warden." It was certainly a great day to be *with* this game warden.

CHAPTER 9

EYES TO
THE SKIES

How right it feels to know a true night sky, how
right to know the dark.

—Paul Bogard, *The End of Night:
Searching for Natural Darkness
in an Age of Artificial Light*

I just learned the official name for the acute condition I've had for the past thirty-five years or so: I'm *ornithophilous*—bird loving. For those of us who live with this, northern Michigan is a primo place to be.

My wife has it too. As a result, we've witnessed countless avian wonders together. Such as coming upon a pair of ring-necked pheasants bug-hunting in a roadside ditch near our Cedar cottage, a first-time sighting of these regal creatures, the male's vivid coloration and feather pattern right out of a fairy tale. Watching beautiful sunburst-colored Baltimore orioles building their gourd-shaped nests along the Boardman-Ottaway River in late May. Seeing several bald eagles fly out of the woods along Good Harbor Bay to climb and soar above Lake Michigan. Spotting a peregrine falcon perched on a dying white pine tree perhaps fifteen yards from our beach chairs along the shoreline of the great lake one mid-September afternoon, who then mesmerized us with its F-16-like maneuvers as it swooped and dove for flying insects, repeatedly returning to the same pine. Incidentally paddling within ten feet of an occupied sandhill crane nest, the two mates resting with their chicks, while kayaking the Cedar River in mid-June. Ascending one of the Brown Bridge Pond stairways one rainy afternoon during Memorial Day weekend (before the dam removal and draining of the pond in 2012) and realizing we had entered a cloud of migrating Cape May and yellow-rumped warblers, stopping to watch, getting drenched, and not caring as they moved through the woods ever northward.

We are incurably happy about our ongoing fascination with bird life.

Because birdwatching continues to grow as a pastime throughout the United States—as of 2021, the U.S. Fish & Wildlife Service estimates as many as forty-five million Americans are into birding[1]—and many species migrate annually to nesting grounds in Michigan, it seemed only appropriate to talk with a northern Michigan expert about the state of birdlife in the region. When I happened to mention this to Tina Greene-Bevington, the owner of Bay Books in Suttons Bay, who, it seems, knows everyone throughout the Leelanau Peninsula, she immediately said, "You need to meet Kay Charter." An email outreach resulted in a visit to Charter's Saving Birds Thru Habitat bird sanctuary on Wednesday afternoon, May 4, 2022.

The Crazy Lady Who Loves Birds

I drove on M-22 just north of Peshabestown, near Omena, made a few turns per Google Maps, which managed to get me close but not exactly to my destination, in the heart of that glacially gifted rolling hill country of which the Leelanau Peninsula is renowned. Orchards and farms and pockets of woods and long two-tracks leading up to homes situated on acres of breathing room, which so many visitors admire and envy, made me forget my irritation at Google for not seeing the job through. Yet I managed, relying on my somewhat rusty sense of direction sans technology. I rolled up to the Saving Birds Thru Habitat's Discovery Center, a one-story building adjacent to the forty-four-acre private bird sanctuary. A Honda CR-V with some years on it sat in the yard outside the building. I parked in the sandy lot and walked into the center. Inside, Kay Charter, an eighty-three-year-old diminutive fireball, awaited. She was masked and insisted that I socially distance, as I had just arrived the previous week from out of state and she was being especially careful about avoiding contracting Covid-19. As I'm in my sixties and recognize my Covid-19 vulnerability, she got no public health compliance complaints from me.

The self-described "crazy lady who loves birds" says, "I'll try to watch my language," though she fails miserably, only adding to her charm. She tells me that the keynote speaker at the tenth anniversary of the dedication of the Discovery Center in 2011, Glen Chown, the executive director of the Grand Traverse Regional Land Conservancy, compared her to Teddy Roosevelt, the twenty-sixth president of the United States. Roosevelt, who established America's National Parks, is Charter's "greatest hero."

About ten minutes later, and now comfortable with one another, we get to the subject at hand. I tell her I like birds, and she emphatically says, "Good. This is a good place to be."

I mention visiting the Arcadia Marsh Nature Preserve the week before. "Oh my gosh, it's fantastic," she agrees. She asks if I saw any trumpeter swans, which I did, as well as mute swans: check. She's no fan of the invasive mutes, of European origin, imported to America beginning in the 1850s.[2] "They're driving down our loon population," she says indignantly. "We need to get rid of all the invasive species, and mutes are terribly invasive. We need to do what's right for the environment for our native species." Straightshooter, that Charter.

Although we haven't known each other for more than fifteen minutes, she makes a frank request: "I wish you could come here and shoot some of the deer that are wrecking my habitat for birds. If you don't have apex predators, you've got a mess." I don't own a long gun, though I do have some outstanding local connections who would be happy to oblige. We move on.

She asks if I'm familiar with Doug Tallamy. I am not; but I'm about to be. She gets up, instructing me to follow her into another room, and begins pulling books from her shelves for me to take as gifts. Tallamy, a professor in the University of Delaware's Department of Entomology and Wildlife Ecology, has written several books that have an avid national following by those fond of nature, including the New York Times Bestseller *Nature's Best Hope: A New Approach to Conservation That Starts in Your Yard* and *Bringing Nature Home: How You Can Sustain Wildlife with Native Plants*, which is in its fifteenth printing as of 2021. "He's the guy that wrote about the importance of native plants to caterpillars, which songbirds need for their young. We didn't understand that before as well as we do now. So when you get rid of caterpillars, it's a whole chain."

Charter refers to herself as "a Perma-Fudgie." She moved here from southern Illinois many years ago. Her connection with the area, like so many Perma-Fudgies, came by marriage, her husband's family having settled nearby on the Leelanau Peninsula around Omena in the middle 1800s.

"In 1992 I had an epiphany. We were living on our forever home on the water; we lived there for two years. We built it ourselves, a beautiful little house. Just over this way on the bay south of Northport." One day in late summer that year while working in her yard, which overlooked a cedar-hemlock swamp, she spotted two winter wrens, one of her favorite birds, active in a nearby brush pile. These evasive wrens are not often seen, though they are heard, belting out a mellifluous flute-like song that belies their size. "And as I sat there, the parents and four fat little carbon copies of the adults came out from under the brush pile." She was overjoyed by the sighting. But as she watched, she realized that these, among other songbirds, were in decline. "And it's because of people like me. My husband and I had built in that habitat."

Habitat destruction is the top factor in bird population decline, with the loss of three billion birds in the United States and Canada since 1970.[3] "So all we can do is what we can do ourselves on our own property, or perhaps try to impact others," she says imploringly.

Despairing about the future of the wrens, she recalls, "I had to do something; I was driven." She approached her late husband, Jim, and announced that she wanted them to sell their dream home "and buy a big piece of inland property and make it a bird sanctuary." Jim was "lassoed into it," she confesses. They searched and found the property Kay wanted, which featured thirteen acres of wetlands and woods with a creek running through it, prime bird habitat. In 1993, they began buying chunks of what would eventually become the current forty-seven-acre sanctuary (which includes the Discovery Center's three acres). In 2001, following the publication of her memoir, *For the Love of Birds*, Saving Birds Thru Habitat was born. "So this came about from my experience with winter wrens who were losing ground and my inability to accept that as an inevitable result for these birds. I wanted to do something."

She recalls, "It didn't take too long to figure out that forty-seven acres wasn't going to save too many birds." So her mission expanded to being a voice for the creatures she seeks to protect. She got in front of classrooms of schoolchildren and reached out to adult audiences. For twelve years, Charter wrote a popular column for the *Traverse City Record-Eagle*, "On the Wing." One notable column encouraged bluebird lovers to use ventilated nesting boxes rather than closed boxes. Should the ambient temperature reach ninety-three degrees or above, she explains, just for one day, then the temperature inside closed nesting boxes will rise to fifteen degrees higher. "The eggs will addle, or the nestlings will die like a dog in a car from heat stress." She received almost two hundred letters from readers who were grateful to know what had been the cause of the bluebird chick mortality and consequently switched to vented nesting boxes. The vented bluebird boxes at her bird sanctuary—all thirty of them—have yet to lose a chick to heat stress, she proudly shares. The only real issue is the highly competitive house sparrows, who try to take over bluebird nests. "You just have to kill them," she whispers, then admits, "I have done that—with no compunction." I believe her.

Although the sanctuary is miniscule in the greater scheme of things, remarkably, the property attracts more than one hundred migratory bird species. About sixty of them will nest on the property in the spring. It may be a small contribution, a modest success. But little victories like this matter.

Since establishing Saving Birds Thru Habitat twenty-two years ago, Charter has witnessed the precipitous decline in songbird numbers. One spring day in 2005, while observing from her bay window in her living room, she counted thirteen species of warblers in just one hour. Regrettably, she says, "I will never see that again. We used to have four or five nesting pairs of Baltimore orioles. Now, at most, one. We don't have veeries [a type of thrush] nesting here anymore; no ovenbirds nesting anymore; no mourning warblers; none of the ground nesters—they're totally gone."

In 2007, she reached out to Tallamy after reading an article he authored in the American Birding Association's magazine, *Birding*. It covered the importance of insects to birds and native plants to insects, essential symbiotic relationships for supporting biodiversity. The etymologist and the bird protector hit it off, and Tallamy and his wife, Cindy, became supporters of Saving Birds Thru Habitat. Charter says that Tallamy "has been a mentor to me," adding, "when I don't know what I'm talking about, I go to Doug."

Then she stops, leans forward, and addresses me as if I'm her student, as if what she has to say is unequivocally the most important thing I'll ever hear. "If you like birds, you need to understand this: you have a responsibility in your own backyard. Conservation begins at home."

Having an abundance of bird feeders, several birdbaths, and hesitating to remove dying trees—bird habitat—I'm already a convert to the cause. Yet Charter's passion for the well-being of wild birds hits me like an altar call, and I'm transformed into a born-again bird conservation evangelist.

Of course, at the heart of our conversation is our mutual love of birds. I tell her about hiking with a friend several times a year who recently asked me why I'm so interested in birds. Charter and I look at each other for a telepathic moment—then burst out laughing.

I tell her how much I love orioles—"I do too!"—and eastern kingbirds, having seen one on the drive up the peninsula today. "Me too! They take no prisoners." The dark gray bird with the notable white-tipped tailfeathers, considered a sizable flycatcher but small as birds go, is fearless, warding off much larger birds such as red-tailed hawks or crows straying into its territory. Then she tells me about a family of northern goshawks nesting nearby. I've seen several of these bird-eating accipiters gliding over fields since I arrived back in northern Michigan in late April. I tell her about my wife being horrified by several predatory bird sightings we've had near our bird feeders, with Cooper's hawks picking off songbirds. I'm fine with nature running its course, referring to the "crime scenes" as hawk-feeding stations. She laughs in ornithophilous agreement.

I broach the issue of the increasing popularity of the region, especially Leelanau County. "People are coming here because it's beautiful; everyone wants to come here," she says. But she doesn't scapegoat visitors for any environmental degradation of the area. "You just can't blame the tourists." We all have skin in this game.

She contends that environmental protection and economic development in northern Michigan and throughout the country doesn't have to be an either/or—it can be a both/and. Housing developments in the region could be designed as ecosystems, a gospel preached by Tallamy, friendly to both humans and the creatures they share the Earth with, she explains while pointing to a nearby hillside that may one day attract development.

Charter combats willful ignorance of the human responsibility to be conservators of nature through her organization's education mission. She believes, though, that "there are just some [people] who are absolutely ineducable." But that doesn't stop her from trying.

"If we can educate people to respect the natural world and treat it as though it's the Mother Earth that it is, that's a lot." She adds, "If we do this, we save the planet."

....

Our interview concludes, and before Charter gets into her car, she invites me to follow her to her nearby home. At her insistence, we take advantage of the restorative warm spring weather (she's no fan of winter) and go for a short walk on her birding trail, crossing the footbridge over Weaver Creek, which courses behind her home. As we walk, she holds my hand for balance and support, a precaution due to her inner ear issue. We pause on the footbridge to watch a healthy-sized bullfrog that's most likely just emerged in the past several days from its hibernation. We hear, then see, a kingfisher, flying by as it makes its territorial racket. She tells me that "right now the peepers [tree frogs] are going crazy. If you come down here in the evening, it's deafening."

We slowly make our way up the hill to a snug two-seater bench. "Let's just sit here for a minute and look at this beautiful vista," Charter gently directs. "I've been wanting to come up here, but I just needed somebody to help me." The bench faces westward toward the back of her house and the creek. Birdland. We talk; rather, she talks, I listen. She discloses that her husband had dementia and went into a care center before he died. She has no debt, but no retirement savings either. "I'm not worried about it," she comments. We sit quietly for a few minutes. "This is just a wonderful piece of property," she then muses aloud. "It really is paradise." I couldn't agree more.

Beaver Island

During our May afternoon together, Charter brought up her collaborations with Pam Grassmick on several Beaver Island birding initiatives, including the development of the Beaver Island Birding Trail. Grassmick, sixty-seven, a born-and-raised islander, went away to college to train for a nursing career, returning years later with her husband, Brad, upon their retirement. They own island property that her family homesteaded in the 1860s.

When a senior scientist with the Nature Conservancy told her twenty years ago that invasive species were the single-biggest threat to the island's ecosystem, well, that did it.

Since then, environmental conservation has been her life's focus, much of it involving promoting the protection and appreciation of birdlife.

Grassmick is the founder of the Beaver Island Birding Festival—Warblers on the Water. Since 2013, the event occurs annually on Memorial Day weekend. The festival, which she envisioned with Charter, draws birders from as far as Texas and California. Since the songbirds are at the height of their spring migration then, she notes, "Every morning there's a new sound: somebody else has moved into the neighborhood. It's fun being able to share it with people."

Having been to the fifty-six-square-mile island—the largest in Lake Michigan—three times myself since 1996, I envy Grassmick's life as a year-round islander. It's an extraordinarily beautiful place.

In August 1996, I sailed there from Charlevoix with my friend Greg on his nineteen-foot Flying Scot, a thirty-two-nautical-miles day sail to St. James on the island's northside. The boat is designed for bay racing, not so much for navigating the open waters of an inland ocean. But, younger then, more impulsive, and not so wise, we did it, arriving at St. James Harbor early that evening, safe and sound, Lake Michigan becalmed and bedazzling the whole way.

The following morning, we made for uninhabited Garden Island, but two miles to the north, where we camped for three days. The sail home *was* eventful, however, though my thrill-seeking captain was in his element. He skillfully maneuvered the seven- to ten-foot waves all the way back to Charlevoix, thunderstorms the night before having stirred up the lake. As the first mate and quite the inexperienced sailor, I bailed my way through the stomach-churning swells and troughs, water coming over the side keeping me busy, a survival meditation. To this day, whenever Captain Greg recounts the story of that crazy voyage, he always mentions that I never puked, a glorious piece of flattery, that.

In October 2000, the two of us again traveled to Beaver Island, this time on the Emerald Isle ferry, a two-hour ride across Lake Michigan. The 130-foot car ferry can carry nearly three hundred passengers, as well as fifteen vehicles, cargo, and has capacity for a semi-truck.[4] We went to check out a ten-acre vacant parcel that was for sale, a short drive from St. James. The ruins of a log cabin stood across the street, supposedly from a one-time Mormon farm. To the south was a corporate retreat center, a contemporary log-constructed building. Most of the property was adjacent to state land, never to be developed, and featured numerous birch trees on gently rolling terrain. An escapist's dream.

While exploring the parcel, we discovered an almost completely silted-in cellar, the home long gone. We also found several antique bottles, one which sits on a bookshelf in my home office. It's as close as I got to owning the property, as my dear wife rejected the idea once I gave my full account. Although she had been to South Manitou Island with me several times and loved it, having experienced that "island consciousness" natural high, this was just too far of a reach. Nice bottle, though, reminding me from time to time of what might have been.

More recently, in October 2021, Greg and I stayed for three days on the island. We rented a room at the Erin Motel, on the waterfront and a short walk from the harbor. Our location came with the added benefit of being within crawling distance of the Shamrock Bar, almost directly across from the motel on Main Street. Although the convenience wasn't lost on us, we behaved.

The following day we roamed the island, renting a Honda Element that qualified for life support. The rattletrap did the trick, however, getting us to where we were going. Our diversions included straying into wild blackberry and raspberry patches and eating our way bearlike through them, picking apples from abandoned orchards, fishing several inland lakes, rockhounding along the Lake Michigan shoreline, and marveling at the booming real estate market. It seemed that a for-sale sign was posted on every possible empty parcel bordering or overlooking Lake Michigan, with construction of a surprising number of dream homes underway. When we had visited in 2000, vacant land for sale was common, yet stayed on the market sometimes for years, and could be bought at the right price. No more. The pandemic had triggered a virtual stampede of people of means looking to get off the mainland from time to time or forever. Those who could afford the escape were making it happen. Although the Discover Beaver Island website states that "Beaver Island has historically been a great middle-class family vacation destination, and it still is,"[5] middle-class homeownership on the water is a thing of the past, a phenomenon well underway on the mainland in northern Michigan and throughout the Great Lakes region.

....

Grassmick characterizes the rising Beaver Island tourism and interest in purchasing property as "an explosion." She adds, "Just like everywhere else, we're seeing an influx of people." The Beaver Island Boat Company (BIBCO), which runs two ferries back and forth between Charlevoix and St. James (most runs handled by the Emerald Isle), reports that in 2021, the company ferried 35,087 passengers (which includes counting a roundtrip as two tickets) and 7,544 vehicles; in 2022, BIBCO transported 37,429 passengers and 6,648 vehicles. Tim McQueer, BIBCO's president and general manager, says he believes the transit company will experience slower increases in volume due to high consumer prices and the pandemic winding down, while expecting an uptick in out-of-state vacationing.

The other option in getting to Beaver Island is by air. The oldest airline of the two serving the island, Island Airways, has been in business since 1945. Originally, it just delivered mail. In the eighties, Island Airways began handling freight and passenger transportation.

Angela LeFevre-Welke, fifty-three, president of Island Airways, reports that "in a typical year, we haul thirty thousand passengers and 1.8 million pounds of freight." They also deliver all the United States Postal Service mail and FedEx and UPS packages to the island, as well as all prescriptions. Their transportation service is the lifeline for the island during winter when the ferry isn't running. Over the past several years, Island Airways has seen a 20–30 percent increase in FedEx and UPS transport. "Beaver Island has discovered the online economy," she remarks, making remote living on the island for the more convenience-oriented kind more doable.

Once the pandemic struck, Island Airways saw a precipitous drop in passengers. Typically, in April they transport 1,400–1,800 passengers. In April 2020, they hauled two hundred. LeFevre-Welke and her husband, Paul Welke, pilot and owner of Island Airways, were wondering how long they would stay in business. "And then the phones started to ring," she says, with callers from all over the country—from California and Washington to Texas and New York—who had homes on Beaver Island. According to LeFevre-Welke, they asked, "Can you get us to our house on the island? We're going to ride out the pandemic there." Once they arrived, many began working remotely. Then real estate on the island really took off, she says, some of it attributable to the "doomsday" type of thinking that islands would be the safest places as the pandemic ravaged the mainland. "People bought property sight unseen." Of those pandemic-inspired newcomers who purchased a home and moved to the island, atypically, just a handful left after a year or two.

....

In advance of our conversation, Grassmick referred me to the "Beaver Island Visitor's Guide," which encourages right-minded behavior—for visitors to care for the island as if they lived there. It contains a leave-no-trace set of recommendations that touches upon waste disposal and proper campfires, as well as an appeal to respect wildlife, fellow visitors, and island residents.[6]

She also sent me a two-page profile, "The Beaver Island Archipelago—Caring for a Lake Michigan Treasure." It echoes the low-impact instructions found in the visitor's guide, and then some. It states that up until recently, the island "has remained a low-traffic zone in terms of tourists and sportsmen. Yet greater public awareness of the region, shifting tourism patterns, and the growth of what some call the 'experience economy' may change that in times to come," noting a "significant spike in summer visitors to Beaver." The profile, which covers the fourteen-island archipelago, stresses not to remove native plants for personal gardening use and not to tamper with "ancient tribal cemeteries" (such as found on Garden Island). It also discourages motorized vehicles from speeding for the sake of wildlife, pedestrian, and bicyclist safety, which will also keep the dirt road dust down.[7]

The problems that are cropping up more frequently now, resulting from increasing people pressure, includes speeding off-road vehicles (ORVs), visitors wandering off trails and damaging flora, and, like Sleeping Bear Dunes is experiencing, off-the-leash dogs causing havoc with shoreline bird nesting. Grassmick wants me to know that rude behavior is not the norm for the island's visitors. "The kind of people that are normally attracted to Beaver Island are nature lovers, people seeking quiet." But the sheer numbers of summer tourists aren't bringing out the best in everyone. An added complication, she tells me, is that incidents of people getting lost on the island are increasing, taxing its limited search and rescue resources. Beaver Island itself has areas with no cell phone coverage, so hikers new to the island should especially keep this in mind.

Beaver Island's vibe is distinctly unique as opposed to that of the mainland. Grassmick, who grew up an islander, says, "We never had to worry about crime; we still don't. Everyone leaves their keys in their cars and their doors open. It's wonderful. People here know each other; they keep an eye on each other." She adds, "People in the sixties, seventies, and eighties really flocked here for just that reason." But they didn't come in the numbers that are being seen today. Beaver Island has been discovered.

Beaver Island's Chamber of Commerce reports that the island's year-round population is about six hundred.[8] Grassmick claims that nearly seven thousand people were on the island for the 2020 July Fourth holiday, a remarkable number given the small size of St.

James. Although such summertime crowds are a windfall for the island's businesses, the price paid is the abnormal congestion. "You can't get through the streets" of St. James, Grassmick attests.

I happened to stumble upon an *Indianapolis Monthly* magazine article from October 18, 2020: "Beaver Island Retreat, In Up-North Michigan." It talks about the actual Beaver Island Retreat that opened in 2019 that offers *glamping*: glamorous camping (which strikes me as an oxymoron), an amenities-rich outdoor camping experience. "Each safari tent is situated on its own 2,500-square-foot glamp site, with a queen-size bed and memory foam mattress, private picnic area, and outdoor kitchenette." And that's not all: "bedside lamps fitted with iPhone chargers" (helpful, if not necessary), "outdoor twinkle lights for ambience" (I prefer the Milky Way, thank you), "and a Bluetooth speaker" (give me crickets, songbirds, and peepers to serenade me).[9] Is this the continuing softening of American culture and ever-encroachment upon nature, or a step in the right, modern, albeit hedonistic direction?

During my October 2021 trip to Beaver Island, although our Erin Motel room door faced the water and Charlevoix, with some light pollution emanating from the eastern mainland, still, the night sky was magnificent. We would take our beers outside, sit on the low seawall, and watch the Milky Way emerge. The stars popped even more dramatically to the west. Because of this incredible nighttime view, in 2020 Beaver Island applied to become an International Dark Sky Sanctuary through the International Dark-Sky Association (now known as DarkSky International), seeking to join a select list of nineteen official Dark Sky locations in the world, ten in the United States.[10] Grassmick notified me in March 2024 that DarkSky had just approved the twelve-thousand-acre Beaver Island State Wildlife Research Area Dark Sky Sanctuary. Indeed, the Sky Quality Measurements (SQM) on the island are outstanding. The SQM scale measures maximum to minimum light pollution, ranging from sixteen to twenty-two. Beaver Island readings consistently achieve scores just under twenty-two SQM, more than surpassing DarkSky requirements.[11] Here, dark nights are precious.

Human pressure isn't the only concern that's getting islanders' attention these days. Climate change, too, is making its presence felt. Grassmick contends that the island is experiencing more ice storms and thunderstorms, and as a result, more electrical outages. The prevailing winds now tend to be easterly, and stronger, she adds. And then there's the fluctuating Great Lakes water levels. Michigan Natural Features Inventory Senior Conservation Scientist Phyllis Higman said in a 2023 *MLive* article that Beaver Island "is starting to see climate change impacts more than ever. And the challenge with that is you're changing the abiotic environment, the temperature, the rains, the severity of the storms in the winter."[12]

A former educational colleague of mine in Indy invited me and Janet to come spend some time with him and his wife at his father's Beaver Island waterfront home on Lake Michigan. Unfortunately, we couldn't get our schedules to jibe. Then in 2020 he showed me photos of his father's property ravaged by high water and Lake Michigan storms. The encroaching water had destroyed his break wall and clawed down his second-floor deck. They put the house up for sale, moved to Florida, and, when last I checked, a year later, the house was still on the market.

The Beaver Island Master Plan, branded as "Resilient Beaver Island," was created in 2017 and updated in 2023 per the Land Information Access Association. "The Master Plan helps shape the future of Beaver Island by summarizing existing conditions and trends, identifying a vision for the future, and prioritizing the actions that should be taken to achieve the community's vision." The plan's vision statement targets the best of both worlds, striking a balance, if not an alliance, between conservation and prosperity:

> In 2045, Beaver Island will be a thriving community: economically diverse, socially vibrant, and environmentally rich. High-quality ecosystems will be preserved and managed in a sustainable way, but also leveraged to support ecotourism and economic development. Historic and cultural resources will help define the Island, telling stories of its rich past and attracting visitors and new residents. There will be a diversity of affordable housing options that meet the needs of all residents and pave the way for changing demographics. A connected network of bike paths, sidewalks, and paddling routes will link recreational assets, community services, and residences.[13]

With the unforeseen impact of the Covid-19 pandemic and the sweeping change ushered in by the remote work movement, Resilient Beaver Island's 2017 vision statement is not only prescient as a roadmap for the future but also reflects the need for careful planning when progress is being courted so intensely. Grassmick comments, "I worry about our island culture changing. You need to have a working waterfront, a workforce. It can't be all retired wealthy people; it's not sustainable." As a planner and promoter of events to draw birders and other nature lovers to the island, she is all about "low-impact recreation." Notably, she adds, "Those kinds of things appeal to the kind of visitors that we want here." Although a tourist destination can aim for a certain type of visitor, controlling who comes and who doesn't is next to impossible.

LeFevre-Welke notes the chamber of commerce's efforts to educate folks on "how to be a kind visitor." The Beaver Island Birding Trail and proposed Dark Sky Sanctuary cater to "really nice visitors," she notes. "Birders are the kindest, least impactful, most thoughtful visitors you ever want to meet. Same with our Dark Sky Park focus. They just want to come and look at the dark sky; they're not going to have a rave in the woods."

Thanks to the island's chamber of commerce's promotional efforts, Beaver Island is clearly on the map for tourism. Fortunately, it's small enough that, with due care, in years to come the island just might get it right. "We've worked really hard on the island to protect our habitat; it doesn't just happen," Grassmick says, and provides me an example of such effort paying off. "On our shoreline, we had about thirty acres of phragmites [an invasive perennial reed grass] growing on it—we don't have any right now. That's what happens if you get on top of things."

....

The resolute Beaver Island environmentalist recommends I get in touch with Sheri Richards, an associate broker with Real Estate One who works out of the Charlevoix/Beaver Island office. She's a forty-six-year-old mother of four boys. Her husband, Adam, is a middle and high school social studies/business education teacher at Beaver Island Community School. They moved to the island in 2009.

My phone call to Richards on the afternoon of February 21, 2023, catches her at the Costco in Traverse City with a full cart. She politely asks if she can call me back once she checks out. I am merciful, having reluctantly accompanied my wife to the consumer warehouse on a number of occasions, always an anxiety-inducing experience. Besides, Costco isn't conducive to interviewing.

She begins our conversation by informing me that "a lot of the [housing] inventory has been bought up over the last few years." In the spring of 2021, seventy-two homes were for sale on Beaver Island. "Today there are sixteen," she reveals. By her count, about 350 homes dot the island's forty-five miles of waterfront along Lake Michigan. Home sales there accelerated in 2019, just before the pandemic, she recalls, "the largest increase since the housing market crash in 2008." She describes the island as being "an ideal place for someone to live and work remotely."

When the pandemic struck, people across the country began to explore the option of working remotely and searched through real estate websites such as Zillow and short-term rental sites like Vrbo. "People would tell me all the time that they found Beaver Island just by exploring on Google Maps," she says. Some callers inquire about available island properties without having their directional bearings. "I can't tell you how many people have reached out to me through Vrbo and asked, 'How far is it to the Tahquamenon Falls?' Well, we're sort of an island, like, you can't really drive there," she laughs. (Tahquamenon Falls is in Michigan's Upper Peninsula.)

Thanks to technological advancements since Richards began her real estate career, virtual showings have proven to be a useful tool for working with potential buyers on the mainland and across the country. Information is available at homebuyers' fingertips without having to make an in-person exploratory trip. These technological conveniences have only accelerated interest in the island.

Beaver Island Boat Company's Tim McQueer says, "Building on the island really took off the last few years and I expect that it will continue." BIBCO not only ferries people and vehicles but supplies of all kinds, as well as construction materials. Richards says that as of February 2023, the island's handful of home-building contractors are booked well into 2026. New property owners who can't wait sometimes bring in their own off-island teams of construction workers, which includes Amish work crews. Whatever the case, Richards notes, "There are a number of projects being worked on all the time."

Although Richards estimates that the average price of a home on Beaver Island is approximately $385,000, many of the newer homes, especially those recently built along the lakeshore, are well beyond the reach of the average family. These are predominantly second homes, vacation properties on Lake Michigan. "Those homes will never be affordable homes," she says.

Richards also has a second business, a short-term rental management company. She says there are roughly fifty short-term rental properties on the island. I mention the controversies surrounding Vrbo and Airbnb on northern Michigan's mainland, especially with poorly behaving renters disrupting the locals' peace. She responds pragmatically, "The reality is, you will always have neighbors who are annoying and do things that you don't like." One of the properties she manages, on an inland lake, had a neighbor who complained to her about renters shooting off fireworks, trashing the lake, and playing loud music. After some investigating, Richards discovered that the homeowner had been there that week. "It wasn't a renter causing all this disturbance—it was your neighbor. People will be people, won't they?" I admire her "que sera, sera" attitude. If only it could be boxed and sold.

Before I get off the call, the Beaver Island real estate broker mentions how interesting "this whole phenomenon is." Specifically, tourist towns throughout the region, such as Traverse City and Charlevoix, as well as Beaver Island, "have all worked so hard to attract people to come north to vacation here. For the last fifteen or twenty years we've been pushing it. They've been so successful that the shoulder seasons have now become almost a year-round experience, at least for Traverse City."

Although she is a Realtor and rental property manager, Richards is also an island resident. She shares her fear regarding an increasing "demand of newcomers." She questions whether there's a solid foundation established to plan for the island's future when it comes to the growth of tourism and interest in building vacation homes. "And of course, we all market it and want commerce," Richards candidly admits. Zoning is not well enforced on the island, she says, which is no doubt attractive to those wanting to build a home there. "The island is so untouched and beautiful. I would hate to see someone come and just take that away in a blink of an eye." Richards characterizes the island as "paradise." Whether you're a native islander, a transplant as she is, or tourist, her observation is absolutely true.

Richards would hate for Beaver Island to become another Mackinac Island. The looming question is, how to keep it that way while accommodating the visitors that mean so much to Beaver Island's economy. She recently served on an affordable housing committee for Beaver Island. The committee had conversations with a sister group on Mackinac. They said, somewhat ominously, "You're about thirty to forty years behind us." During the summer, tourists swarm Mackinac Island (where, interestingly, automobiles are not permitted and horse-drawn carriages and bicycles predominate), long a tourist destination. The 388-room Grand Hotel there has been in business since 1887 (and recently underwent an extensive remodeling).[14] According to the Mackinac Island Tourism Bureau, the island hosts more than one million visitors each year.[15] Yet residents fearing the worst for Beaver Island a la Mackinac Island aren't being realistic, maintains LeFevre-Welke. "We're thirty-five miles out on the lake; we're a two-hour ferry ride. We couldn't be more polar opposite."

Richards finishes our talk by telling me that living on the island is unimaginable. To those who try to get her impression, she says, "You know, you've just got to be here." When there are only six-hundred-plus locals in midwinter and the cold winds are howling and the lake effect snow is relentless, the romantic attraction of island life for someone who has relocated there may be short-lived; or perhaps, it's just perfect. Then she gives me a clue as to what it's like to call Beaver Island home: "On some nights, it feels like the Milky Was is pressing down like a blanket. It's incredible."

Star Party

When we co-owned a lakeside cottage on Spider Lake southeast of Traverse City in the early 2000s, I never knew that an observatory was in the vicinity, so close to North Garfield Road. Yet twenty years later, I'm driving uphill after turning south off Brimley Road, making my way toward Northwestern Michigan College's Joseph H. Rogers Observatory, which sits about 250 feet higher than the surrounding area and is located approximately six miles south of the NMC campus.[16] I'm going to my first "star party."

I've been invited by Jerry Dobek, astrophysicist and head of NMC's science and astronomy departments, to visit the observatory during its monthly public open house, or star party. Members of the Grand Traverse Astronomical Society are gathering when I arrive about 9 p.m. on Friday, August 5. Older men are ambulating into the hilltop building. Darkness is coming. (A clear dark sky is a must for a successful star party. Otherwise, the worst can happen, as the society's November 12, 2022, Facebook post sadly announced: "Family Night canceled due to clouds.")[17] But optimum stargazing darkness takes a while to advance during the northern Michigan summer, as Traverse City is located just below the 45th parallel.

As I walk into the observatory with a society member, I tell him that I'm here to speak with Dobek about light pollution's effect on the region. Without hesitating, he says, "Light pollution. Oh my God, yes. You need to talk to Jerry."

Dobek could have played a cameo role on *The Big Bang Theory* and fit right in. He's wearing a black Hubble Space Telescope T-shirt with an image of Saturn. His longish, gray, mildly wild hair is seventies vintage. Although I'm a bit concerned that he might be a brainiac like Dr. Sheldon Cooper and respond to my questions in astronomical technobabble, Dobek knows how to smoothly dumb it down for mere Earthlings like me. He also has a dry sense of humor, exemplified in his answer to my question inquiring about his age: "I have been on your planet now for 64.5 revolutions around the Sun."

As soon as I take a seat in the observatory's classroom, Dobek instinctively approaches the chalkboard and begins explaining light pollution, using rapidly composed dry-erase marker sketches to help illustrate proper lighting to avoid/mitigate "light trespass." As he lectures, I glance about the room. Several Celestron and Meade telescopes are here and there, as well as planetary models. Twelve ancient Dell desktop computers sit atop tables along one wall. Eyes front, I remind myself. Twenty minutes later and me a bit wiser we go outside, as darkness is descending and the volunteers are setting up their telescopes for the public to stargaze. It's clear but hazy due to the high humidity; not ideal night sky viewing, but it will do.

As I look to the west toward Chums Corners, near the intersection of U.S. 31 and M-37, I see the glow of Turtle Creek Stadium about four miles away, home of Traverse City's minor league baseball team, the Pit Spitters. Some impressive commercial grade fireworks are going off. It's a celebration marking the last home game of the season. It's pretty. It adds to the ambiance for the fans—and to the light pollution for sky watchers.

The array of telescopes is now set up. A bespectacled volunteer enters the outdoor viewing area, wearing bib overalls and a flannel shirt, with a bushy gray beard and unkempt hair. Asked how he's doing by a fellow society member, he says, "I'm here. I guess that's good." Then he looks around, points upward toward the southwest sky, and announces, "And for you new people here, that's the moon." Everyone laughs. To the north, the handle of the Big Dipper is beginning to materialize. I'm hoping to see a Perseid meteor or two, as the annual shower has been going on for weeks now, and we're approaching its peak. The bright half-moon isn't helping, though, bleaching out some of the sky. I look toward the meteor shower's radiant—the point of origin—in the constellation of Perseus, near Cassiopeia—the "W" constellation in the north sky. Nothing. At least, not yet.

A young father has brought his two children to the star party. A volunteer tries to encourage the youngsters to look through a sixteen-inch telescope, but their shyness is winning. Eventually, with the prodding of dad, the youngest boy, about four, steps up the short ladder and peers through the eyepiece. He's sees craters on the moon for the first time. "Wow!" he effuses, delighted by the celestial view. The society's star parties can draw up to sixty visitors. Tonight, there are less than ten. And they're getting a lot of attention from the society members, who freely share their passion for astronomy. Attendees are "fairly knowledgeable about astronomy, or would like to be," Dobek tells me.

I learn that the observatory's largest telescope gathers 4,096 times as much light as the unaided eye, meaning stars and planets appear about 4,100 times brighter through the optical magnification. Dobek explains, "We can see small craters on the moon—not the flags left there [by American Apollo mission astronauts]—and galaxies out to about two hundred million light years. The latter may appear as faint fuzzy smudges, but they are detectable." In a small act of engineering genius, he transfers the images of heavenly bodies captured on a fourteen-inch telescope behind the observatory to a security camera connected to the telescope, then shows them to sky watchers across the country participating via Zoom videoconference.

The volunteer in the flannel shirt walks over and hands me a DVD with a content note written in black Sharpie: "NOVA, July 13, 2022: Ultimate Space Telescope." It contains photos from the James Webb Space Telescope. "You won't believe these images," he says, conveying his sense of awe as he distributes copies to each visitor.

....

Dobek confirms that light pollution has indeed grown worse above Traverse City and Grand Traverse County over the past several decades. More people, more lights. He says that light pollution really became noticeable, and problematic, in the eighties.

The NMC astronomer is one of the three founding members of the International Dark Sky Association. The impetus was to help develop city ordinances to regulate lighting to mitigate light pollution. "Left on their own, Earthlings—I mean, humans—are self-destructive," he quips. "So they have to have guidance, which means we need to have rules and regulations, ordinances and zoning."

In 1989, Dobek wrote the first lighting ordinance for a Michigan township (White-water Township in Grand Traverse County), which he claims is his best because it's so simple. "You can hand it to an eight-year-old, and he can read the ordinance and understand what it means. Basically, it defines what's a bulb, what's a fixture, and what's meant by full cutoff—shining light downward" (not the light-polluting outward or upward directions).

Dobek also assisted Garfield Township, just south and west of Traverse City, with standards for LED billboards. "They're extremely bright and overpower the sun during the daytime," he explains. "They don't have to be so bright at night, as all they have to overpower is the moon and car headlights." He proudly notes, "What we did in Garfield went national as far as a standard for billboard illumination for LEDs." Dobek's near-obsession with keeping the night sky viewable has led him to author or co-author fifty-three lighting ordinances in Michigan alone, as well as assist with those developed for several other states.

"Enforcement is the biggest issue: if you have an ordinance, you've got to get people out there to enforce it. This seems to be the biggest hurdle. And the education piece that goes with it. People are not aware that their lighting is a problem until you tell them or educate them." More lighting isn't better lighting. It's all about "visual acuity," he emphasizes. Targeted, just-enough, downward lighting is key.

....

In 2022, I stayed at our cottage in Cedar from late April through mid-October. Every night I paused to look up at the night sky. On the clearest of nights, the Milky Way would emerge in all its glittering grandeur. Most of my neighbors have modest outdoor lighting or turn off all their lights once they turn in. Eventually, it's densely black. The night critters are noisy; they're in their element. Some of our guests from ever-glowing Indy are disturbed by the Up North night, as they're so accustomed to the city's pervasive darkness-combatting street and security lights. In Indianapolis, the Milky Way is no-where in sight, other than the primary constellations. During the Perseid Meteor Shower, which runs from mid-July through most of August, I sit on my deck in Cedar and peer through the opening in the towering sugar maples that surround our cottage, waiting for those cosmic streaks of white, and I'm never disappointed. It had been decades since I saw a Perseid in Indianapolis, that is, until August 2020, when driving had curtailed dramatically, thanks to the pandemic, and consequently, so did the collective vehicular light glow and air pollution. Still, seeing the Milky Way from Indy remained out of the question, as it does yet today. I mention this to Dobek. City folks, he says, "don't know what they're missing because they never had a chance to experience it."

The less-light evangelist provides a mini-lecture on LED, low-kelvin, solar-powered, full-cutoff lighting that's being installed at the Historic Barns Park's 110-foot parking lot near The Village at Grand Traverse Commons. The energy-efficient, dusk-to-dawn, 3000 kelvin lamps with 2250 lumen LED fixtures have almost no carbon footprint. "After twenty-five years, you may have to replace the battery," he says. These cooler temperature, downward-casting lights are a boon to those concerned about preserving dark skies. Dobek says this "color-corrected temperature" lighting is devoid of the warmer blue light that disrupts humans' circadian patterns and disturbs birds and plant life. Once this night-sky-friendly outdoor lighting is fully in place at the Historic Barns, Dobek, who's been talking with several township planners in the region, will use this project as an example to get his point across. He enthuses, "Here's the best part: in this parking lot, I walked over by my Jeep and there's an eighteen-foot light; I was about sixty-five feet away from that light. I looked up and I found five of the seven stars in the Little Dipper. I'm in a lit parking lot, and I can look up at the sky and see stars. This is the way we need to do it."

These custom outdoor LED lights aren't cheap—as of this writing running about $4,000 apiece. But they have an estimated thirty years of life and use no electricity, so the cost-benefit equation is advantageous in the long run.

Dobek is point-blank about the peril that lies ahead should the region not pay attention to light pollution: the Milky Way "is going to be gone." Farther north, the Headlands International Dark Sky Park, several miles east of Wilderness State Park and just two miles from Mackinaw City, is at risk due to outdoor lighting in both Mackinaw City and Petoskey. He says they are "becoming problem areas." Meanwhile, in a positive development, Dobek is working with Sleeping Bear Dunes National Lakeshore to get it designated as an International Dark Sky Park, which will include the Manitou Islands. "It will be the largest

Dark Sky Park east of the Mississippi River," he says. Each late summer and early fall, the National Lakeshore is a star party location for the Grand Traverse Astronomical Society.

....

Dobek, who first taught as an adjunct in 1987 and became a full-time instructor in 2001, teaches three astronomy courses: a stellar class, a planetary class, and in the summertime, Observational Astronomy. I ask if his students have changed over time in their understanding of astronomy upon entry into his courses. "Yes. Some of it good; some of it not so good. Lots of misconceptions and preconceptions. I try to teach them the basics. Sometimes it's difficult to get them to understand what causes the phases of the moon, regardless of going over it time and time again. Invariably, they can't get it in their heads that it's the Earth that's blocking the light from reaching the moon. And seasons: seasons occur because of the tilt of the Earth. They have this thing about distance that they will just not let go of."

Yet I'm convinced that one thing his students will come away with is a greater appreciation for the wonders of the night sky, and that he will hammer home how light pollution threatens that extraordinary view in northern Michigan, and how to contribute to keeping the night sky dark and the Milky Way prominent. Dobek's proselytizing is essentially a message of hope.

The NMC astronomy professor believes that most people are reasonable when they learn they've been shining too much light in their neighborhoods, invading other people's space and reducing the visibility of the night sky. "When you go talk to your neighbors and say, 'Okay, the lights that you're using are becoming obtrusive, and I'd like to enjoy the nighttime sky,' more than 75 percent of them will go, 'Wow, I didn't realize.' And they'll work with you on it." As is ever his refrain, "It's an education process."

In a follow-up email, Dobek tells me that he grew up watching all the space launches, and is still watching: from Alan Shepard Jr., the first American in space, to today's SpaceX rocket launches. (He even met Shepard while the former astronaut was in northern Michigan filming a commercial for AT&T.) As a child, he was curious as to how dragonflies at night could move so fast, and his mother explained that he was seeing shooting stars—meteors—not flying insects. This childhood revelation only increased his fascination with science. He's been staring into telescopes since the age of seven, when he received his first at Christmas. Dobek's father constantly told his mother, and not derogatorily, "That kid's got nothing but space in his head." Now look what he's doing: getting the word out about how to reduce light trespass in northern Michigan and preserve that spectacular night sky view.

....

As the clock approaches 11 p.m., I take my leave of the star party. When I drive into Cedar, it's dead, though business security lights are ablaze. When I reach Manor Green, my neighborhood, there are no streetlights, my headlights torching a path through the dark. One residence has a campfire going, a home that's now a short-term rental. Since most of the workweek is done, some TV screens are aglow in otherwise darkened homes. I sit on an Adirondack chair on our deck, eyes to the stars. In just a few minutes, as if match-lit, a meteor streaks across the sky, gone in a flash. I smile in wonder, just as our ancient ancestors surely did. Then keep watch for just one more.

The Greatest Toy Store in the Galaxy

In mid-May 2022, I visited the Enerdyne science and nature store in Suttons Bay for a scheduled interview with store owner Dick Cookman. (Enerdyne is the conjoining of two scientific terms: "*Ener* relates to energy," he explained, "and *dyne* is the unit of force in the metric system.") He directed me to a small, nondescript back room, and I wore a mask, as all Enerdyne employees and customers must, a protocol Enerdyne has maintained throughout the pandemic. Cookman, who is in his later years, was double-masked. He's a scientist, so his care regarding viral transmission was no surprise. Surprisingly, the interview went just twenty minutes, which was all the time he allotted—he needed to meet with a customer.

I return on a Monday in mid-July, Cookman's usual day off, to have one of his salespeople show me around to get that unique Enerdyne experience. Unexpectedly, Cookman is there, preoccupied behind the optics counter, which features telescopes, field scopes, and binoculars, perhaps "the largest selection in the Midwest," he informs me later. "Me again," I announce through my mask, breaking his concentration. "I'm here to bother you with some more questions, if you have a few minutes." I'm unsure what to expect.

Bespectacled, he smiles through his masks, his bushy white beard protruding beneath them, slowly rises, straightening out to his over six-foot height, and says warmly, "You're no bother." He's wearing an unbuttoned short-sleeved collared shirt with a black T-shirt beneath it depicting constellations, Orion in the center of his chest. For the next half hour or so I'm a child again, captivated by Cookman's wonderland store and its myriad entrancing items.

As we get started with my guided tour, I ask if people are paying more attention to science nowadays. "Some people. And then you've got all the anti-science people out. They come in and I ask them to put on a mask and they say, 'Well, I don't wear a mask.' And when they leave, we say, 'good.' I consider it to be a pretty neat way of having a cover charge."

Enerdyne's business hasn't suffered since the start of the pandemic; in fact, it was helped by the outbreak. "People didn't have anything to do, so they would think, 'I always wanted a telescope. And now I can't go out to parties and stuff, so maybe I'll pursue astronomy or birdwatching or whatever.'" I ask his thoughts on climate change. He says, "When you bring up climate change, it's like masks." Enough said.

What's the best-selling stuff for the kids? "It's all over the map," Cookman answers. "We don't carry a lot of toys but a lot of kits." He refers to Enerdyne's extensive inventory of books, kits, tools, and fossil and rock specimens as "Playthinks," with the aim of developing curious minds' scientific understanding of the Earth and the universe. The kits are "toys you have to build yourself. That's probably the top seller amongst the kids' stuff." Regarding adults, "we like to think we have toys for all ages."

I observe that Enerdyne embodies Cookman's lifelong passion for science. "Oh, yeah," he confirms. About halfway through his thirty-year astronomy, geology, and environmental science teaching career at Northwestern Michigan College, he and his wife, Pat, opened the store. "My wife ran it for a long time. Then when I retired, I came on full time." I comment that I'm not sure this really qualifies as work. He chuckles knowingly. And he's had a great run. As of 2023, Enerdyne, is in its forty-second year of operation.

"The philosophy behind the store is that when a lot of kids take a science class, it turns out to be a vocabulary class, and they don't really do science," Cookman explains. "The reason we have this place is to show them how much fun science is." Science learning should be hands-on, he insists. Then, ever ready with a joke, he asks, "You know what they call a person who plays with toys all day long? A scientist."

Cookman leads me behind the optics counter. "Have a look through this scope." It's a large Celestron. "You can easily see the other side of the bay." I can indeed. The clarity is remarkable as I watch a windsurfer cruising out on Suttons Bay. "You might be able to see some chairs over there. That's over two miles away." All day long Cookman is the mild-mannered seller of science. He enhances my experience with the scope by providing ever more detail. "That's a thirty-one power. It's set up as a spotting scope." It's ideal for birders looking at species that are far away, I suggest while marveling at the scope's reach. He nods. I'm not buying today, but when I decide on acquiring a spotting scope, I know exactly where to go to get all my questions answered. And to leave some significant cash behind.

....

Cookman serves as the astronomer on the autumn evening tall-ship schooner sails for Inland Seas Education Association in Suttons Bay. "I introduce people to the constellations, sort of using them as a theme to delve rather deeply into astronomy. So when we talk about Scorpius, I can talk about Antares as a red super giant, and from there we can get into things like neutron stars and black holes and supernovas. And every one of those constellations has something going on; it has a whole story attached to it in terms of the science behind it." I ask him an obvious question—if he's geeked about the first batch of James Webb Space Telescope images. He pipes up, "Yeah, yeah. In a few places on the Internet, they put what the Hubble did on a particular object and then right below or above it they posted the new ones—and there's a huge, huge difference," he says with childlike glee.

I ask Cookman to show me around the rocks. But there are rocks, and then there are stones. "Stones have been worked by humans; rocks haven't," he informs me as we approach the glass display cases in the back of the store. Once they've been polished, then they're stones, such as the lustered agates and rose quartz I find myself immediately admiring. "We do have, of course, lots of Michigan stuff, mainly from the UP." There are hunks of labradorite with fantastic striations of vibrant blue. Samples of the quartzite and jasper conglomerate puddingstone. Globs of shiny native copper, which when mined didn't have to be smelted to remove impurities. And otherworldly amethyst and citrine geode towers.

Cookman is eager to talk about his sodalite specimens. "They glow in the dark. They're finding them around here too." This surprises me, as I was under the impression that "Yooperlites," as they're nicknamed, are found only along the shores of Lake Superior. Yooperlites are detected in the dark by using UV (ultraviolet) flashlights to illuminate the fluorescent veins of sodalite in feldspar rocks. It looks like lava. They were initially "discovered" by a rockhounding Yooper (a resident of Michigan's Upper Peninsula). His finds were analyzed and confirmed by geologists at Michigan Technological University in 2018.[18] Now even the Pure Michigan tourism and travel website promotes the latest thing in Great Lakes rock hunting—a uniquely nighttime undertaking.[19]

Then we move to the fossils. "Okay, this guy right here was a straight nautiloid. They lived back in the early Paleozoic, four hundred million years ago or so. Their modern descendant is the chambered nautilus. Basically, they're related to the squid and the octopi. Each year, they would build their shell out a little farther and move into the new abode and build a wall behind them, and all the walls are set to create individual chambers connected by this large tube called a siphuncle. Like the musical group Garmin and Siphuncle." He just can't help himself, as he concludes his overview of the straight-shelled nautiloid.

Next, we examine his trilobite fossils. Although I've found fragments of trilobites in southern Indiana on a school outing with my son, Matt, decades ago while climbing the side of a steep roadcut caked with fossils, I've never touched an intact specimen. I am touching one now—a several-inches-long trilobite Phacops fossil, a marine arthropod that lived during the Paleozoic era (541–252 million years ago).[20] It's for sale, along with others, ranging from $15 to $24. I'm tempted. But buying a fossil strikes me as strange. Finding them is more than half of the fun.

"Here's a Petoskey stone," he indicates. I'm well acquainted with the fossilized stone, having brought hundreds of them back to our cottage, out on loan from Mother Nature. However, this is the biggest I've seen yet, nearly the size of a basketball. As with this specimen, some of the store's rocks, stones, and fossils are for display only, part of the Cookmans' private collection. I imagine that their home must be another version of Enerdyne.

The store also carries a slew of nature books and guides. Fiftieth anniversary copies of Rachel Carson's iconic *Silent Spring* are prominently displayed. John McPhee titles are near the geology display cases, as is Simon Winchester's *Krakatoa: The Day the World Exploded: August 27, 1883*, the story of a catastrophic volcanic eruption in Indonesia. Notably, Enerdyne offers books that tell visitors where to go hiking in the region, such as *The Trails of M-22* and *On the Trails of Northern Michigan*. I almost cringe. Almost. Telling visitors exactly where to go to experience the best that northern Michigan's outdoors has to offer is almost disturbing. Decades ago, when I began to explore the area, there were no books disclosing these prime locations. Nor was there Google Maps to geolocate these places for us. We had to find them ourselves, relying on our own instincts and curiosity, as well as a little help from some local friends. Discovery seemed to be a higher art form then. But I remind myself that I'm falling into the trap of generational bias. The concept of discovery is a constant; how we go about it changes with advancements in technology.

As we meander about the store, I'm suddenly taken back thirty-five years to when I purchased a package of glow-in-the-dark plastic star cutouts from Enerdyne on our first visit to Suttons Bay in 1988. When we returned to Indy, I adhered them to my then-six-year-old son's bedroom ceiling, setting up patterns reflecting the Big Dipper, Cassiopeia, and Orion. Each evening we "stargazed" together for a few minutes before his bedtime.

"Did you see this?" Cookman asks invitingly. He shows me the constellation projector that will cover ceilings with impressions of sixty thousand stars. I find myself uttering "wow" a lot during this visit. The slowly rotating star field occasionally displays a meteor blazing across its projection range. It also has alternative disks that can show the constellation figures from Greek and Roman mythology. My wallet is humming; I gotta get out of here.

Cookman tells me he's lived all over the Western Hemisphere, much of his travels occurring when he was young, his father a freelance civil engineer for international hire. As for Leelanau County, he says, "I haven't really found another place that exceeds this area in terms of natural beauty. And the people up here are pretty good people." He characterizes Enerdyne's clientele as being "fairly educated, they're interested in the outdoors, and we share a lot of interests."

As I leave, I spot a photo of two flying saucers floating above Enerdyne, on display at the optics counter. "I can't believe that happened here," I blurt, laughing at the photoshopped image. Cookman remarks, "I tell people that they hover right over Jefferson Street and materialize right about where you are. Then they pull out their probes, and I'm in for three hours of unmitigated pain."

CHAPTER 10

EVERY DAY IS EARTH DAY

In 1855 . . . an Indian chief, a leader of the Cayuse of what is now Oregon, refused to sign a treaty because he felt that it excluded the voice of the Earth: "I wonder if the ground has anything to say?" he asked.

—Amitav Ghosh, *The Nutmeg's Curse:*
Parables for a Planet in Crisis

I t's early April. We're just a few weeks out from Earth Day on the twenty-second of the month. I'm old enough to remember the inaugural Earth Day, which took place in 1970. I was fourteen years old, a ninth grader at Belzer Junior High School in Lawrence, Indiana, a suburban community just northeast of Indianapolis. Back then, my three-packs-a-day, gas-guzzler-driving parents could never be accused of being environmentalists. Although we were taught not to litter, beyond that, we received no training about taking care of Mother Earth. Earth Day, however, as enthusiastically promoted by our bell-bottomed teachers, planted a seed. I ended up marrying an environmentalist, one of those tree-hugging socialist libs who keeps me ever conscious of my responsibilities to the planet, though complain on occasion that I do, personal ecoterrorist that she can be.

I've always been attracted to water and the creatures who call it home. Even here in central Indiana. I've fished in the often chocolate-colored water of the White River, though never keeping the caught catfish, suckers, carp, or smallmouth bass for eating, their bodies containing toxins, notably PCBs (polychlorinated biphenyls) and mercury. The river is saturated with farm runoff throughout the growing season, thus its typically opaque appearance. It's also contaminated by high levels of *E. coli* (*Escherichia coli*) bacteria, making swimming a strongly discouraged activity. Once, during a party at a house on the White River in the eighties, I impulsively decided to swim across it. The river was in its shallow summer pool stage, reaching no more than five feet deep at our northside location. It took me less than ten minutes to cross and return. When I emerged, my body had broken out in an itchy red rash. That was the first and last time I would swim in that stream. Decades later, the White River is still polluted, and advisories warning about eating its fish remain in place.[1]

When I return to northwest lower Michigan each spring, I use any excuse I can to get near the fresh water. To see and float on it, wade and swim in it. I marvel at all of it: Lake Michigan, inland lakes, rivers, even three-foot wide, twelve-inch-deep creeks, cold and clean enough for brook trout to thrive. Northern Michiganders cherish their waters and support the many nonprofit organizations that do their best to keep them ecologically healthy for all of us, forever. Those with an environmentalist's heart think that every day should be Earth Day. Shouldn't we all?

River Walk

When I first heard the term, I was puzzled: what the heck is a "baykeeper"? In the fresh-water playground that is northern Michigan, one should know such things. Therefore, I reached out to the Watershed Center Grand Traverse Bay to see if I might spend some time with theirs.

So I could truly understand her role, Heather Smith, the Watershed Center's baykeeper since 2016, invited me to a "walk and talk" along the Boardman-Ottaway River on a sunshiny mid-June morning in 2022. We rendezvous at the Traverse Area Recreational Trail where the river enters Boardman Lake. Although we haven't met before, I recognize her from the center's website's staff photo. Her blonde ponytail sticks out from beneath her baseball cap as she looks about in her dark sunglasses for the writer who's just a few minutes behind, parking not that easy to come by in the congested area.

We get acquainted while taking in the view of the Boardman-Ottaway, standing on an abnormally perfect patch of weedless lawn. Then Smith suggests we get on with our walking and talking, moving toward the riverbank path. Along the way, we'll pass condominiums and apartments crowding the shoreline, visit the Union Street Dam, the location of the proposed FishPass, and make our way over to Hannah Park. Smith knows the area well, regularly monitoring the Boardman-Ottaway for signs of water quality concern. Part of her role involves public presentations, so she speaks in layperson's terms for me, providing clear explanations of foreign terminology before I even have to ask for translation.

"The term 'baykeeper' comes from the Waterkeeper Alliance, a global water advocacy nonprofit," she explains. The alliance's aim is for "swimmable, fishable, and drinkable water." There are more than three hundred waterkeepers across the globe that advocate for clean water, ensuring that local and federal clean water laws are upheld. Smith's "hyper-local-scale" focus is on the Grand Traverse Bay watershed, roughly 976 square miles in northwest lower Michigan, including most of Grand Traverse, Leelanau, Kalkaska, and Antrim counties.[2] Smith reports that the watershed holds 9.9 trillion gallons or 8.97 cubic miles of water.

Launched in 1994, the Watershed Center, with a staff of four and a cadre of volunteers, monitors the embayment's water quality, ever on the lookout for threats that could jeopardize it, and Smith's in-person observations are a significant part of that effort. The center develops and implements watershed protection plans, which includes water pollution prevention and habitat protection measures. As well, it provides guidance for streambank restoration and stormwater management projects. The center also offers expert environmental consultation on commercial and residential developments to reduce their impact on the watershed, including advice on erosion mitigation and habitat protection.[3]

The Watershed Center's baykeeper also focuses on policy and advocacy efforts. Smith presents at local planning commission, township board, and city commission meetings to ensure that zoning ordinances are followed by developers and ecologically friendly best practices are used on projects that stand to impact the watershed. Take coal tar sealants, for example, used on driveways and parking lots. "Coal tar versus asphalt-based sealants have a really high concentration of polycyclic aromatic hydrocarbons, or PAHs," she explains. "We encouraged our state agency, the Department of Environment, Great Lakes, and Energy (EGLE), to do some studies on the Boardman-Ottaway River here, looking at PAHs and riverine sediments. And they were really high. They're toxic to aquatic life and are a human health concern; it's a carcinogenic compound." So the Watershed Center collaborated with Traverse City's leadership in developing a ban on the sale and use of coal tar sealants, assisting with developing language for a public relations campaign. This effort included contacting sealant companies in the region to encourage safer alternatives.

Part of Smith's job is to respond to citizen concerns. One frequent call involves dead fish washing up on homeowners' lake frontage, and they want to know why. She had numerous calls about this in early June, most attributable to the alewife die-off during the spring spawning season, a natural occurrence (though much more pronounced than usual in 2022). Or they're concerned about erosion and want advice. Or they want to know what the plant life is growing along their shoreline. Or how concerned should they be about microbeads (tiny plastic particles found in, for example, body washes and toothpastes) in the bay.[4] Or are there any safe weedkillers to use along waterfront property. "I want people to have a better understanding of our water bodies, our rivers, lakes, streams, and wetlands," she says, welcoming all such queries that contribute to keeping Grand Traverse Bay and its tributaries clean. Although she presents to K-12 students about her role with the Watershed Center, adult outreach is foremost on her agenda. "Most of the public education explaining ecological processes is for adults, citizens who are making decisions about their shoreline." Optimistically, she adds, "Maybe people are starting to pay attention."

Smith understands that many township board members and planning commissioners are not experts on riparian matters. That's her wheelhouse, and she's happy to meet with these officials to explain the stakes and provide helpful advice to aid in their policy development and decision making.

Within the Grand Traverse Bay watershed there are forty-four townships in eleven municipalities. So due to the Watershed Center's few staff members, she has to be strategic about where to focus her energy. Worth noting, not all developers are receptive to her environmentally responsible suggestions, so diplomacy is critical. "We have to be very careful about giving our seal of approval. We won't say we're supportive of this development; we'll say we're supportive of these shoreline trees."

....

I tell Smith that in preparing for our walk, I read most of the three-hundred-plus pages "Coastal Grand Traverse Bay Watershed Plan," published in May 2021. Though it was highly informative, I found it disturbing, given the number of threats to the watershed from stormwater, erosion, sedimentation, invasive species, toxins, and pathogens, even thermal pollution.[5] Smith sympathizes with me. "It is spooky and can be depressing thinking about it." She continues, "By far the biggest threat in our region is the immense development pressure. That's the biggest threat on aquatic habitat and water quality." She says the center "has to walk a very fine line. We're not anti-development; we just want to promote ecologically sensitive development. Everybody up here is here for the water. We value water. But why isn't water in the center of that decision-making process?"

A big part of the public awareness challenge is the ever-clearing cerulean blue water of Grand Traverse Bay, courtesy of the invasive zebra and quagga mussels. "People just generally think that we don't have a problem here," she comments. "We do. If we're not going to do anything and just do that status quo development and behavior, then it's going to be too late. We're going to have Lake Erie on our hands, and then it's going to take decades to undo that. So we want to preserve and protect what we have now."

Smith explains how important riparian vegetation is. People tend to want to clean up "this unruly, unkempt, unmanaged vegetation." The center hears this from residents, municipal staff, commissioners. Yet there isn't enough woody debris in the river system because of the removal of shoreline trees. "The natural progression is that a tree falls into the river and provides habitat, then algae colonize the woody substrate, and it becomes a source of food for the invertebrates, which of course are providing food for fish. It's such an important part of our river systems that we just don't see a lot of in our very developed spaces." The conversion process is challenging, especially in convincing those shoreline property owners who value manmade aesthetics over the workings of nature.

The setback issue is sometimes daunting as well. Many buildings are within twenty-five to fifty feet of the Boardman-Ottaway, yet some are but ten feet away. This wide variance is largely due to the lack of a state law regulating the shoreline-to-structure distance. "For instance, I would like to see all buildings, impervious surfaces, and other structures be ideally three hundred feet back from the riverbank," Smith indicates. However, she admits, "that's not realistic." On the section of the river we're now walking, most setbacks average around twenty-five feet. Waterfront "chem-lawns" are common, their fertilizer, herbicides, and insecticides washing into and contaminating the river. Yet some communities, she says, have landscaping ordinances for properties along the water, permitting only Michigan native species and forbidding invasive species.

"One of the things the city is working on right now is a riparian buffer zone," she says, "a series of ordinance provisions that would help establish some rules with what we call the water's edge setback." The Watershed Center has been in conversations with the city for several years in promoting the development of buffer zone regulations. Such setback ordinances would cover boardwalks (some of which she refers to as "boardwalks to nowhere"), decks, patios, parking lots, and maintained lawns. These decisions are "really complex," she says, especially when they involve multiuse developments in light of what's best for the river's ecology.

Smith points toward a "hardened shoreline" featuring sheet piling. The water's energy cannot be absorbed by the piling, so spring snowmelt will pour more water into the river and bounce along, its energy causing erosion. This specific area, she says, looks nice and she likes the bit of vegetation that remains, but significantly, mature trees have been removed. "It's that desire to create this very manicured look. We see it everywhere in landscaping and land use." She adds, "This British idea of the lawn has totally ruined so many of our waterways and our waterbodies."

The zero-lot-line crowding of shorelines is a common phenomenon along Grand Traverse Bay and becoming more frequent along inland lake properties, she comments. "Oftentimes, people that come from a more urban area may not understand the importance of keeping the trees or not totally making an artificial shoreline, putting in artificial sand beaches." This out-of-sync-with-nature mindset creates additional problems. The center sometimes receives complaints about trees and bushes blocking riverfront views and wanting them removed. Property owners with their first septic systems often don't know that the fields need to be pumped out periodically. Further, some short-term rental property owners stretch occupancies beyond their homes' capacities, which can contribute to freshwater contamination from overwhelmed septic systems. This, says Smith, is a growing problem in the watershed.

We pass several stormwater drains that empty into the river. There are many such outlets entering the Boardman-Ottaway and Grand Traverse Bay, she explains, locations for problems with *E. coli* and other pathogens that come from fecal contamination. During the summer, it's not unusual for public beaches in Traverse City to be under *E. coli* warnings immediately following a rain event, as stormwater drain outlets can be found in those locations, thereby flushing the bacteria into the bay. *E. coli* can cause diarrhea, stomach cramps, and vomiting.[6] Such notifications from the Grand Traverse County Health Department often surprise visitors, as the bay's clarity is so striking. Notably, *E. coli* water contamination can be attributed not just to human sources but also to other animals, such as raccoons and Canadian geese.

....

We walk along the Union Street Dam, the proposed site of FishPass. I ask if the fish in this stretch of the river are safe to eat. She diplomatically refers me to the "Eat Safe Fish Guide." I look it up online. For the Boardman-Ottaway upstream of the Union Street Dam, the only warnings—and just for mercury—pertain to northern pike, suckers, and walleye.[7] Being a trout angler, I receive the news with a sense of mixed relief.

Along the way, Smith mentions some of the Watershed Center's success stories, most notably the center's partnership with Munson Medical Center regarding stormwater management and how constructed sections of wetlands help treat runoff from the impervious asphalt pavement throughout the hospital campus. As a result, the water quality of Kids Creek, a tributary of the Boardman-Ottaway, is rebounding. Munson has also installed green roofs to assist with stormwater management. These roofs provide a host of other benefits, including contributing to biodiversity and reducing the heat generated by urban environments.[8]

Smith, who is "thirtyish" and the mother of two young daughters, and who also grew up on West Grand Traverse Bay, takes off her figurative baykeeper's hat to share her view that her generation is more focused on ecological issues than others, such as mine—boomers. As younger generations rise to leadership positions, more environmentally friendly development and building design is occurring, she maintains. "This new push for green infrastructure and low impact has really gained a lot of traction in the last ten years." I won't argue that my parents' generation, and that of my own, haven't made a mess of things. Her commentary is not falling on deaf ears.

In downtown Traverse City, we walk on a sidewalk next to condominiums built in the past few years. We stop as I show her one of my former favorite salmon-fishing spots. This once-preferred location, which I used to fish in relative solitude midweek without any competition, is now overshadowed by multistoried condominiums. There is an easement, she tells me, so I wouldn't be trespassing, but this is little consolation. Smith says sympathetically, "It's definitely that balance between providing access and respecting the environment." Riverside property is in especially high demand in Traverse City. Cynically, she adds, "Every square inch has to be utilized."

An hour and a half later, now back at our vehicles, Smith says the Watershed Center has been "really pushing for this idea of coastal resiliency and really focusing on planning efforts at the municipal level to ensure that we're ready to withstand and recover from what's going to happen in the Great Lakes' future, with water levels and coastal flooding and climate change and more intense storms." The expectation is more dramatic variability between water level highs and lows, with faster fluctuations. Once again, there's no statewide standard for setbacks on the Great Lakes, though individual communities set their own standards. This is tricky business, given the fluctuating water levels, especially seen in recent years and the near-record highs in 2020. Building waterfront homes during low-water years can be deceiving—and costly—once the Great Lakes rise. Commonsensically, Smith suggests, "If we can just realize that we need to step back from the Great Lakes; we just really need to allow the lakes to breathe."

Holy Is the Land

Northern Michigan has rebounded dramatically from the lumber industry's denuding of the pine forests in the late 1800s. Yet concern for the future of the area's natural resources keeps people like Glen Chown, executive director of the GTRLC, motivated to protect as much land as possible. Chown intends to "make good on the promise of forever" in preserving large tracts of land for future generations, which, he emphasizes, "is our most sacred trust with our supporters in the community."

In mid-May 2022, I meet Chown at the site of the conservancy's new headquarters, about a mile and a half south of East Grand Traverse Bay. It's an active construction site, with workers wearing hardhats as they go about their business, heavy machinery crawling about, and dust coating my just-washed pickup truck. No complaints, though. Pickup trucks should be filthy, even those owned by white-collar workers with soft, keyboard-pounding hands like mine.

The main attraction—the Conservation Center—is taking shape, with the exterior walls and roof in place. Inside, however, there's much work to be done. Chown is talking with the project manager when I arrive and waves to me as he wraps up his conversation. We shake hands. He's exuberant. I ask him how often he stops by to check on progress. "Lately, a lot; I'm just too excited." I get the impression his unrestrained excitement about the work and growth of the conservancy is nothing new, given the organization's ever-expanding footprint in the five-county Grand Traverse region. If anyone who's entering the field of nonprofit management needs a walking/talking example of what being "mission driven" means, look no further than Glen Chown. He lives and breathes it.

Chown is the first and only executive director to lead the GTRLC, launched in 1991. To date, the nonprofit has worked to protect more than forty-six thousand acres of land and nearly 150 miles of northern Michigan lake, river, and stream shoreline throughout the region.[9]

Dressed as if he's prepared for a hike, which he is—wearing a baseball cap, shorts, hiking boots, and a fern-green, short-sleeved button-down GTRLC shirt—the tall, talkative, Energizer Bunny–like Chown takes me on a walking tour of the property. The 204-acre parcel, formerly the Mitchell Creek Golf Course, still has deer stands, dilapidated now, dotting the area, where the previous owners used to allow friends and family members to hunt. We traverse open space now brimming with autumn olive, a pesky and tenacious invasive species. The $13 million Mitchell Creek Meadows: The Don and Jerry Oleson Nature Preserve, home of the Conservation Center, will feature goats that will take care of the olive bush invaders, Chown says. "They'll strip them and wipe them out. No herbicides.

It's the organic way and free labor. Who doesn't love goats?" he laughs. I ask who the goatherd will be. "Probably me," he answers jokingly, though I wouldn't be surprised. I don't yet know it, but we're heading for Vanderlip Creek, which flows into Mitchell Creek, a tributary of East Grand Traverse Bay.

At the creek, Chown tells me in a hushed, reverent tone that where we're standing is "a sacred spot" that one of his colleagues found while scoping out the property in 2019. The babbling brook is enchanting. Shafts of sunlight pour through openings in the low cedar-dominated canopy. We stand still for a few minutes. Eventually, we see several brook trout facing upstream beneath an undercut on the opposite bank, opportunistically waiting for their next meal to drift by. Although Mitchell Creek has suffered from environmental degradation due to commercial and residential development, Chown tells me this branch is "very clean, especially for how urban the area is." In days to come, he envisions school-children visiting the preserve to learn about watersheds and how to protect them, and to take water samples from the creek "and treat it as a classroom." We wait a few more minutes, both of us in no hurry to leave, observing fish time.

As we begin our return to the center, Chown turns around and points up to the ridge east of us above the creek—and to the active bald eagle nest just below it. He says the new conservancy property boasts six thousand feet of creek frontage. And he already wants to expand this preserve. The ridge property is for sale for several million dollars. "If you know anyone who wants to buy a ridge and donate it to us, we can use their help," he suggests, completely serious, ever trolling for possibility. There is no denying that Chown is a salesman. And what he's selling is what money can buy: permanent protection of natural settings that otherwise would be lost to development. He foresees the ridgetop property being targeted for housing. And why not: the view from there takes in Grand Traverse Bay in its entirety and Old Mission Peninsula. He's ever motivated by an underlying urgency to conserve all he can.

The conservancy is well positioned to act quickly in making land purchases. Its "quick-strike fund" enables it to show immediate interest in desirable conservation properties, with speed being critical in the current hot real estate market. "Usually, the developers have a lot of contingencies," he explains. "We don't, other than doing an environmental survey of everything we buy, of course. But we can do that very quickly." The other major contingency is financing. When the conservancy has its financing lined up, it can approach landowners of prime property before Realtors can get to them. One benefit of selling to the conservancy is the elimination of Realtor commissions when engaging the nonprofit directly. There's also a possible tax deduction involved against capital gains if the property is sold at a discount. And importantly, many landowners don't want to see their land developed. The conservancy is ready to accommodate their wish.

Chown is a visionary who believes nothing is beyond reach. For example, the conservancy plans to invite environmental speakers to give talks at its new digs. He asks me to name a famous environmentalist. I feel like I'm suddenly on *Jeopardy*. Greta Thunberg, the young, world-famous environmental activist from Sweden, immediately comes to mind. "Greta—yeah!" he congratulates me as if I answered correctly. "If she comes and does a whole thing on saving the planet, we can use all of this space," he says as we reenter the center and the area destined for conferences. "I really should have her out." I suspect that Chown could indeed secure Thunberg as a guest speaker appearing at the Conservation Center. I don't think the man has ever taken no for an answer.

Chown proudly shares that the Conservation Center is intended to be fully climate neutral. He refers to the project as a pioneering effort that will feature "the first water reuse system in all of Michigan." The rainwater harvesting system will collect water from the center's roof then filter and distribute it for irrigation and flush toilets. Outside, a solar array has been installed, which adjusts to the angle of the sun; it can also collect energy below reflected from snow. Smart electric panels will monitor, manage, and conserve solar energy. An electric geothermal heat pump system will heat and cool the building. Special protective glass with patterns visible to birds and undetectable by humans will help prevent avian mortality.[10] Electric vehicle charging stations will be installed. The grounds will also have a hiking trail system open to the public.

A greenhouse is also part of the plan. The conservancy has a partnership with the Smithsonian Institution, he says, which involves saving rare orchids—Michigan has more than fifty orchid species[11]—many of which are victims of the biodiversity crisis. The greenhouse will assist in native plant restoration, a key undertaking at GTRLC preserves. And the conservancy will put it to use in growing organic vegetables to support its work in providing nutritious produce to local food pantries to help combat food insecurity.

Conservancy supporters come from many age groups and demographics, often bearing little resemblance to the classic and much maligned tree-hugging stereotype. Says Chown, "It's all over: left wing, right wing, independents." Significantly, major donors tend to be snowbirds, multigenerational families, and "summer people"—tourists and other seasonal property owners. "They look at us as an organization that's preserving the context for these multigenerational traditions and experiences," he notes. Protect the watersheds, protect the farms, protect visitors and locals' favorite scenic views. When, like me, you come from a place that gives a backseat to nature, that rampantly develops land with little concern for nature's place in the scheme of things, and you experience northern Michigan's arresting great outdoors, pocketbooks are easily opened.

Although the conservancy is focused on land acquisition and protection, because its territory is the Grand Traverse region, this necessarily includes water as well. "If you survey the American people about their number one environmental issue, it's clean water," he asserts. "It trumps everything else. It cuts across all political lines; it's totally nonpartisan. It's like motherhood and apple pie."

....

After more than thirty years at the helm of the conservancy, Chown is finding his second wind. "We're not done," he declares with bold optimism. He imagines that the conservancy's holdings could grow to perhaps two hundred thousand acres over the next fifty-plus years. "Our prioritization maps show that if we're going to have the forests all connected and the watersheds all protected and lots of farmland protected, it's a lot more acreage. So, we've got to think ahead."

Out of concern for climate change, the conservancy established the 2051 Committee. Its role is to project out thirty years, "to think big and long term," he says. "We're focused on nature-based solutions to climate change. How do we get habitats like [Mitchell Creek Meadows] to function more efficiently? How do we keep forests intact? How do we restore habitats, so they store more carbon in the soil, like our grasslands?"

A serious climate change response calls for "a big protection piece," Chown maintains. "You have to protect corridors for plants and animals, the connector pieces between state forestlands and conservancy nature preserves. So that allows us to be a major player in addressing climate change in a way that: a) the public can feel good about because it's not controversial; and b) they feel like they can actually do something here. None of them are going to go and negotiate in Paris" (in reference to the United Nations' Paris Agreement on climate change). "None of them are going to drive to West Virginia and persuade [Sen.] Joe Manchin to get rid of his coal interests. But they can help us plant trees. They can write checks to help us buy important tracts of forests."

(Note: The Conservation Center opened on schedule in January 2023).

Climate Change Refuge in the Making

"While the Earth warms and America crumbles and a war is turning Ukraine to rubble and death, here in Benzie we're together. We're troubled like everyone we know. We're also safe." This is an excerpt from a post on journalist Keith Schneider's website, ModeShift, from a piece entitled "Moving to Benzonia."[12] For the past five years, Schneider and his wife, Gabrielle, had been spending much milder winters, by northern Michigan standards, at her home in Somerset, Kentucky, and the warmer months in his home of more than twenty years, in Benzonia, in Benzie County. "I don't need to be in Kentucky in the winter; I love winter," he declares, a sentiment commonly expressed by northern Michiganders who live here year-round. "We're finally back here full time, which is just groovy to me." He says he has but one understandable requirement from his transplanted wife: "Just promise to keep the heat on."

Schneider, sixty-seven, has had a long, esteemed career as a journalist, often covering environmental science and biotech, including more than forty years writing for the *New York Times*. He now serves as the senior editor and chief correspondent for Circle of Blue, a nonprofit with the tagline "Where water speaks." The Traverse City–based environmental news organization publishes journalism covering climate change, with an emphasis on the interrelated topics of "water, food, and energy."[13] In 1995, Schneider launched the Michigan Land Use Institute, a nonprofit located in Traverse City as well. It's now known as the Groundwork Center for Resilient Communities. The center promotes building environmentally conscious, clean, and economically sustainable communities, which includes advocacy for farming's central role in providing healthy, locally sourced food.[14]

I catch Schneider by phone while he's driving, just getting underway with a lengthy road trip. He's glad I called—to talk about an interconnected triad of some of his favorite subjects: the environment, climate change, and northwest lower Michigan—and to keep him company for a while.

Schneider had the good fortune to be interviewed by *the* Bob Woodward in the early eighties and ended up turning down a job as a suburban reporter for the *Washington Post*. By then, he was already being acknowledged for his quality journalism, receiving the George Polk Award (formerly awarded to such notables as Walter Cronkite, Edward R. Murrow, and James Baldwin), and writing for major publications. At the age of twenty-nine, he was hired by the legendary Abe Rosenthal to work out of the *New York Times* Washington bureau in the eighties.

Early in our conversation, Schneider interprets my project as having a significant political component, a focus I have intentionally tried to avoid, preferring a more middle-of-the-road approach. Different instincts guide us. He bluntly shares his views, relating that the political environment in Michigan is not helping the state in terms of its economy. "Michigan has developed a national reputation for being the Mississippi of the north," he states. But things are looking up, he says, with the current Democratic governor, secretary of state, and attorney general (and as of the 2022 election, the state's senate and house are controlled by Democrats). He also notes Leelanau County as being one of the rare conversions of a rural county from red to blue during the 2020 presidential election. A few minutes later he winds down with "I'm just saying that in northern Michigan, you have these bright blue town centers and then bright red rural areas. And Traverse City is so green—I call it the leftist Taliban up there. They're so doctrinaire about everything left." I can't help but laugh—and loudly. "I could go on and on," he says good humoredly. "Anyway, what do you need from me?" he asks, laughing.

Environmentalism is in Schneider's journalistic blood. His interest in the field took off when he covered the Three Mile Island nuclear powerplant accident—a partial meltdown of a reactor—that occurred on March 28, 1979, near Middleton, Pennsylvania.[15] In the same breath he tells me, "The history of environmentalism is the history of disaster." According to Schneider, a recent presidential administration, led by a former reality TV program host, helped lay the groundwork for such future disasters, diminishing environmental policy as a priority as well as undermining the credibility of science in the early critical stages of the pandemic. Add climate change to the topical mix in talking with a renowned environmental journalist, and it's nearly impossible to put some appreciable distance between politics and the environment. For him, it's just naturally inseparable.

"We're in this era when Mother Nature is putting more [reciprocal] pressure on the planet," he says. "There's a relationship between that and Michigan and the upper Midwest being attractive as a place to move to evade that ecological pressure. I'm not sure it's started yet; it's hard to measure; it's all anecdotal." Which has been my research experience. Climate migration into northern Michigan appears to be at a trickle right now. Emphasis on *right now*.

Migrating Up North "is clearly attractive to people in our [boomer] generation because we have the time and the money to get here," Schneider comments. "But I'm not clear that it's yet a real thing among young people because they still have to make a living and raise their families." Schneider says that school enrollments in the Grand Traverse region present no evidence of such a migration, as public-school enrollments continue to decline or remain static at least since 2000.

Traverse City Area Public Schools (TCAPS) Superintendent John VanWagoner confirms that assessment, saying that enrollment during the 2021–2022 school year came in at 9,200 pre-K-12 students, as expected. (The TCAPS district, with sixteen schools, is approximately three-hundred square miles, covering Grand Traverse County and parts of Leelanau and Benzie counties.)[16] TCAPS enrollment is down about 1,600 students from its pre-Covid peak, VanWagoner indicates. He expects this trend to continue for at least the next handful of years due to several factors, including an ebbing birth rate in the region. "If you look at our census and everything it points to, we simply have an older median population in Grand Traverse County." Another factor that's impacting TCAPS more than its neighboring school districts is affordable housing, especially within Traverse City itself, he notes. The sticker shock inherent in the housing affordability crisis tends to convince young families to look to surrounding counties for more viable options.

So the evidence isn't in just yet regarding climate migrants/refugees as being "a real thing," Schneider observes, "but clearly, for the future it is."

Schneider explains what's generally occurring environmentally in northwest lower Michigan as being three dimensional. First, the Great Lakes region is less subject to the consequences of climate change that have increased over the past century, such as wildfires and intensifying storms and flooding. This makes the region "less hazardous to live in." The hazards that the area is expected to experience, however, involve dramatic swings of heavy rain and protracted periods of drought. He adds that this is what climatologists have been "uncannily" predicting for years now. "No group of human beings has ever been as accurate in predicting the future over the long term as climate scientists, as American climate scientists, in particular, led by James Hanson." In 1988, Hanson warned Congress about the greenhouse effect and global warming. He is the author of *Storms of My Grandchildren: The Truth About the Coming Climate Catastrophe and Our Last Chance to Save Humanity*. The very first sentence in the book's preface maintains that stark theme: "Planet Earth, creation, the world in which civilization developed, the world with climate patterns that we know and stable shorelines, is in imminent peril. . . . The startling conclusion is that continued exploitation of all fossil fuels on Earth threatens not only the other millions of species on the planet but also the survival of humanity itself—and the timetable is shorter than we thought."[17]

The second dimension brings up the lesson of the lumber industry's destructive impact on northern Michigan's woodland ecosystem in the late nineteenth century. "Virtually every acre of old-growth virgin forest was cut in our region and across the state to build Chicago and Denver . . . and produced an environmental calamity in our rivers," he says. (Of note, Michigan's lower peninsula's white, jack, and red pine forests played a major role in the rebuilding of Chicago after the Great Chicago Fire in 1871.) "They battered our rivers, completely changing their ecology." Due to the colossal clearcutting, the lumber industry made itself obsolete in Michigan, and so moved westward to states like Minnesota.[18] Eventually, however, thoughtful environmental stewardship came into play. Nature knows how to recover, and the forests returned, largely under the care of state and federal forestry agencies that took over and revegetated the cutover lands and patiently replanted and managed them for decades. Schneider avers, "The landscape, as we've seen over the last 120 years, has a really amazing capacity to heal."

And the third dimension, he explains, is that Michigan evolved to become an environmental champion. Over the years, the Michigan Legislature and a series of environmentally progressive governors "passed the world's leading ecological safety statutes." Of course, there was an economic component, with legislation centering on economic development while emphasizing recovering and protecting the state's natural resources. This legislation significantly changed northwest lower Michigan's resource-based economy, converting it from an extraction focus to that of safeguarding natural resources. As a result, the tourist economy dramatically expanded. Meanwhile, a series of dunes, wetlands, and river protection legislation was passed. Says Schneider, "So you had nature healing and public policy protecting and clearing up the air. Lake Michigan became crystal clear, absolutely beautiful, which encouraged shoreline development. And the other piece is, the region preserved the coastline, from Ludington to Northport." State and federal wilderness areas were protected, and nature conservancies stepped in to enhance governmental conservation efforts. Schneider says the Michigan Department of Natural Resources and Department of Environment, Great Lakes, and Energy deserve considerable credit for these advances. "Michigan has more public land than any state east of the Mississippi," he states. Approximately 4.6 million acres of public land are owned by the state's residents. This includes 3.9 million acres of forestland, 360,000 acres of parkland, and 364,000 acres of state game and wildlife areas.[19]

Although certain areas like northwest lower Michigan are experiencing growth, the state's population as a whole is declining. According to the annual United Van Lines National Movers Study, in 2022, Michigan ranked fourth in the nation in the number of outbound moves United handled, with 58 percent, or 2,453, going out of state. (Due to population decrease, Michigan has lost five congressional seats since 1980.)[20] The main reasons for leaving Michigan, per the study and in order, were family (33 percent), job (30 percent), and retirement (26 percent).[21] "We're still an outmigration area," Schneider underscores. "And housing prices and affordability and jobs are not helping us become a migration [destination] state; but climate change is. Climate change is going to change all that."

For decades, Americans have been moving for climate reasons—to literally find their place in the sun as a choice and not a forced move. Evidence the Sunbelt's exploding population, with retirees leading the rush to Florida and Arizona. According to the U.S. Census Bureau, the Sunshine State "now is the nation's fastest-growing state for the first time since 1957."[22] Nevada and Arizona aren't far behind. In anticipation of climate change–inspired population shifts, the American Society of Adaptation Professionals, located in Ypsilanti, Michigan, is developing scientific models, with a special focus on migration to the Great Lakes region. Beth Gibbons, the society's executive director, portentously offers, "The really important piece we need to know is what is the threshold that matters for people to pick up their heads from the dinner table and say, 'You know what? I can't stay here anymore.'"[23]

Water Warrior

If you want to learn about protecting the water of the Great Lakes from a public interest law standpoint, Jim Olson is your go-to guy. Olson, who founded the nonprofit For Love of Water (FLOW) in 2011, is a nationally recognized environmental champion of the Great Lakes watershed and ecosystem. In agreeing to my emailed request for an interview, he added, "Even without the onslaught of migration, climate change and growth have already pushed Traverse City and the region beyond preparation." I was eager to hear more.

We meet in mid-June for lunch at one of his haunts, the Red Door Coffee House in quiet Lake Ann. He's wearing a baseball cap, flannel shirt, blue jeans. He drives a Toyota Prius, of course. I decide not to tell him I'm driving a pickup truck. Given the sharply rising gas prices in the summer of 2022, the extensive amount of driving I'm doing throughout northern lower Michigan, and my desire to reduce my carbon footprint, after my lunch conversation with him, my environmental guilt over my gas-guzzler is reaching crisis proportions.

The lunchroom tables are almost echo-chamber empty. A group of four talkative thirtysomethings bustles in, deciding, of course, to sit right next to us at an adjacent table, which hampers my hearing of the soft-spoken seventy-seven-year-old. But once he starts sharing his grave view of the emerging future for the region, a hush comes over our neighbors. They're now eavesdropping on Olson's storm warning of things to come, especially, he maintains, if planning for climate change impacts on the region continues to be largely ignored.

Olson opened a law practice in Traverse City in 1972 and became enamored with the public trust doctrine as it applies to environmental law. Soon after, several prominent Traverse City leaders walked into his office wanting to contest the sale of the property at the mouth of the Boardman-Ottaway River to Holiday Inn. Olson was engaged to represent them, relying on the Michigan Environmental Protection Act and the public trust doctrine. He explains the doctrine as "the principle that when the states joined the union (Michigan became a state in 1837), the states took title of all the submerged lands up to the ordinary high-water mark, wherever that may be. . . . And it's held in public trust, and there is a duty not to allow it to be impaired or alienated or sold or transferred primarily for private purposes. Every citizen has a paramount right to use and access those waters for fishing, navigation, swimming, sanitation, drinking water, and sustenance. That's a pretty powerful directive."

Although technically Olson did not prevail in the case, the experience furthered his interest in environmental law. He thought he would practice law for a decade or so then get a law school teaching gig. But environmental cases kept coming his way. "I realized I could learn more and teach more and do more of what my passion was in the courtroom—in representing citizen groups in fighting these powerful interests. So I had to make a choice, and it was a tough one. And I've been on this path ever since."

....

FLOW came into being after the documentary *For Love of Water* premiered at the State Theater on Front Street in downtown Traverse City on November 16, 2008. The film portrayed the global water crisis, and Olson appeared in it. After the showing, the standing-room-only crowd continued the evening with a community conversation at the nearby City Opera House, with dignitaries such as the film's director, Irena Salina, former Michigan Gov. Bill Milliken, author of *Great Lakes for Sale* Dave Dempsey, Michigan Citizens for Water Conservation (MCWC) President Terry Swier, northern Michigan poet Michael Delp, other local environmental activists, and Olson himself, who addressed the gathering.[24] Olson spoke about the MCWC's lawsuit in 2000 against Nestlé to prevent the Perrier Group, a Nestlé subsidiary, from diverting groundwater from the Little Muskegon River in Mecosta County for its bottled water product, Ice Mountain. An appealed decision favoring the MCWC, whom Olson represented, eventually led to a determination reducing the number of gallons per minute (gpm) to be taken by Nestlé (averaging 125 gpm during the summer and 218 gpm the rest of the year, down from 400 gpm).[25]

The Opera House was packed as well, Olson recalls. "They all came to the Opera House instead of going home after the film. It was amazing. And we had this town hall meeting." The upshot of that discussion and the groundswell of support for something to be done on a practical level—"not to prevent the use of water but to prevent the control, ownership, and sale of water"—planted the seeds for the eventual establishment of FLOW as a nonprofit in 2011.

....

As we dig into the present and future of the Great Lakes Basin in light of climate change, Olson brings up the "obsolete designs" of storm and flood probability of return periods. Case in point: on April 13, 2023, Fort Lauderdale, Florida, experienced rainfall of biblical proportions: 25.95 inches within twenty-four hours, with some areas of the city reporting 20 inches in just six hours. Dan DePodwin, director of forecast operations for AccuWeather, said the rainstorm was a one in one- to two-thousand-year event.[26] Fort Lauderdale can only hope.

Then the environmental law expert takes the impact of increasing weather event intensity even further. "It's not just water infrastructure and waste structure and combined sewage overflows—it's the very essence of dealing with stormwater drainage and soil erosion and sedimentation control. And we're not prepared for it." The physical forces unleashed by the more frequent and powerful storms that are occurring are dramatic, Olson emphasizes. "And then you combine that with human forces, and you have a crisis on your hands—a devastating crisis. That's how I see the climate piece of this and how it plays out: it's a very big deal. We're existentially facing the end of the planet and very severe suffering by our children and grandchildren."

He calls climate change "the predominant force on the planet right now in terms of human impact," adding darkly, "it's devastating, and it's not going to get better."

When Olson talks about the wave of climate migration he foresees coming to the region, he suggests more noticeable numbers will be on the move here over a stretch of years in conjunction with global warming's increasing severity and repercussions, should they play out. First will be the affluent, then those that can—the upper-middle classes, then those that must from a survival standpoint—those who live on the edge economically. This could be a landscape-altering influx, he posits, comparing the possibility to the massive human migrations now underway across the globe: in Africa, the Middle East, Central America, and Europe, the latter largely caused by the Syrian Civil War and the Russia-Ukraine War.

This reminds me of the *National Geographic* August 19, 2019, issue that's been gathering dust on my office desk. The cover shows a woman in a sari carrying a worried child as she wades in knee-deep water. It says, "A World on the Move: Seas rise, crops wither, wars erupt. Humankind seeks shelter in another place." Paging through the lead piece, I learn that "the United Nations estimates that more than a billion people—one in seven humans alive today—are voting with their feet, migrating within their countries or across international borders."[27] This anxious mega-movement is staggering in its implications. And practically impossible to imagine happening here in the United States. It seems farfetched, the stuff of science fiction. Even so, sci-fi writing of the highest caliber has often proven to be remarkably prescient. As Olson says, humans struggle with adjusting to change. Yet, "nature migrates. Wildlife migrates." People migrate. And despite our change-resistant natures, "we've been adjusting right along, for better or worse."

Because Olson believes that climate migration to the area will eventually accelerate, he insists the need for planning is now. He believes that current "infrastructure design, engineering, and development relies on obsolete standards, with very little attention to direct or cumulative impacts on controlling water, natural or artificial systems, not to mention similar systemic problems. Add migration from climate change, and it will be disastrous."

Olson refers me to the Environmental Law & Policy Center's 2019 report, *An Assessment of the Impacts of Climate Change on the Great Lakes*. The comprehensive study, coauthored by U.S. and Canadian climatology experts, elucidates a series of impacts already occurring in the Great Lakes Basin: increasing air temperatures (at a rate exceeding national averages), heavier precipitation and flooding (notably, a 10 percent increase in precipitation from 1901 to 2015, compared to a 4 percent increase nationally during the same period), more extreme weather, decreasing crop yields, summertime heat waves and air pollution affecting urban residents, and threatened water quality due to waterborne pathogens affecting the Great Lakes watershed.[28] Alarming as these trends are, compared to the East and West coasts and the Southwest, the Great Lakes is considered by environmental scientists to be "one of the safe havens," tells Olson. Come-visit-and-bring-money campaigns such as that promoted by Pure Michigan will advance "migration as an economic moneymaker and increase of gross domestic product," he says, adding suggestively, "we know what happens with too much PR."

According to FLOW's founder, the lack of urgency for climate change planning comes down to "local communities not accepting the reality of what's happening. You know, don't look up. They'll talk about it, and they're aware of it, and they want to see good things, but nobody is willing to dig down deep enough and ask the right questions about how much water is there going to be, how much are we using now, what are we going to use in the future." He contends, "We have no idea. We need a major data collection in Traverse City and every watershed on this planet, but particularly in the Great Lakes Basin. We need to understand what's happening and what's going to happen, and we need to redesign, building in the climate change predictions." Ultimately, what Olson is pleading for is the development of comprehensive climate change response plans for the region. Incoming population projections. Housing needs and infrastructure adjustments. Watershed impacts. How families already struggling from economic pressures will be able to survive, a problem already rearing itself in the shortage of affordable housing and rising real estate taxes and gas prices. "So you have this complete breakdown, and it's happening in our community, and it has been for some time."

Perhaps the difficulty in planning for what the region might look like by 2050 and even later into the twenty-first century as a result of global warming can be blamed on a sense of being overwhelmed by the very thought of it. Jake Bittle, author of *The Great Displacement: Climate Change and the Next American Migration*, sums it up like this: "The range of possible outcomes on the question of climate change is so large as to be almost unfathomable."[29] Curiously enough, the terms "Great Lakes" and "Michigan" do not appear in the book's index.

Yet Olson believes there is a simple answer as to what to do now to prepare for days to come. "I would offer this: I think communities and farmers and people who are environmental- and conservation-minded should be talking. We need to be on the same page. This is not a battle between ourselves." He notes that fortunately, so much of Michigan's land is state owned, keeping it unavailable for development.

Then there's the 2008 Great Lakes-St. Lawrence River Basin Compact signed by the governors of the eight contiguous Great Lakes states and includes the Canadian provinces of Ontario and Quebec. In short, it bans most new diversions of water outside of the basin, with proposals close to or straddling inside the basin's range subject to approval. Of concern, an increasing number of "allowable" diversions, such as the Waukesha, Wisconsin, diversion, have been occurring. The Compact Council's signatory states and Canadian provinces approved the Waukesha diversion in 2016. Olson commented then that this allowance "threatens the integrity of the compact's purpose and its prohibition on diversions."[30]

The Sunbelt's thirst is only growing as the Colorado River continues to shrink. On Tuesday, April 11, 2023, the Biden administration proposed to cut water allotments from the river "delivered to California, Arizona, and Nevada by as much as one-quarter." Of course, this is a huge ask of states that rely on the Colorado River for drinking water and agricultural irrigation, which affects forty million Americans, two Mexican states, and 5.5 million agricultural acres. A further complication: millions of homes and businesses receive power from the hydroelectric dams on Lake Mead and Lake Powell, lakes whose levels have dropped precipitously and whose electricity-generating turbines may soon not have the hydraulic power to run them.[31] (Something of a reprieve has been granted by Mother Nature due to the historic snowfall in the Rocky Mountains during the winter of 2022–2023, with reservoir levels rising as a result. This buys some time but doesn't alleviate the longer-term water shortage problem.)[32]

Despite the compact's existence, a federal government intervention on behalf of drought-stricken Sunbelt states isn't out of the question. Olson notes, "The diversion ban pressure is increasing." The ban could backfire, in a sense, by causing people to move to the Great Lakes region, "to come here because the water can't go anywhere else," he says. "It's a very inconsistent position: if you don't want people here and you're going to maintain the diversion ban, how long is the politics elsewhere in the country going to put up with that? Don't come and don't take the water. And people are trying to survive. It's not going to work; that's not a good policy."

Olson says language exists in the compact that calls for its review every five years to look at "what's coming, and one of the things they should be looking at is climate change—and they're not dealing with that." He stresses that much more proactivity is needed, examining the number of people moving into the basin, water usage now, and projected usage based upon expected population increase. Olson asks the difficult circumstantial question about those states thirsting for more water: "How do we insist that they use water conservation in their own place?" From a human decency standpoint, he adds, "And if it's not possible, how do we help them adjust?"

Being a realist runs the risk of being called a pessimist, or worse yet, a doomsayer. Yet Olson is for raising awareness based upon proven climate science and acting decisively upon what is learned. This requires hope. "That's where I am," he says, spending his waking hours inspiring people to action. He paraphrases a New Testament letter entry, Romans

5:3–4: "Endurance builds character, which gives us a hope." His hope is embodied in the very reason he started FLOW: "to solve problems."

(Postscript: A few weeks after meeting with Olson, I traded in my beloved Honda Ridgeline pickup truck on a significantly higher mileage CR-V Hybrid.)

Weather Report

While watching the weather on northern Michigan's 9&10 News one late afternoon in early September 2022, I decide to reach out to the station's chief meteorologist, Tom O'Hare, to see if he can recommend a climatologist to interview about climate change in the region. He writes back suggesting a professor at Michigan State University but offers another option: "As for a more localized feel on the changes, I think we could talk about what's been going on." He invites me to meet him at Cast Iron Kitchen on U.S. 31, just south of Traverse City.

I approach the only person seated at what looks like a bar—and soon will be, according to the sassy and fun young waitress, who will end up waiting on us. "Tom?" I ask, and the meteorologist rises to shake my hand. He could easily be mistaken for an athletic and impeccably put-together guy in his forties; except that he's an athletic and impeccably put-together guy somewhere in his fifties. I don't probe for his exact age, as I assume that may be a closely guarded industry secret.

O'Hare speaks rapidly yet clearly with a friendly, confident voice that's easy to follow, reflective of his years as a TV weatherman, the last eighteen spent with the Doppler 9&10 Weather Team. We order coffee and talk about—what else?—the weather.

The interview takes place in mid-September, and I begin by commenting that it seems we've been experiencing a traditional northern Michigan summer this year, with comfortable warm days and cool, sleep-enhancing nights. "To me it was," he concurs. "It was great; it was perfect. And the numbers all came out to being roughly a normal summer. The only exception is that early on we were dry for about a month or so." This throwback to what used to be the norm, weatherwise, points to the subject of consistency. "That's the biggest thing: consistency of being warm or cold. And moisture—we're not seeing as much of it as we have in the past." What they are seeing is more unusual weather patterns. "For instance, the last two years we haven't had a good frost until November or December.

Last year [2021], we didn't have a frost advisory issued or freeze warning at all because we never had cold enough weather until it was normal, until November or December. He calls this repeat abnormality "bizarre"—which the phenomenon of climate change certainly is.

Whenever Doppler 9&10 Weather runs a climate change/global warming story, the station can count on receiving pushback from some viewers. "Most of the times it's like 'BS, it's not happening.'" O'Hare finds this uncritically thinking response unfortunate, attributing it to, unsurprisingly, partisan politics: liberals who generally accept climate change versus "drill, baby, drill" far-right conservatives.[33] Folks in the latter category aren't seeing the big picture, aren't perceiving the long view, and tend to only be interested in the here and now, he explains.

For those who question whether climate change is real, NASA has a blunt answer: "There is unequivocal evidence that Earth is warming at an unprecedented rate. Human activity is the principal cause."[34] *The Intergovernmental Panel on Climate Change 2023 Synthesis Report* seconds that: "Human activities, principally through emissions of greenhouse gases, have unequivocally caused global warming." The report further states, "Widespread and rapid changes in the atmosphere, ocean, cryosphere and biosphere have occurred. Human-caused climate change is already affecting many weather and climate extremes in every region across the globe."[35]

The remarkably unseasonable Michigan winter of 2023–2024 should give climate change deniers pause. Multiple annual winter events throughout northern Michigan were canceled due to lack of ice and snow. This includes a first: the cancellation of "Michigan's shortest fishing season"—spearfishing for sturgeon on Black Lake. (In 2023, the season lasted sixty-five minutes before the DNR-set limit was reached; the year before, it ended in thirty-six minutes).[36] And more: the cancellation of the forty-eighth North American Vasa races (cross-country skiing, fat bike, and snowshoe races), the Michigan Snowmobile Festival in Gaylord, and the Interlochness Ice Fishing Contest, among others.

I comment that some longtime northern Michigander families I know who, when it comes to mentioning anything about climate change, are—and he suddenly cuts me off: "Opinionated?" I tell him I try to avoid engaging in a political argument as it pertains to weather. "Yeah, that's the best thing," he agrees. Weather politicized, weather weaponized, human fabrications. For weather—to coin a trite though apropos term in this case—is what it is. While under the ever-increasing influence of eight billion people and counting.

One noticeable weather trend O'Hare's been observing over the past few years is that northern Michigan summers and winters tend to last longer. "So it seems like the cool air lasts a bit longer and then it jumps into summer really fast. And winter is slower to get here now." As well, every few years the region has what he refers to as a "good winter," meaning snowy and cold. His meteorological instincts tell him that good winters will become more infrequent. So much so that when a friend was recently about to buy a new snowmobile, O'Hare, a snowmobiler himself, talked him out of it. "Snowmobile season is going away," he believes. "There will still be some snow to some degree. But the amount of snow we used to have twenty years ago, don't expect that consistency." When meteorologists start talking like this, snowmobile dealers beware.

Northern Michigan's Climate Migration, an Open Question

One look at Jon Allan's resume and it's crystal clear why several of my environmental subject expert interviewees recommended him as a source for my research. Allan, sixty-five, perhaps best described as an environmental science, strategy, and policy polymath, is currently with the University of Michigan's School for Environment and Sustainability, serving as a senior advisor and senior academic and research program officer. His work focuses on "the intersection of ecological, economic, social, and cultural value. He seeks to understand and influence the rate at which the region is adopting and implementing the principles of a sustainable and just society."[37] He also runs a freshwater/Great Lakes environmental and natural resource management strategy consulting firm, the Jon W. Allan Group. Previously, he was the director of Michigan's Office of the Great Lakes from 2012 to 2019.

Allan serves on several esteemed scientific boards, including the National Oceanic and Atmospheric Administration (NOAA) Science Advisory Board and as co-chair of the International Joint Commission's Great Lakes Water Quality Board. In 2020, the Water Quality Board enlisted LimnoTech, an environmental science and engineering firm out of Ann Arbor, and the RAND Corporation to conduct an extensive study on what the future looks like for the Great Lakes region over the next three decades, comprehensively examining the utility of the world's largest group of freshwater lakes. The final report—*On the*

Great Lakes Horizon: Scenarios, Opportunities, Threats, and Responsive Governance—was published in late March 2023. Significantly, the report also explores the potential impact of climate migration.

"Climate migration for us isn't just about numbers of people coming; it's about who's going to be forced out of where under what circumstances, whether it's environmental or conflict driven," Allan begins our Zoom conversation. "Those are the two [main] sources of diasporic movements of people. . . . So what's the likelihood that we'll see large movements of people by mid-century? I think it's pretty high." Yet this pertains to global human migration. Specifically, what does this bode for the Great Lakes Basin?

"The jury for me is still out as to whether they'll show up in the Great Lakes region," he responds. "I think we will be a recipient of some percentage of some of the repacking of North America." This, he believes, will largely involve boomerangers returning to northern Michigan, an anomaly in light of the state's otherwise overarching outbound population movement. "For me, the dominant narrative is sort of coming home. . . . It's people coming back."

I share some of my observations gleaned from working part time at Cottage Books in Glen Arbor during the summer of 2022. Notably, quite a few patrons came from the Chicagoland area, with some families owning seasonal homes over the course of generations in Glen Arbor (thus Glen Arbor's nickname "Little Chicago"). Allan asserts that this uniquely intra-Midwestern migratory movement "is by invitation and familiarity. We send a lot of kids out into this world, and now those kids are in their fifties, sixties, seventies, and eighties with some means. That's who I think will come back." That they have, and will continue to, though in what numbers due to climate change–related factors remains to be seen.

On the Great Lakes Horizon depicts a series of long-term scenarios on how the Great Lakes' fresh water is withdrawn and used for drinking and bathing, waste processing, irrigation, and recreation—what Allan refers to as "the demand function." These scenarios also prompt questions of identity and how that stands to shift in coming years as the region evolves. "Who are we? Who will be here? And what will we believe?" he poses in his professorial manner. As well, how will water quality be protected and maintained? And what will be the actual impact of climate change on the region? Allan says it's not enough to estimate a count of Michigan's incomers over the next fifty years; there needs to be a much deeper dive. For instance, when newcomers arrive, where will they settle? "Where will they find community? Will they be welcomed—or not—in some fashion? And then what will they believe when they get here?"

Though the people living in the Great Lakes Basin are emotively connected to the region—as are the many repeat visitors and seasonal homeowners like me—those who come in future days may not necessarily be drawn here by love of an awe-inspiring scenic location. They may well be fleeing threatening changes in climate, yearning for ready access to fresh water, and, of course, seeking new career opportunities. So this local appreciation must somehow be defined and shared, Allan suggests, or the values long held dear by inhabitants of the region could deteriorate if not disappear. "Are we creating systems to curate care? Or are we going to erode systems that link us to the underlying value that we currently hold with the Great Lakes? That's the question of the day," he stresses.

He indicates that Michigan has hundreds of square miles that are ripe for reinvention. Near-ghost towns dot the state's map. (Allan is spot on: I drove through quite a few myself in late September 2023 when Google Maps' "Avoid Highways" feature apparently self-activated, and I found myself meandering from Cedar to Ann Arbor, though not unhappily so.) "Kids have left, parents have stayed. But they are nonviable; I drive through them all the time. Yet they have infrastructure. At what point does that look interesting to a community somewhere else that's looking to create their own enclave?"

I bring up the recent settlement of Amish families in Manistee County, as of 2018.[38] Allan comments that it isn't too farfetched to imagine immigrants from as far as India making their way to northern Michigan and breathing life into slowly dying small towns. Reinvigoration of large-scale metropolitan areas is already occurring along the Great Lakes. Take, for example, cosmopolitan Toronto, Allan submits, where ethnic groups migrating there are transforming the city. Toronto government officials are planning and preparing for *millions* more to come, he says.

Allan is frustrated by the certitude some have in the regional environmental conservation nonprofit sector that northern Michigan Great Lakes communities are destined to become climate migration meccas. "The underlying issues are much more rich, deep, and need exploration." He further explains, "So yes, we may get some wealthy retirees who want a physical hedge, meaning go buy a place on Beaver Island so I can get access to water in the Apocalypse. I'm going to hedge my bets around access to water if I have enough money to buy two or three places. But I'll also push out the community that needs to tend my garden and clean my house—I'll push them off the water. They can go live in Wolverine, right?" (Wolverine is in central northern Michigan, approximately fifty-five miles from St. James on Beaver Island.)

This gentrification has been in progress for some time in the region, though it accelerated dramatically during the pandemic. Allan has spent a lot of time in Maine and has seen this phenomenon play out there too. "Same thing. Too much money pushing everyone else out." Still, the wealthy vacation homeowners and relocated retirees of means need their homes cleaned, their grass cut, their leaves blown and disposed of, their yards landscaped, their gutter debris removed, their restaurant meals and cocktails prepared and served. This marked demographic shift calls for these now affluent communities to preserve if not further develop affordable housing to enable service workers to live near their customers and places of employment. "It's one thing to buy paradise," says Allan, "it's another thing to service paradise."

Having the opportunity to work with impoverished urban families in Indianapolis during my public education career was a godsend in raising my awareness of the widening socioeconomic divide between the Haves and the Have-Nots. I'm no longer blind to poor folks in my vicinity, wherever I may be. This includes Leelanau County and the Grand Traverse region at large, where for years I had my tourist blinders on. "And you're understanding their politics of hate and discontent," Allan comments on my epiphany. "You're understanding now what's driving it." I do indeed.

I grew up in working-class neighborhoods in Lawrence, Indiana. Although in the sixties and seventies there were pockets of wealth in this northeast-side suburb of Indianapolis, most notably in subdivisions near Geist Reservoir, for the most part, the city was predominantly comprised of middle- and lower-middle-class families. When I started working in restaurant bars on the northside of Indianapolis, my Lawrence friends would derogatorily refer to "north-siders" with some choice words. Then when I began dating a North Central High School graduate, my former Lawrence Central High School classmates, now young adult friends, half-seriously called me a traitor (that is, until they met my soon-to-be wife, who bedazzled them with her charm and beauty). North-siders represented the college-educated, moneyed, privileged class. Although that wasn't entirely accurate, by comparison, my friends had none of those advantages. They were envious, resentful, even hateful. Provincialism has its roots in the consumingly frustrating lack of access, whether by birth or other circumstances, to a better life.

Allan continues, "So our study hasn't determined how many people are going to come and live in the next community or not. It is to drive a set of thematics around what will determine whether [the Great Lakes region is] attractive." A key to being an attractive area in which to relocate is how capitalized the target area's economy is. Much of the wealth of vacation homeowners in the region is not "endogenous wealth," he notes; it's money made elsewhere. Allan says this type of gentrification fueled by imported money has already occurred, for example, in Seal Harbor and Camden, Maine. "We see it all throughout the coastline where the boatbuilders can't afford to be on the water. Now there's an irony: if you're a lobsterman or a boatbuilder, you can't afford to be on the water. Tell me how that works." Nonetheless, he agrees with the progressive economic interests in the Grand Traverse region, such as Traverse Connect, in promoting the relocation of technology-oriented businesses to the area and diversifying the local economy. "I do think for long-term viability Traverse has to have a more vibrant, year-round, nontransient, nonrecreational, and noncottage industry."

Allan contends that the Great Lakes region is not attracting the type of investment that it should. In a meeting focused on sustainable investments in the region with the Norwegian Sovereign Wealth Fund's money managers, Allan and David Naftzger, executive director of the Great Lakes St. Lawrence Governors and Premieres, asked the Norwegian representatives about their interest in investing some of the fund's nearly $1.3 trillion in the Great Lakes. "What was their answer? *'The Great what?'*" The Great Lakes not only didn't appear on their radar screen as a fertile investment opportunity, but the Norwegians also had no idea they even existed. In an understatement, Allan says, "So our stewardship of 20 percent of the world's fresh water is a little thin." That money won't be coming here, he laments. "We're not interesting. We're not attracting sustainability-driven, ESG-driven [Environmental, Social, and Governance] wealth." Moreover, "we're not showing anybody that we're worthy of an investment. . . . We're not showing that we're planning ahead for the eventualities of this changed world. And if we're not even attracting capital, what's the likelihood that we're going to attract people if we don't have capital underneath it to grow an economic capacity?" Drawing an accurate picture of the region's next three decades per the LimnoTech/RAND Corporation report's detailed SWOT-like analysis [Strengths, Weaknesses, Opportunities, and Threats] is, well, complicated.

What Michigan does have, though, as Allan points out, is agriculture: it's the second-most diverse agricultural state in the country.[39] Much of Michigan's fruit and vegetable growing happens north of Grand Rapids and runs up to the tip of northern lower Michigan, which includes the Grand Traverse region's cherry country. He states that "eighty-five percent of Michigan's food farm production is sent to other states for processing." So plant it, grow it, ship it out, "and let somebody else benefit from the economic value of turning it into a product," he criticizes.

To correct this loss of millions of dollars getting exported to other states for them to realize greater profit there, the West Michigan Food Processing Initiative has been created. "[It's] an economic transition from a high-carbon to a low-carbon economy around the sustainable development of food and food processing capacity," Allan explains. "Let's do the value-add of something we know how to do: grow stuff. But let's figure out how to blanche it, package it, freeze-dry it, juice it, bottle it—whatever the processing side is. And let's take a little bit of that economy and internalize it in West Michigan and grow an economy around something we know that is already part of the regional landscape. It's slow work, but I think they're starting to make a difference and attract capital in a very unique way." West Michigan already has a significant history of food processing, with industry giants like Gerber and Kellogg's having a well-established footprint there, accounting for 43 percent of the state's food processing jobs. With the majority of Michigan-grown crops shipped to processors in other states, only to be returned to Michigan grocery stores as processed food products, the room for growth is exponential.[40]

Allan points out that at least 85 percent of the 4,530 miles of coastline along the Great Lakes "is privately owned and managed at the township level. That's a tyranny of a lot of small decisions: where to put your house, siting decisions, zoning decisions." Migration, as it stands to impact these areas, deserves a dedicated, ongoing conversation to align communities in managing such potential sea change. "It's very hard to see these large-scale, slow-moving risk amplifiers . . . and help communities that would rather not think about it." Fortunately, he says, fewer and fewer of them are in denial. So now it's a question of what to do about it. "It's a communitarian problem in an individualistically aligned world.

And this is going to be a problem. It's not the number of people. It's about the choices we make about where those people go."

....

After my interview with Allan in mid-October 2022, I found myself pondering one statement in particular that he made: "All of us are the consequences of movements of people." Such as my Irish forebears arriving at Ellis Island in New York City and making their way to northeastern Pennsylvania generations ago. My parents relocating us to Indianapolis in 1966. My northern Michigander friends whose European ancestors sailed into Good Harbor Bay in the 1850s. The Polish families that settled in Leelanau County beginning in 1870 seeking a new life, largely as farmers, while establishing new communities such as Cedar.[41] Now, generations later, their descendants claim these towns as their own, with an understandable sense of prideful originality. Before them, however, were the First Peoples, who themselves migrated to the region thousands of years earlier. Humans, as Allan observes, are a migratory species and will leave their homelands whenever under duress to seek safety and opportunity, a place to put down new roots. And whenever that relocation occurs, change is inevitable as the newcomers leave their own mark on the places they now call home.

EPILOGUE

We need hiking trails, not water parks; public
land, not shopping centers. It must be easy for
some people to forget WHY this is a popular
tourist destination. It's not because of the
shopping opportunities, but because of the
lakes, rivers, beaches, woodlands, and fresh
air.

—Jerry Dennis

In mid-December 2021, Janet and I temporarily relocated from our Midwestern home in Indianapolis to Redington Beach, on Florida's Gulf Coast near St. Petersburg. We stayed for six weeks on the barrier island, Sand Key, working remotely during the Covid-19 pandemic's most fraught days and mixing in some vacation time. This was our first taste of "snowbirding." My wife loved it. She's third generation Syrian, and it's in her genetic makeup to be drawn to sun and warmth. Me? My Irish genes prefer something a bit cooler. Admittedly, it's hard to argue with near-constant sunshine and temperatures in the mid-seventies most days—in winter. And it was no imposition to having steps-away access to the Gulf of Mexico across the street. As well, wearing shorts, a T-shirt, and sandals every day is something a guy could get used to. I was also fascinated by the subtropical biodiversity of Florida, its flora and fauna, especially the wildlife: the shorebirds and osprey, the reptiles that belong—such as the ubiquitous alligators and plodding gopher tortoises; and the ones that don't—delightfully ugly green iguanas and many of the proliferating species of sporadically sprinting geckos. Well, I soldiered on and suffered through it.

The people are, of course, of greatest intrigue in the Sunshine State. The locals have had a lot of practice with out-of-staters, including "Silver Tsunami" permanent relocators and seasonal migrants and tourists of all ages. It's a hospitable state, for the most part. People freely say hello and strike up a chat with little prodding, especially those of a more venerable age. And as long as the conversation doesn't stray into an oppositional political exchange, which is easy to do down Florida way, that Margaritaville attitude of dreamy coexistence can stay intact.

So, we returned in the winter of 2022, snowbirding becoming something of an annual habit now, once again staying in Redington Beach for a longish respite, despite my obligatory protestations. We take some twisted delight when we're away and a snowstorm is bearing down on the home front, which is far more typical in northern Michigan than Indianapolis, whose winters have continued to become milder, most noticeably over the past five years or so. Precipitous temperature drops, heavy snow, and howling high winds are most amusing when sunbathing in the subtropics and out of harm's way. And yet I miss the existential thrill of such storms, the preparations, the vigil, the survival, the lending a neighbor a helping hand.

In 2022, our son, Matt, and his wife, Kelli, and their two young boys came down for a week's vacation in early February. One evening we decided to order a few pizzas from a nearby restaurant. It was just a few miles from the rental house, and its cozy bar carried Tampa's Cigar City Brewery's Jai Alai India Pale Ale on tap, one of Matt's favorites. So we volunteered to pick up the pizzas, allowing us to work in a pint or two in the process. Win-win.

It was Tuesday, just after 6 p.m., when we arrived. As we walked in, Matt nudged me and said, "Hey, there's Bo Schembechler."

"I'll be damned," I responded, playing along but laughing at the resemblance. "And I thought he was dead."

The lookalike of the iconic University of Michigan head football coach, who ran the U of M program from 1969 to 1989,[1] wore a letter jacket and baseball cap in the official maize-and-blue school colors. He had a nearly empty beer in front of him, and his companion, a dignified-looking older woman, was drinking a glass of white wine. The other ten or so barstools were empty. We left a chair between us and the couple, exchanging hellos as we settled in and ordered our Jai Alais. Then Matt told the gent that he mistook him for Bo Schembechler, and the two erupted in laughter. As we waited for our to-go order, a casual conversation with the couple ensued.

Such a small world: they were from Traverse City. The northern Michigan snowbirds were in their late seventies, boyfriend and girlfriend. He owned a flooring business and had "tried to retire" several times. The glut of homebuilding and remodeling in the region prevented that, and he preferred to be hands-on during such boom times. It also got him out of the house for some socialization, which his partner acknowledged with a nod.

As for her, she was a successfully retired Traverse City Area Public Schools teacher. I inquired what she thought of the ever-increasing number of tourists flocking to the Grand Traverse region over the past decade as well as the pandemic-caused inpouring of property seekers. She leaned toward me and whispered, "I can't stand it. I've lived in Traverse City all my life. It just keeps getting worse. It's just not like it used to be." She reached for her glass, and I did the same.

"How long you two here for?" I asked.

"Got here in January," Schembechler's doppelganger responded. "Be back in Traverse in late March. I'd stay longer, but hell, my business needs me as we gear up for the spring." Our pizzas were ready a few minutes later, and we bid the couple goodbye.

As we drove back to the house, I mentioned to Matt how interesting it was to hear complaints about all the tourists and newcomers to the Grand Traverse region from two northern Michiganders who were sitting out the winter along Florida's Suncoast. "I wonder what native Floridians think about the annual snowbird migration?" I asked.

"Pretty weird, isn't it," Matt answered. "But we're all a bit hypocritical and self-absorbed, you know? Most of us don't really think about how our choices and behaviors factor into the bigger picture. I guess that's just the American way." He got no argument from me.

....

On our return trip to Indy in mid-February, Janet called attention once again to the gigantic Confederate battle flag rippling majestically in the north Florida breeze, just off Interstate 75. There were other smaller versions of the rebel flag flying in southern Georgia we would spot from the highway as well, along with the occasional good ol' boy wind-whipped banners extending from imitation monster pickup trucks with suspension lift kits. "I can't believe people are still putting up those awful flags," she said, appalled. "That shouldn't be allowed."

"The war of northern aggression will never be over for some people," I responded. Maybe they're just making a strong statement about all the damn Yankees invading every winter. Or maybe they're just proud to be racists. Or they're just sore losers. Or all of the above; who knows. Nationalistic flags, banners, signs, T-shirts, and caps are visual claims on territory and statements on identity. Humans mark and defend turf. And they're not always willing to share.

Though there are yard signs in rural northern Michigan brazenly stating, "My Governor Is an Idiot" in reference to "that woman from Michigan," Gretchen Whitmer,[2] I've yet to see a flag declaring allegiance to a kind of border-wall mindset intended to send a strong message to visitors and moneyed migrants that they're not wanted Up North. Far from it.

Good thing. Given the pressures of the pandemic, environmental degradation, headline-grabbing big city crime—often of the violent kind—and, for some, the gravitational pull of home, many of them are deciding to take up residence. So the question, posed to me by a burnt-out local shop owner at the Leland Township Library following a book presentation I gave in midsummer 2021, remains: *what should we do?*

The United States remains a free country. State borders are open. Further, after decades of "half-the-pay-by-the-bay" employer exploitation, real economic opportunity with competitive compensation can now be found in northern Michigan. And certainly, it is stunningly beautiful here: you can't get views like this just anywhere. Once you've seen it, you're forever smitten. You can't help but tell your friends, tell your extended family, tell your coworkers all about it. Unlike the rest of the state, Boomers are retiring here in waves. Prosperous young people are relocating to the region for an unparalleled lifestyle—because they can. Then these settlers encourage others to come and join them, to make a new life here in an almost unimaginably spectacular part of the world. A new northward expansion. So, the word is out, and there's no taking it back.

Now what?

Those in the tourism-serving industry, state and local governments, and the region's chambers of commerce will continue to promote and welcome growth in northern Michigan. Managing that—with a unified vision that keeps environmental protection front and center—is paramount. Fragmented self-interest will only lead to a confused approach that will threaten precious natural resources and risk the region losing its identity as a paradise on Earth worth visiting, living in, and safeguarding for generations to come.

....

One evening in Redington Beach last January, I was scanning Netflix for some mindless entertainment. Instead, I came across an arresting autobiographical nature documentary, *David Attenborough: A Life on Our Planet*, released in 2020. Attenborough, ninety-three years old at the time of the documentary's making, calls it his "witness statement." It's the distinguished naturalist's warning to us all about global warming and human overpopulation and the rapidly accelerating species extinctions. Of the many quotable lines throughout the film, this stood out most to me: "We need to rediscover how to be sustainable, to move from being apart from nature to becoming a part of nature once again."[3] Less consumption; more active appreciation. *Together.*

Here in northern Michigan, overpopulation seems improbable—except for the annual summer tourist spike. This is a short-lived circumstance that remains vital to small business survival throughout the entirety of the year. Yet as so many environmental groups headquartered in the region and its members know well, human impact can quickly cause the area's ecological integrity and balance to deteriorate—as the ever-increasing Great Lakes invasive species, and biological attempts for nearly the past sixty years to mitigate if not eliminate them, attest. What people come north for can quickly go south, so to speak, without an active respect for nature and the responsibility of all to be good stewards of the Earth. Every one of us has an obligation to ensure that what we value most in northern Michigan stays intact: *Pure Michigan* forever.

So, if you're visiting northern Michigan, thinking about moving here, have recently migrated to the area, are boomeranging your way back, or have lived here since birth (or long enough to earn your Up North citizenship credentials—and it isn't just getting a Michigan driver's license and mailing address), I do have some simple advice. It's gleaned from the collective input of my generously forthcoming interviewees and my nearly forty years Up North experience of having been a former tourist, seasonal visitor and property owner, and now fortunate enough to live half of the year here in God's country. For your consideration:

1. Always. Be. Nice.
2. For those of you who are older and wiser, remember, at one time you weren't. So be patient with those who aren't—yet—and model the way.
3. Become a perpetual student of nature. And bring your kids and grandkids with you.
4. Life is a miracle, time is short, and the Earth needs you *now*. We are all called to be good stewards of the planet, wherever we may find ourselves—like northern Michigan.
5. And did I mention, be nice?

ACKNOWLEDGMENTS

As mentioned in the introduction, a series of conversations with Traverse City writer Dave Dempsey led to the concept of this book. Throughout the research and writing process, Dave provided invaluable support. He recommended interviewees and made key introductions, reviewed several chapters that benefited significantly from his attention, and checked in on me periodically to see how things were progressing and to offer encouragement. A career-long environmental policy expert with a special emphasis on the Great Lakes, Dave agreed to share his perspective on the Grand Traverse region's environmental challenges as they apply to the book's focus. As they say in Indiana in the folksiest of high compliments, he's good people.

JoAnne Cook, chief appellate judge for the Grand Traverse Band of Ottawa and Chippewa Indians and an in-demand speaker on Anishinaabek history, tradition, and culture, not only agreed to an interview but also kindly reviewed chapter two, "An Indigenous Perspective," upon my request. JoAnne's clarifications were essential improvements.

And of course, my deepest thanks to all my interviewees. The list reached nearly eighty, including many experts in their respective and varied fields. Just one of my requests for an interview was turned down, which speaks to northern Michiganders' affinity for this unparalleled place as well as their inclination to be kind. Even though some of the interviews didn't appear in the book—only due to length restrictions—all of those I spoke with contributed to its outcome. This book would have never happened were it not for their enthusiastic responses.

Sue Boucher, former owner of the iconic Cottage Books in Glen Arbor, hired me as a very part-time employee during the busy summer season in 2022. I'm not sure I was all that much help, as her regular employees ran circles around me. But the gig gave me greater insight into visitors' regard for and knowledge of the region, especially those seasonal folks who return to the Glen Arbor area year after year. Those many casual interactions, as the credit card commercial says, were priceless.

Others who provided help along the way include Betsy Myers and Katheryn Carrier, reference librarians at the Traverse Area District Library's main branch, who assisted in directing me to historical texts about the region; Kim Kelderhouse, executive director of the Leelanau Historical Society Museum, who cheerfully did the same when I dropped by unannounced one rainy late May day; and Heather Shaw, who previously served on the Traverse City Planning Commission and provided me a list of potential interviewees to consider, along with background information on some of the most critical issues facing the Grand Traverse region.

My dear friend Dan Landwerlen got me out of the house on timely occasions, giving me needed social breaks from the solitude of book writing (including field trips involving adult beverages), always welcome diversions. Dan is indeed a good soul.

Writers must have people in their lives who believe in them, in their creative aptitude, in their ability to tell an engaging story by breathing life into a unique collection of words. Such is the case with my wife of more than forty years, Janet Walker Mulherin. She reviewed the book throughout its many stages, offering diplomatic commentary on the weaker areas that needed reconsideration. That's not an easy thing for a partner to do, but she did it with love.

I greatly appreciate the editorial team at Michigan State University Press, who made the publishing experience as painless as possible. Their expert guidance and positivity in shepherding the process made everything right.

Finally, to anyone else I might have neglected to recognize, well, you know how grateful I am and how much you mean to me.

NOTES

Preface

1. "Fast Facts—Great Lakes," National Oceanic and Atmospheric Administration, https://coast.noaa.gov/states/fast-facts/great-lakes.html#:~:text=The%20Great%20Lakes%20span%204%2C530,percent%20of%20the%20Canadian%20population.

Chapter 1. A Migration Story

1. Sandra Serra Bradshaw, "A Historic Journey through Leland's Fishtown," *Glen Arbor Sun*, July 16, 2021, https://glenarborsun.com/a-historic-journey-through-lelands-fishtown/.

2. Nell Greenfieldboyce, "Light Pollution Hides Milky Way from 80 Percent of North Americans, Atlas Shows," *All Things Considered*, NPR, June 10, 2016, https://www.npr.org/sections/thetwo-way/2016/06/10/481545778/light-pollution-hides-milky-way-from-80-percent-of-north-americans-atlas-shows.

3. Jayden Kennett, "Shooting, Attempted Robbery Leaves Indianapolis Funeral Director

Dead," *Indianapolis Recorder*, August 8, 2022, https://indianapolisrecorder.com/shooting-attempted-robbery-leaves-indianapolis-funeral-director-dead/.

4. Joe Schroeder, "Attendees Pepper Sprayed after Fight Breaks Out During Indy Funeral," *Fox59*, September 10, 2022, https://fox59.com/indiana-news/attendees-pepper-sprayed-after-fight-breaks-out-during-indy-funeral/.

5. Leo Sands, "Indianapolis: Dutch Commando Dies after Shooting outside US Hotel," *BBC News*, August 30, 2022, https://www.bbc.com/news/world-us-canada-62712298.

6. Jacob Burbrink and Courtney Spinelli, "Downtown Indy Safety Concerns Prompts Starbucks Closure," *Fox59*, October 14, 2022, https://fox59.com/news/downtown-indy-safety-concerns-prompt-starbucks-closure/.

7. Joe Schroeder, "Indiana Announces 'Air Quality Action Day' for Sunday," *Fox59*, September 17, 2022, https://fox59.com/indiana-news/indiana-announces-air-quality-action-day-for-sunday/.

8. "Northwest," U.S. Climate Resilience Toolkit, https://toolkit.climate.gov/regions/northwest. "Southwest," U.S. Climate Resilience Toolkit, https://toolkit.climate.gov/regions/southwest. "The Southeast's Productive Coastal Zone," U.S. Climate Resilience Toolkit, Coastal Impacts, https://toolkit.climate.gov/regions/coastal-impacts.

Chapter 2. An Indigenous Perspective

1. Edward Benton-Banai, *The Mishomis Book* (Minneapolis: University of Minnesota Press, 2010), 94–96.

2. Benton-Banai, *The Mishomis Book*, 93.

3. Benton-Banai, *The Mishomis Book*, 93.

4. Josh Monroe, "Traverse City Will See New Signage around Town," *9&10 News*, January 20, 2022, https://www.9and10news.com/2022/01/20/traverse-city-will-see-new-signage-around-town/.

5. Wilbert B. Hinsdale, *Archaeological Atlas of Michigan* (Ann Arbor: University of Michigan Press, 1931), 3, https://quod.lib.umich.edu/g/genpub/1265156.0001.001. Emily Modrall says that Hinsdale compiled all the archeological/historical information he could find about Michigan, motivated by his concern that such sites, including Native burial mounds and

villages, were rapidly disappearing from the face of Michigan, most of which had already vanished by 1931. Notably, the Anishinaabek trails he identified crisscrossed much of the upper Midwest, particularly along the Great Lakes and into northeastern Canada and the United States.

6. David Lyden and Josh Monroe, "Special Report: Secrets of Holy Childhood, Part 1," *9&10 News*, November 8, 2021, https://www.9and10news.com/2021/11/08/special-report-secrets-of-holy-childhood-part-1/.

7. Matthew L. M. Fletcher, *The Eagle Returns: The Legal History of the Grand Traverse Band of Ottawa and Chippewa Indians* (East Lansing: Michigan State University Press, 2012), 87.

8. "Agriculture & Food Sovereignty," Grand Traverse Band of Ottawa and Chippewa Indians, https://www.gtbindians.org//agricultural.asp.

9. "American Indian Urban Relocation," Educator Resources, National Archives, August 15, 2016, https://www.archives.gov/education/lessons/indian-relocation.html.

10. Patti Brandt Burgess and Sierra Clark, "'Stolen': Grand Traverse Band Seeks Its Day in Court for the Theft of Reservation Lands," *Traverse City Record-Eagle*, December 21, 2020, https://www.record-eagle.com/news/grand-traverse-band-seeks-its-day-in-court-for-theft-of-reservation-lands/article_64ed04b6-3e4a-11eb-82be-bbfad2fb4f41.html.

11. Burgess and Clark, "Stolen."

12. "2020 Decennial Census Data," U.S. Census Bureau, https://data.census.gov/cedsci.

13. "U.S-31/M-72 (Grandview Parkway) in Traverse City Substantially Complete, Fully Open," Michigan Department of Transportation, https://www.michigan.gov/mdot/news-outreach/pressreleases/2024/10/28/us-31-m-72-in-traverse-city-substantially-complete-fully-open.

14. Marc Schollett, "Traverse City Proposal 1 Knocked Down by Voters," *UpNorthLive*, November 10, 2022, https://upnorthlive.com/news/local/traverse-city-proposal-1-knocked-down-by-voters.

15. "Commercial Fishing Safety: National Overview," National Institute for Occupational Safety and Health, Centers for Disease Control and Prevention, October 1, 2021, https://www.cdc.gov/niosh/topics/fishing/nationaloverview.html.

16. "2000 Great Lakes Consent Decree FAQs," Michigan Department of Natural Resources, https://www.michigan.gov/dnr/-/media/Project/Websites/dnr/Documents/Fisheries/TCU/2000_GLConsent_Decree_FAQs.pdf?rev=07856e4323ed4a699581ccee080c95ba.

17. Nara Schoenberg, "Lake Michigan Water Levels Are Expected to Stay Well Below the

Near-Historic Highs of 2020," *PHYS.org*, August 12, 2022, https://phys.org/news/2022-08-lake-michigan-near-historic-highs.html.

18. Kurt Williams, "Invasive Mussels Challenge Commercial Whitefish Fishing in the Great Lakes," *Michigan Bridge*, June 24, 2019, https://www.bridgemi.com/michigan-environment-watch/invasive-mussels-challenge-commercial-whitefish-fishing-great-lakes.

19. Dan Egan, "How Invasive Species Changed the Great Lakes Forever," *Milwaukee Journal Sentinel*, September 2, 2021, https://www.jsonline.com/in-depth/archives/2021/09/02/how-zebra-mussels-and-quagga-mussels-changed-great-lakes-forever/7832198002/.

20. Fletcher, *The Eagle Returns*, 117–118.

21. Fletcher, *The Eagle Returns*, 119.

22. "History of State-Licensed Great Lakes Commercial Fishing," Michigan Department of Natural Resources, Michigan.gov, https://www.michigan.gov/dnr/managing-resources/fisheries/business/commercial/history-of-state-licensed-great-lakes-commercial-fishing.

Chapter 3. Welcome Wagon

1. Whitney Amann, "A Look Behind National Cherry Festival's 'Go for the Gold Commemorative Pin Program,'" *9&10 News*, July 5, 2022, https://www.9and10news.com/2022/07/05/a-look-behind-national-cherry-festivals-go-for-the-gold-commemorative-pin-program/.

2. "History of Cherries," National Cherry Festival, https://www.cherryfestival.org/p/get-cherries/history-of-cherries.

3. Christian Glupker and Paul Isely, *The Economic Assessment of the 2022 National Cherry Festival* (Allendale, MI: Grand Valley State University, October 2022), 4, https://scholarworks.gvsu.edu/cgi/viewcontent.cgi?article=1010&context=eco_otherpubs.

4. National Cherry Festival, *National Cherry Festival: Generations of Fun* (Traverse City, MI: Mission Point Press, 2016), 6.

5. "Exactly Where We Should Be," *Midwest Living*, Fall 2022, inside cover advertisement for Traverse City Tourism.

6. "About Traverse City Tourism," Traverse City Tourism, https://www.traversecity.com/about-traverse-city-tourism/.

7. Craig Manning, "Growing Pains: Traverse City Tourism CEO Talks New Hotels, Demand, Labor Shortages, and Growth Opportunities," *Traverse City Ticker*, November 20, 2022, https://www.traverseticker.com/news/growing-pains-traverse-city-tourism-ceo-talks-new-hotels-demand-labor-shortages-and-growth-opportunities/.

8. Brian Manzullo, "Short's Brewing Co. Again Calls Out 'Jerk' Customers, Says They Are as Relentless as Ever," *Detroit Free Press*, July 29, 2022, https://www.freep.com/story/entertainment/nightlife/2022/07/29/shorts-brewing-company-bellaire-rude-customers/10182111002/.

9. Lara Moore, "Due to Mistreatment of Our Servers," Facebook, July 24, 2022, https://www.facebook.com/larah.spasoff/posts/5615951471771867.

10. E. Campbell, *Beauty Spots in Leelanau* (Leland: Leelanau Historical Society Museum, 1901).

11. Grand Rapids and Indiana Railway, *Take the G.R.&I. to All Points on Grand Traverse Bay*, poster, Leelanau Historical Society Museum.

12. "Railroad: Grand Rapids & Indiana Railroad," MichiganRailroads.com, https://www.michiganrailroads.com/railroads-in-history/461-g-h/3478-grand-rapids-indiana-railroad.

13. "What Is Traverse Connect?," Traverse Connect, https://traverseconnect.com/about/.

14. Survey-EDGE, *Event Economic Impact, 2021* (Traverse City: Traverse City Horse Shows, 2021), https://traversecitysh.wpenginepowered.com/wp-content/uploads/2021/12/2021-Final-Econ-Report-12-6-web.pdf.

15. Grant Piering, "Michigan's Creative Coast: Keenan & Kristen's Story," Michigan's Creative Coast, https://michiganscreativecoast.com/create/careers-industries/remote/.

16. "Northern Navigators," Michigan's Creative Coast, https://michiganscreativecoast.com/explore/northern-navigators/.

17. "Diversity, Equity, Inclusion & Belonging: DEIB Committee Positioning Statement," Traverse Connect, https://traverseconnect.com/diversity-equity-inclusion-belonging-committee/.

18. Amy Tikkanen, "US Airways Flight 1549," *Britannica*, https://www.britannica.com/topic/US-Airways-Flight-1549-incident.

19. Cherry Capital Airport, "Highlights," in *Cherry Capital Airport Annual Report* (Traverse City: Cherry Capital Airport, September 2023), https://tvcairport.com/wp-content/uploads/2023/10/2023-TVC-Annual-Report.pdf.

20. Real Estate One, Jack Lane Team, https://www.jacklaneteam.com.

21. Craig Manning, "Will Traverse City Real Estate Remain Insulated from Larger Forces This Time Around?," *Traverse City Ticker*, July 31, 2022, https://www.traverseticker.com/news/will-traverse-city-real-estate-remain-insulated-from-larger-forces-this-time-around/.

22. "Line 5 Overview," Michigan Department of Environment, Great Lakes, and Energy, https://www.michigan.gov/egle/about/featured/line5/overview.

23. Sheri McWhirter, "Traverse City's Historic Wind Turbine Retired, Makes Way for Solar Panels," *MLive*, August 3, 2022, https://www.mlive.com/public-interest/2022/08/traverse-citys-historic-wind-turbine-retired-makes-way-for-solar-panels.html. The towering wind turbine, decommissioned in spring 2022, had been a renewable energy landmark for years along M-72. It's been replaced by a solar panel field that continues to expand.

24. Jordan Travis, "Mayor Carruthers Steps Down after Years in Traverse City Government," *Traverse City Record-Eagle*, November 2, 2021, https://www.record-eagle.com/news/local_news/mayor-carruthers-steps-down-after-years-in-traverse-city-government/article_f57f6c40-3b4b-11ec-b509-9f30df9e6299.html.

Chapter 4. Settlers

1. Ian James, "Western megadrought Is Worst in 1,200 Years, Intensified by Climate Change, Study Finds," *Los Angeles Times*, February 14, 2022, https://www.latimes.com/environment/story/2022-02-14/western-megadrought-driest-in-1200-years.

2. Rex Weyler, "How Much of Earth's Biomass Is Affected by Humans?," Greenpeace, July 18, 2018, https://www.greenpeace.org/international/story/17788/how-much-of-earths-biomass-is-affected-by-humans/.

3. Christine Smallwood, "The Climate Novelist Who Transcends Despair," *New York Times Magazine*, October 6, 2022, https://www.nytimes.com/2022/10/06/magazine/lydia-millet-dinosaurs.html?searchResultPosition=2.

4. "Who Was Thornton W. Burgess?," Thornton W. Burgess Society, https://thorntonburgess.org/who-was-thornton-w-burgess.

5. "St. Joseph Church," St. Rita-St. Joseph Parish, https://strita-stjoseph.org/index.php/st-joseph/.

6. "About Seattle," Seattle Office of Planning & Community Development, https://www.

seattle.gov/opcd/population-and-demographics/about-seattle#population.

7. Bob Burkey and JoAnne (Nachazel) Burkey, *Descendants of Wencil Nachazel & Miscellaneous Items January 2002*, family history document, 3, 35.

8. Burkey, *Descendants of Wencil Nachazel & Miscellaneous Items*, 35, 47.

9. Burkey, *Descendants of Wencil Nachazel & Miscellaneous Items*, 47–48.

10. Jacob Wheeler, "Leelanau County's Iconic Bicentennial Barn Gets Enthusiastic New Owners with Local Roots," *Glen Arbor Sun*, February 19, 2021, https://glenarborsun.com/leelanau-countys-iconic-bicentennial-barn-gets-enthusiastic-new-owners-with-local-roots/.

11. *Boardman Review* 19, Summer 2022.

12. Mark Torregrossa, "Crazy Snowfall Totals Last Winter: Over 22 Feet of Snow in 2 Michigan Cities," *MLive*, August 14, 2014, https://www.mlive.com/weather/2014/08/season_snow.html.

13. "Programs & Properties," Traverse City Housing Commission, https://www.tchousing.org/programs-properties/riverview/.

14. Northwest Michigan Coalition to End Homelessness, https://www.endhomelessnessnmi.org.

15. "Quick Facts, Grand Traverse County, Michigan," U.S. Census Bureau, https://www.census.gov/quickfacts/grandtraversecountymichigan.

16. Chris Zollars, "Before and After Photos of Traverse City's Converted Mental Hospital," Michigan Radio Newsroom, March 19, 2013, https://www.michiganradio.org/business/2013-03-19/before-and-after-photos-of-traverse-citys-converted-mental-hospital.

17. "Central State Hospital," Encyclopedia of Indianapolis, https://indyencyclopedia.org/central-state-hospital/.

Chapter 5. A Taste of Northern Michigan

1. Jordan Travis, "Biden Visits King Orchards with Governor, Senators," *Traverse City Record-Eagle*, July 3, 2021, https://www.record-eagle.com/news/local_news/biden-visits-king-orchards-with-governor-senators/article_4b5194ee-dc48-11eb-b5c9-03ccb70cc9ed.html.

2. Mike King and Spencer Milbocker, dirs./eds., "Feast or Famine," YouTube video, March 23,

2020, https://www.youtube.com/watch?v=NIR54P7NQ4I.

3. Ben Logan, "The Future of Line 5: Engineering under Lake Michigan," Michigan Engineering, University of Michigan, May 6, 2021, https://news.engin.umich.edu/2021/05/the-future-of-line-5-engineering-under-lake-michigan/.

4. John King, "As the Anniversary of Enbridge's Refusal to Shut Down Line 5 Approaches, Groups Press Biden Admin," *Michigan Advance*, May 10, 2023, https://michiganadvance.com/2023/05/10/as-the-anniversary-of-enbridges-refusal-to-shut-down-line-5-approaches-groups-press-biden-admin/.

5. Thomas Benn, "Largely Forgotten, Migrants Toiled Where Others Wouldn't," *Glen Arbor Sun*, September 18, 2003, https://glenarborsun.com/largely-forgotten-migrants-toiled-where-others-wouldn't/.

6. Alice C. Larson, Michigan Interagency Migrant Services Committee, Michigan Department of Health & Human Services, "Table One: Michigan Update MSFW Enumeration Profiles Estimates, Final," in *Michigan Migrant and Seasonal Farmworker Enumeration Profiles Study 2013* (Lansing: State of Michigan Interagency Migrant Services Committee, June 2013), 32, https://farmworkerlaw.org/sites/default/files/2018-10/numbers2013.pdf.

7. "Fact Sheet #26G: H-2A Housing Standards for Rental and Public Accommodations," Wage and Hour Division, U.S. Department of Labor, November 2022, https://www.dol.gov/agencies/whd/fact-sheets/26g-housing-standards-for-rental-and-public-accommodations-H-2A.

8. Neil MacFarquhar, "Sweet Cherries, Bitter Politics: Two Farm Stands and the Nation's Divides," *New York Times*, June 6, 2021, https://www.nytimes.com/2021/06/06/us/michigan-masks-covid-farm-stands.html.

9. "Humble Beginnings," Cherry Republic, https://cherryrepublic.com/discover/history/.

10. Andrew Moore and Andrew Pritchard, "Four Hikers Complete Trek to Manitou Island," MyNorth.com, March 11, 2014, https://mynorth.com/2014/03/four-hikers-complete-trek-to-manitou-island/.

11. J. A. Craves and D. S. O'Brien, "Michigan Checklist," Michigan Odonata Survey, 2023, https://www.michodonata.org/michigan-checklist/.

12. Jillian Manning, "Sara Harding Takes The Lead on Climate, Community, & Charitable Giving at Glen Arbor's Cherry Republic," *Leelanau Ticker*, September 19, 2022, https://

www.leelanauticker.com/news/sara-harding-takes-the-lead-on-climate-community-charitable-giving-at-glen-arbors-cherry-republic/.

13. Kurt Luedtke, "Please Don't Come to Leelanau County," *Glen Arbor Sun*, August 4, 2020, https://glenarborsun.com/please-dont-come-to-leelanau-county/.

14. Leelanau Peninsula Wine Trail, https://lpwines.com.

15. "The History of MAWBY Winery: 50 Years of Sparkle," MAWBY, https://mawby.wine/history.

16. Craig Manning, "ALICE in Wonderland: How Leelanau's Paradise Status Hides Staggering Levels of Near-Poverty," *Leelanau Ticker*, February 9, 2022, https://www.leelanauticker.com/news/alice-in-wonderland-how-leelanaus-paradise-status-hides-staggering-levels-of-near-poverty/.

17. Craig Manning, "Larry Mawby Wants to Help Solve Leelanau County's Affordable Housing Puzzle. Here's How." *Leelanau Ticker*, January 24, 2022, https://www.leelanauticker.com/news/larry-mawby-wants-to-help-solve-leelanau-countys-affordable-housing-puzzle-heres-how/.

18. "About," SCORE Traverse City, https://www.score.org/about.

Chapter 6. Invasive Species

1. *Yellowstone*, "One Hundred Years Is Nothing," season 5, episode 1, directed by Taylor Sheridan, Viacom International Inc., Paramount Network, 2022, https://www.paramountnetwork.com/shows/yellowstone.

2. "One Hundred Years Is Nothing."

3. "Leelanau County Statistics," Leelanau County Government, updated August 24, 2022, https://www.leelanau.gov/leelanaustats.asp.

4. Phil Monahan, "Classic Fish Facts: Brown Trout (Salmo Trutta)," *Orvis News*, October 19, 2016, https://news.orvis.com/fly-fishing/classic-fish-facts-brown-trout-salmo-trutta.

5. Cortney Brown, "UpNorthLife: Michigan Sees Increase in Fly Fishing Anglers," *UpNorthLive*, April 29, 2021, https://upnorthlive.com/news/local/upnorthlife-michigan-sees-increase-in-fly-fishing-anglers.

6. Garret Ellison, "Dam Collapse: $6.3M Lawsuit Claims Botched Traverse City Project

Worsened April Flooding," *MLive*, May 21, 2013, https://www.mlive.com/news/2013/05/dam_collapse_63m_lawsuit_claim.html.

7. Dan O'Keefe, "Great Lakes Migrants: More Than Just Salmon," Michigan State University Extension, Michigan Sea Grant, December 5, 2014, https://www.canr.msu.edu/news/great_lakes_migrants_more_than_just_salmon. Great Lakes salmon are more accurately considered potamodromous fish in that they do not typically travel to salt water—the Atlantic Ocean—from their freshwater streams of birth during their lifetimes, later returning to freshwater streams for spawning, which anadromous salmon do. Rather, their behavior "involves moving from one freshwater habitat to another as a regular part of the life cycle," O'Keefe says, never entering saltwater. Whether anadromous or potamodromous, salmon being allowed to head upstream on the Boardman-Ottaway River would tamper with the health of the trout fishery.

8. Al Simpson, "It's 'Getting Western' on Montana's Madison River," Al's Point of View, Simpson Fly Fishing, August 8, 2021, https://simpsonflyfishing.com/its-getting-western-on-montanas-madison-river/.

9. Beth Milligan, "What's Next for Building Height, FishPass in Traverse?" *Traverse City Ticker*, October 31, 2022, https://www.traverseticker.com/news/whats-next-for-building-height-fishpass-in-traverse-city/.

10. "FishPass Project to Commence," City of Traverse City, April 8, 2024, https://www.traversecitymi.gov/news/fishpass-to-commence.html.

11. "FishPass Project to Commence."

12. Beth Milligan, "$6.4 Million in Federal Funding Awarded to FishPass Project," *Traverse City Ticker*, April 14, 2020, https://www.traverseticker.com/news/64-million-in-federal-funding-awarded-to-fishpass-project/.

13. Andrew Muir, Daniel Zielinksi, and Marc Gaden, *FishPass: Project Overview* (Ann Arbor: Great Lakes Fishery Commission, October 2019), 5, http://www.glfc.org/pubs/pdfs/research/FishPass_Project_Overview_02_28_2019.pdf, 6, 3.

14. Barry Lopez, *Embrace Fearlessly the Burning World* (New York: Random House, 2022), 44.

15. Craig Welch, "Earth Now Has 8 Billion People—and Counting. Where Do We Go from Here?," *National Geographic*, November 14, 2022, https://www.nationalgeographic.com/environment/article/the-world-now-has-8-billion-people.

16. "A River Reborn," Conservation Resource Alliance, October 14, 2021, https://www.rivercare.org/project/boardman-watershed/a-river-reborn/.

17. Muir, Zielinksi, and Gaden, *FishPass*, 7. My emphasis.

18. Michael Livingston, "DNR Looks to Increase Salmon Stocking in Lake Michigan," Interlochen Public Radio, September 15, 2022, https://www.interlochenpublicradio.org/ipr-news/2022-09-15/dnr-looks-to-increase-salmon-stocking-in-lake-michigan#.

19. Michigan Department of Natural Resources Fisheries Division and Law Enforcement, *2020 Annual Report on Implementation of 2000 Consent Decree for 1936 Treaty-Ceded Waters of the Great Lakes* (Lansing: Michigan Department of Natural Resources, May 2021), https://www.michigan.gov/dnr/-/media/Project/Websites/dnr/Documents/Fisheries/Mgt/2020ImpleentationReport.pdf?rev=484f65a4b5494ce49e3b92f1240bc049.

20. "Old Milwaukee Beer Commercial, 1988," YouTube video, https://www.youtube.com/watch?v=Ga6E63rFW-U.

21. "13 Weird Boating Superstitions," Bass Pro Shops Boating Centers, https://www.bassproboatingcenters.com/blog/boating-superstitions.html. There are many online references to this superstition that had its start in the Caribbean sometime in the 1700s.

22. Keith Matheny, "Smeltdown: Small Fish Continues Great Lakes Vanishing Act," *Detroit Free Press*, April 4, 2015, https://www.freep.com/story/news/local/michigan/2015/04/04/great-lakes-smelt-decline-lake-michigan-invasive/25292463/.

Chapter 7. America's Most Beautiful Place

1. "Sleeping Bear Dunes Voted 'Most Beautiful Place in America,'" *ABC News*, August 16, 2011, https://abcnews.go.com/Travel/best_places_USA/sleeping-bear-dunes-michigan-voted-good-morning-americas/story?id=14319616.

2. Sally Barber, "Port Oneida Book Shines Light on the Heritage Farm Community," *Traverse City Record-Eagle*, May 24, 2019, https://www.record-eagle.com/news/arts_and_entertainment/port-oneida-book-shines-light-on-the-heritage-farm-community/article_a8a0c2eb-a443-54ee-b2b1-4f06b95b5d97.html.

3. "Carsten Burfiend Farm," National Park Service, Sleeping Bear Dunes National Lakeshore,

Michigan, https://www.nps.gov/slbe/planyourvisit/poburfiendcarsten.htm.

4. Melissa Anders, "President Obama Signs Sleeping Bear Dunes Wilderness Legislation into Law," *MLive*, March 13, 2014, https://www.mlive.com/lansing-news/2014/03/obama_signs_sleeping_bear_dune.html.

5. Brian C. Kalt, *Sixties Sandstorm: The Fight over Establishment of a Sleeping Bear Dunes National Lakeshore, 1961–1970* (East Lansing: Michigan State University Press, 2001), 24.

6. Kalt, *Sixties Sandstorm*, 98.

7. "2020 Decennial Census," U.S. Census Bureau, https://www.census.gov.

8. "Visitor Spending Effects—Economic Contributions of National Park Visitor Spending," National Park Service, Social Science, https://www.nps.gov/subjects/socialscience/vse.htm.

9. Bingham, Emily, "Sleeping Bear Dunes' 2022 Visitor Count Marks Lowest Total in 8 Years," *MLive*, April 7, 2023, https://www.mlive.com/news/2023/04/sleeping-bear-dunes-2022-visitor-count-marks-lowest-total-in-8-years.html#:~:text=According%20to%20the%20National%20Park,National%20Park%20Service%20sites%20nationwide.

10. "Lake Michigan at Near-Record High Water Levels," National Weather Service, January 13, 2020, https://www.weather.gov/lot/LakeMichiganHighWater. According to NOAA data, Lake Michigan's water level rose six feet between January 2013 through November 2019. The record high was recorded in the summer and fall of 1986.

11. "Piping Plover Overview," U.S. Fish and Wildlife Service, https://www.fws.gov/species/piping-plover-charadrius-melodus.

12. "Mission Statement," Friends of Sleeping Bear Dunes, https://friendsofsleepingbear.org.

13. "Sleeping Bear Heritage Trail," National Park Service, Sleeping Bear Dunes National Lakeshore, Michigan, https://www.nps.gov/slbe/planyourvisit/sbht.htm.

14. Kerry Kelly, Friends of Sleeping Bear Dunes, *2022 Beach Patrol Summary Report* (Empire, MI: Friends of Sleeping Bear Dunes, September 2022).

15. *Breaking Away,* directed by Peter Yates, 20th Century-Fox, 1979, https://www.imdb.com/title/tt0078902/.

16. "Rising Sun Shipwreck and Nameboard," National Park Service, Sleeping Bear Dunes National Lakeshore Michigan, updated December 1, 2020, https://www.nps.gov/slbe/planyourvisit/rising-sun.htm.

17. Theodore J. Karamanski, "Chapter Three: Changes on the Land; The Early Management of Sleeping Bear Dunes National Lakeshore, 1971–1977," in *A Nationalized Lakeshore: The*

Creation and Administration of Sleeping Bear Dunes National Lakeshore (Washington, D.C.: National Park Service, 2000), http://npshistory.com/publications/slbe/adhi/chap3.htm.

18. Kalt, *Sixties Sandstorm*, 100.

Chapter 8. Protecting Paradise

1. Jacob Wheeler, "Borkovich, Fellow County Sheriffs Defy Gov. Whitmer, Claim They Will Selectively Enforce State's Social Distancing Executive Order," *Glen Arbor Sun*, April 15, 2020, https://glenarborsun.com/borkovich-fellow-county-sheriffs-defy-gov-whitmer-claim-they-will-selectively-enforce-states-social-distancing-executive-order/comment-page-1/.

2. Ted Roelofs, "Michigan's 'Constitutional Sheriffs' Vow to Keep Voters Safe at Polls," *Bridge Michigan*, October 14, 2020, https://www.bridgemi.com/michigan-government/michigans-constitutional-sheriffs-vow-keep-voters-safe-polls.

3. Craig Manning, "Living in Luxury in Leelanau: Million-Dollar Homes, Waterfront, and Open Land Drive the Market," *Northern Express*, October 14, 2023, https://www.northernexpress.com/news/feature/living-in-luxury-real-estate-in-leelanau/#:~:text=By%20Craig%20Manning%20%7C%20Oct.,income%2C%20and%20median%20home%20values.

4. Pat Bauer, "The Andy Griffith Show," *Britannica*, updated March 7, 2024, https://www.britannica.com/topic/The-Andy-Griffith-Show.

5. Networks Northwest, *Seasonal Population Study for Northwest Lower Michigan* (Traverse City: Networks Northwest, October 2022), https://www.networksnorthwest.org/userfiles/filemanager/49nwypzbp28vz3voy6gk/.

6. Billy Currington, "People Are Crazy," track 5 on *Little Bit of Everything*, Mercury Records, 2008.

7. Beth Milligan, "Healthier Drinking Culture Plan Tabs Short, Long-Term Solutions; Public Input Next," *Traverse City Ticker*, September 14, 2021, https://www.traverseticker.com/news/healthier-drinking-culture-plan-released-public-input-sought/.

8. Amy Hubbell, "Index Crimes Jump in Sheriff's Annual Report," *Leelanau Enterprise*, April

6, 2023.

9. Hubbell, "Index Crimes."

10. "The Latest Leelanau County Blotter & 911 Call Report," *Leelanau Ticker*, December 20, 2023, https://www.leelanauticker.com/news/the-latest-leelanau-county-blotter-911-call-report-60/.

11. U.S. Coast Guard, "Coast Guard Warns of Consequences for False Mayday Calls, after Two Calls Sunday," news release, March 18, 2019, https://content.govdelivery.com/accounts/USDHSCG/bulletins/2379c9c.

12. "CO Biweekly Reports," Michigan Department of Natural Resources, September 18–October 1, 2022, https://www.michigan.gov/dnr/managing-resources/laws/cobiweekly.

13. "CO Biweekly Reports."

14. "CO Biweekly Reports."

15. "Mission Statement," Michigan Department of Natural Resources, Missions and Commissions, https://www2.dnr.state.mi.us/publications/pdfs/harbor_guide/missions_commisions.htm.

16. "2020 Decennial Census," Search, Northport village, Michigan, U.S. Census Bureau, https://www.census.gov/search-results.html?q=Northport%2C+Michigan&page=1&stateGeo=none&searchtype=web&cssp=SERP&_charset_=UTF-8.

17. Frank Morris, "The Pandemic Pushed People Outside and Now, Some Companies Hope They Stay There," NPR, March 25, 2021, https://www.npr.org/2021/03/25/979221924/the-pandemic-pushed-people-outside-and-now-some-companies-hope-they-stay-there.

Chapter 9. Eyes to the Skies

1. Robin Catalano, "Could a Birding Boom in the U.S. Help Conservation Take Flight?," *National Geographic*, September 2, 2021, https://www.nationalgeographic.com/travel/article/could-a-boom-in-us-birding-help-fund-conservation.

2. "Mute Swan," All About Birds, https://www.allaboutbirds.org/guide/Mute_Swan/.

3. "State of the Birds 2022," North American Bird Conservation Initiative, https://www.stateofthebirds.org/2022/.

4. Patrick Sullivan, "Summer People: A Northern Michigan Island Ponders Opening Up for Tourist Season," *Northern Express*, May 16, 2020, https://www.northernexpress.com/news/feature/summer-people/.

5. "Visiting the Island—FAQs," Discover Beaver Island: America's Emerald Isle," Beaver Island Chamber of Commerce, https://www.beaverisland.org/visiting-the-island/.

6. Beaver Island Chamber of Commerce, *Beaver Island 2021–2022 Visitor's Guide* (Beaver Island: Beaver Island Chamber of Commerce, 2021), https://www.beaverisland.org/wp-content/uploads/2021/06/20-21-BI-Visitors-Guide.pdf.

7. Pam Grassmick, "The Beaver Island Archipelago—Caring for a Lake Michigan Treasure" (unpublished manuscript, February 18, 2023), Microsoft Word document, February 18, 2023.

8. "Discover Beaver Island: America's Emerald Isle," Beaver Island Chamber of Commerce, https://www.beaverisland.org.

9. IM Editors, "Beaver Island Retreat, in Up-North Michigan," *Indianapolis Monthly*, October 18, 2020, https://www.indianapolismonthly.com/lifestyle/travel/beaver-island-retreat-in-up-north-michigan.

10. "All International Dark Sky Places," DarkSky International, https://darksky.org/what-we-do/international-dark-sky-places/all-places/?_select_a_place_type=international-dark-sky-sanctuary.

11. Cynthia Johnson, "Application for International Dark Sky Sanctuary Designation," Beaver Island Association & Beaver Island Chamber of Commerce, https://www.beaverislandassociation.org/wp-content/uploads/2021/02/BIDSS-Application-2021-01-24.pdf.

12. Sheri McWhirter, "Beaver Island Is a Pristine Environmental Haven. Will It Last?," *MLive*, August 6, 2023, https://www.mlive.com/public-interest/2023/08/beaver-island-is-a-pristine-environmental-haven-will-it-last.html.

13. Land Information Access Association, Resilient Beaver Island, *Beaver Island Master Plan 2023* (Traverse City: Land Information Access Association, April 20, 2023), 12, 14.

14. "About Grand Hotel, Mackinac Island," Grand Hotel, Mackinac Island, Michigan, https://www.grandhotel.com/our-story/grand-hotel/.

15. "10 1/2 Mackinac Island Fun Facts," Mackinac Island Tourism Bureau, https://www.mackinacisland.org/blog/10-%C2%BD-mackinac-island-fun-facts/.

16. "Rogers Observatory History," Northwestern Michigan College, https://www.nmc.edu/resources/observatory/history.html.

17. Grand Traverse Astronomical Society, Facebook, November 12, 2022, https://www.facebook.com/profile.php?id=100070342042618.

18. Aleanna Siacon, "Glowing, Fluorescent 'Yooperlites' Found in Michigan's Upper Peninsula," *Detroit Free Press*, September 10, 2018, https://www.freep.com/story/news/local/michigan/2018/09/10/yooperlites-lake-superior-beach-michigan/1258276002/.

19. Steph Castelein, "A Guide to Finding Michigan's Yooperlites," Pure Michigan, https://www.michigan.org/article/guide-finding-michigan-yooperlites.

20. "Paleozoic," Youth and Education in Science, U.S. Geological Survey, https://www.usgs.gov/youth-and-education-in-science/paleozoic.

Chapter 10. Every Day Is Earth Day

1. Emily Hopkins, "The Truth about the White River," *Indianapolis Star*, September 23, 2019, https://www.indystar.com/in-depth/news/environment/2019/09/23/white-river-getting-cleaner-but-is-it-safe/2164251001/.

2. "Grand Traverse Bay Watershed," The Watershed Center Grand Traverse Bay, https://gtbay.org/gt-bay-watershed/.

3. "What We Do," The Watershed Center Grand Traverse Bay, https://gtbay.org/what-we-do/.

4. "What Are Microplastics?," National Ocean Service, National Oceanic and Atmospheric Administration, https://oceanservice.noaa.gov/facts/microplastics.html.

5. Sarah U'Ren, *Coastal Grand Traverse Bay Watershed Plan May 2021* (Traverse City: The Watershed Center Grand Traverse Bay, May 2021), https://gtbay.org/wp-content/uploads/2022/11/GT-Coastal-Bay-Plan_FINAL_May-2021__with-figures_for-distribution.pdf. If you want to understand how imperiled a watershed can be, and how resilient Mother Nature is—with a little help from friends like the Watershed Center Grand Traverse Bay—this report is well worth the read.

6. "*E. coli* Symptoms and Causes," Mayo Clinic, https://www.mayoclinic.org/diseases-conditions/e-coli/symptoms-causes/syc-20372058.

7. Michigan Department of Health and Human Services, *Eat Safe Fish Guide, Northwest Michigan 2023* (Lansing: Michigan Department of Health and Human Services, 2023), Grand Traverse County, 30, https://www.michigan.gov/mdhhs/-/media/Project/Websites/mdhhs/DEH/Eat-Safe-Fish/Documents/NW_EAT_SAFE_FISH_GUIDE_-_NORTHWEST_MI_WEB.pdf?rev=534ac3216b4f4a73977547ff53270e0e&hash=8643E7E7DCAD80634C1DAA9BF0345D61.

8. "Green Roofs," U.S. General Services Administration, https://www.gsa.gov/governmentwide-initiatives/federal-highperformance-green-buildings/resource-library/integrative-strategies/green-roofs.

9. "About GTRLC," Grand Traverse Regional Land Conservancy, https://www.gtrlc.org/about/about-gtrlc/.

10. "Green Features," Grand Traverse Regional Land Conservancy, https://conservationcenter.gtrlc.org/green-features/.

11. Carly Simpson, "In Search of Wild Orchids in Michigan," *Traverse, Northern Michigan's Magazine*, June 4, 2018, https://mynorth.com/2018/06/wild-orchids-in-michigan/.

12. Keith Schneider, "Moving in to Benzonia," *ModeShift*, April 17, 2022, http://modeshift.org/419/moving-in-to-benzonia/.

13. Circle of Blue, https://www.circleofblue.org.

14. "About," Groundwork Center for Resilient Communities, https://www.groundworkcenter.org/about-25th-anniversary-year/.

15. "Backgrounder on the Three Mile Island Accident," U.S. Nuclear Regulatory Commission, updated November 15, 2022, https://www.nrc.gov/reading-rm/doc-collections/fact-sheets/3mile-isle.html.

16. Traverse City Area Public Schools, https://www.tcaps.net/schools/.

17. James Hanson, *Storms of My Grandchildren: The Truth About the Coming Climate Catastrophe and Our Last Chance to Save Humanity* (New York: Bloomsbury USA, 2009), ix.

18. Courtney Woody, "Lumbering Michigan," *Blue: Michigan's Waterfront Lifestyle Magazine*, November 7, 2022, https://www.mibluemag.com/the-pike/lumbering-michigan.

19. "Your Public Lands," Michigan Department of Natural Resources, https://www.michigan.gov/dnr/managing-resources/public-land.

20. Todd Spangler, "Michigan to Lose Another Seat in Congress as Population Moves West and South," *Detroit Free Press*, April 26, 2021, https://www.freep.com/story/news/politics/elections/2021/04/26/michigan-congressional-seats/7388701002/.

21. "United Van Lines 46th Annual National Movers Study Reveals Where and Why Americans Moved in 2022," United Van Lines, January 2, 2023, https://www.unitedvanlines.com/newsroom/movers-study-2022.

22. Marc Perry, Luke Rogers, and Kristie Wilder, "New Florida Estimates Show Nation's Third Largest State Reaching Historic Milestone," U.S. Census Bureau, December 22, 2022, https://www.census.gov/library/stories/2022/12/florida-fastest-growing-state.html.

23. Keith Schneider, "Water Could Make the Great Lakes a Climate Refuge. Are We Prepared?," *Bridge Michigan*, February 16, 2021, https://www.bridgemi.com/michigan-environment-watch/water-could-make-great-lakes-climate-refuge-are-we-prepared.

24. For Love of Water, Facebook, November 16, 2021, https://www.facebook.com/flowforwater/posts/10159556309066236/?paipv=0&eav=Afa3d8HzCVi-6oaGfINzCkLyFxW1cd1bm9onMnRUD1bi0QsofpWJXw3jQ8ebZANFa4E&_rdr.

25. Jim Olson, "A Remembrance: Terry Swier: A Michigan Water Warrior," FLOW blog post, December 16, 2021, https://forloveofwater.org/a-remembrance-terry-swier-a-michigan-water-warrior/.

26. John Bacon and Jorge L. Ortiz, "'Once in Every 1,000–2,000 Years': Storm Swamps Fort Lauderdale with 25 Inches of Rain; Updates," *USA TODAY*, April 13, 2023, https://www.usatoday.com/story/news/nation/2023/04/13/fort-lauderdale-flood-airport-live-updates/11655448002/.

27. Paul Salopek, "Walking with Migrants," *National Geographic*, August 2019, 45.

28. Donald Wuebbles et al., *An Assessment of the Impacts of Climate Change on the Great Lakes*, (Chicago: Environmental Law & Policy Center), 1–2, https://elpc.org/wp-content/uploads/2020/04/2019-ELPCPublication-Great-Lakes-Climate-Change-Report.pdf.

29. Jake Bittle, *The Great Displacement: Climate Change and the Next American Migration* (New York: Simon & Schuster, 2023), 251.

30. Dave Dempsey, *Great Lakes for Sale* (Traverse City, MI: Mission Point Press, 2021), 69.

31. Christopher Flavelle, "Biden Administration Proposes Evenly Cutting Water Allotments from Colorado River," *New York Times*, April 11, 2023, https://www.nytimes.com/2023/04/11/climate/colorado-river-water-cuts-drought.html.

32. Trevor Hughes, "Water Levels Are Going Up in the West's Massive Reservoirs. Has the Water Crisis Been Averted?," *USA TODAY*, April 29, 2023, https://www.usatoday.com/story/news/nation/2023/04/29/lake-powell-lake-mead-water-levels-going-up-how-high-they-go/11736349002/.

33. Glenn Kessler, "'Drill, Baby, Drill' and Other Nonsensical Trump Claims about Inflation," *Washington Post*, February 16, 2024, https://www.washingtonpost.com/politics/2024/02/16/drill-baby-drill-other-nonsensical-trump-claims-about-inflation/.

34. "Evidence: How Do We Know Climate Change Is Real?," NASA Global Climate Change, https://climate.nasa.gov/evidence/.

35. Core Writing Team, Hoesung Lee, and José Romero, eds., *Climate Change 2023 Synthesis Report: Summary for Policymakers* (Geneva: Intergovernmental Panel on Climate Change, 2023), 4, 5, https://www.ipcc.ch/report/ar6/syr/downloads/report/IPCC_AR6_SYR_SPM.pdf.

36. Tanya Wildt, "DNR Cancels Black Lake Sturgeon Fishing Season in Michigan," *Detroit Free Press*, February 2, 2024, https://www.freep.com/story/news/local/michigan/2024/02/02/black-lake-sturgeon-fishing-season-michigan-2024-canceled-dnr-ice-conditions/72448995007/.

37. "Jon W. Allan," Audubon Great Lakes, https://gl.audubon.org/contact/jon-w-allan.

38. Patti Brandt, "Signs of Amish: New Community Welcomed into Manistee," *Traverse City Record-Eagle*, September 1, 2019, https://www.record-eagle.com/news/local_news/signs-of-amish-new-community-welcomed-into-manistee/article_390c77ca-c428-11e9-8763-0334adccdc22.html.

39. Beth LeBlanc, "Michigan Farmers Enjoy State's Diverse Agriculture," *Detroit Free Press*, August 22, 2016, https://www.freep.com/story/news/local/michigan/2016/08/22/michigan-farmers-enjoy-states-diverse-agriculture/89092478/.

40. "Planting the Seeds of Connectivity," West Michigan Food Processing Association, https://www.westmichfoodprocessingassn.com/infrastructure.

41. Linda Beaty, "Leelanau's Early Polish Settlements," *Glen Arbor Sun*, July 20, 2015, https://glenarborsun.com/leelanaus-early-polish-settlements/. To get a sense of the rich Polish heritage of Leelanau County, there's no better cultural experience than the annual four-day Cedar Polka Fest each August. The event draws about ten thousand people for the beer, kielbasa, and, of course, polka dancing aplenty.

Epilogue

1. Jan Schlain, "More Than a Football Coach," University of Michigan Human Resources, https://hr.umich.edu/more-football-coach.

2. Chris Solari, "'That Woman from Michigan' Shirt Is Hot Seller for Farmington Hills Business Owner," *Detroit Free Press*, March 31, 2020, https://www.freep.com/story/news/2020/03/31/that-woman-from-michigan-shirt-whitmer-trump/5096223002/.

3. *David Attenborough: A Life on Our Planet*, directed by Alastair Fothergill, Jonnie, Hughes, and Keith Scholey, Netflix documentary, 2020, https://www.netflix.com/title/80216393.